# Demonic
# Grounds

# Demonic Grounds

*Black Women and the Cartographies of Struggle*

KATHERINE MCKITTRICK

UNIVERSITY OF MINNESOTA PRESS

MINNEAPOLIS • LONDON

Quotations from "Dis Place—The Space Between," from Marlene Nourbese Philip, *A Genealogy of Resistance and Other Essays* (Toronto: Mercury Press, 1997), are reprinted here with the permission of the poet.

Published by the University of Minnesota Press
111 Third Avenue South, Suite 290
Minneapolis, MN 55401-2520
http://www.upress.umn.edu

Library of Congress Cataloging-in-Publication Data

McKittrick, Katherine.
    Demonic grounds : Black women and the cartographies of struggle / Katherine McKittrick.
        p. cm.
    Includes bibliographical references and index.
    ISBN 13: 978-0-8166-4701-9 (hc)
    ISBN 10: 0-8166-4701-1 (hc : alk. paper)
    ISBN 13: 978-0-8166-4702-6 (pb)
    ISBN 10: 0-8166-4702-X (pb : alk paper)
    1. Women, Black—America—Social conditions. 2. African diaspora. 3. Human geography—America. 4. Geography—Psychological aspects. 5. Slavery—America—History. 6. Women slaves—America—History. 7. Women, Black—America—Political activity. 8. Women, Black, in literature. 9. America—Race relations. 10. America—Geography—Psychological aspects. I. Title.
    E29.N3M38 2006
    305.48'89607009—dc22                                                    2005035148

Printed in the United States of America on acid-free paper

The University of Minnesota is an equal-opportunity educator and employer.

12 11 10 09 08 07 06        10 9 8 7 6 5 4 3 2 1

For Zilli

# Contents

# Geographic Stories

I don't want no fucking country, here
or there and all the way back, I don't like it, none of it,
easy as that.

—DIONNE BRAND

When Dionne Brand writes, she writes the land. Her important collection of poetry *Land to Light On* is a map. But this map does not easily follow existing cartographic rules, borders, and lines. *Land to Light On* provides a different geographic story, one which allows pavement to answer questions, most of the world to be swallowed up by a woman's mouth, and Chatham, Buxton—Ontario sites haunted by the underground railroad—to be embedded with Uganda, Sri Lanka, slave castles, and the entries and exits of Sarah Vaughan's singing. And Brand gives up on land, too. She not only refuses a comfortable belonging to nation, or country, or a local street, she alters them by demonstrating that geography, the material world, is infused with sensations and distinct ways of knowing: rooms full of weeping, exhausted countries, a house that is only as safe as flesh. Brand's decision, to give up on land, to want no country, to disclose that geography is always human and that humanness is always geographic—blood, bones, hands, lips, wrists, this is your land, your planet, your road, your sea—suggests that her surroundings are speakable. And this speakability is not only communicated through the poet, allowing her to emphasize the alterability of space and place, to give up on land and imagine new geographic stories; in her work, geography holds in it the possibility to speak for itself. Brand's sense of place continually reminds me that human geography needs some philosophical attention; she reminds me that the earth is also skin and that a young girl can legitimately take possession of a street, or an entire city, albeit on different terms than we may be familiar with. So this philosophical attention is not only needed because existing carto-graphic rules unjustly organize human hierarchies *in place* and reify uneven geographies in familiar, seemingly natural ways. This attention is also needed because, if we trust Brand's insights, these rules are alterable and there exists a terrain through which different geographic stories can be and are told.

*Demonic Grounds* is, in its broadest sense, an interdisciplinary analysis of black women's geographies in the black diaspora. It seeks to consider what kinds of possibilities emerge when black studies encounters human geography. Drawing on creative, conceptual, and material geographies from Canada, the United States, and the Caribbean, I explore the inter-play between geographies of domination (such as transatlantic slavery and racial-sexual displacement) and black women's geographies (such as their knowledges, negotiations, and experiences). This interplay interests me because it enables a way to think about the place of black subjects in a diasporic context that takes up spatial histories as they constitute our pres-ent geographic organization. The relationship between black populations and geography—and here I am referring to geography as space, place, and location in their physical materiality and imaginative configurations—allows us to engage with a narrative that locates and draws on black his-tories and black subjects in order to make visible social lives which are often displaced, rendered ungeographic. Black histories where, for exam-ple, progress, voyaging, and rationality meet violence and enslavement are worked out in geography, in space and place, in the physical world. Geog-raphy's and geographers well-known history in the Americas, of white masculine European mappings, explorations, conquests, is interlaced with a different sense of place, those populations and their attendant geog-raphies that are concealed by what might be called rational spatial colo-nization and domination: the profitable erasure and objectification of subaltern subjectivities, stories, and lands. Let me give a telling example to outline the ways in which progress and exploration are entwined with a different sense of (black) place. The ships of transatlantic slavery mov-ing across the middle passage, transporting humans for free labor into "newer worlds" do not only site modern technological progression, which materially moves diasporic subjects through space, that is, on and across the ocean, and on and across landmasses such as Canada, the United States, the Caribbean; these vessels also expose a very meaningful struggle for freedom *in place*. Technologies of transportation, in this case the ship, while materially and ideologically enclosing black subjects—economic objects inside and often bound to the ship's walls—also contribute to the formation of an oppositional geography: the ship as a location of black subjectivity and human terror, black resistance, and in some cases, black possession.

But the landscape, our surroundings and our everyday places, the vessels of human violence, so often disguise these important black geographies; they can hide what Sylvia Wynter calls "the imperative of a perspective of struggle."[1] Geography's discursive attachment to stasis and physicality, the idea that space "just is," and that space and place are merely containers for human complexities and social relations, is terribly seductive: that which "just is" not only anchors our selfhood and feet to the ground, it seemingly calibrates and normalizes where, and therefore who, we are. The slave ship, as a materiality, contains and regulates; it hides black humanity because it "just is" and because those inside, bound to the walls, are neither seeable nor liberated subjects. As Olaudah Equiano writes, the ship was a location of suppression upheld, in part, by black grief and death; it hid and suffocated human cargo and curtailed resistances. His memories of the slave ship suggest that its materiality—above and below the deck—in part disguised human terror.[2] The imperative perspective of black struggle is undermined by the social processes and material three dimensionalities that contribute to the workings of the geographies of slavery: the walls of the ship, the process of economic expansion, human objectification, laboring and ungeographic bodies, human-cargo. The "where" of black geographies and black subjectivity, then, is often aligned with spatial processes that *apparently* fall back on seemingly predetermined stabilities, such as boundaries, color-lines, "proper" places, fixed and settled infrastructures and streets, oceanic containers. If space and place *appear* to be safely secure and unwavering, then what space and place make possible, outside and beyond tangible stabilities, and from the perspective of struggle, can potentially fade away.

Geography is not, however, secure and unwavering; we produce space, we produce its meanings, and we work very hard to make geography what it is. *Demonic Grounds* reveals that the interplay between domination and black women's geographies is underscored by the social production of space. Concealment, marginalization, boundaries are important social processes. We make concealment happen; it is not natural but rather names and organizes where racial-sexual differentiation occurs. To return to my earlier example, the slave ship is not stable and unchanging; it is a site of violent subjugation that reveals, rather than conceals, the racial-sexual location of black cultures in the face of unfreedoms. The physicality of the slave ship, then, contributes to the *process* of social concealment and dehumanization but, importantly, black subjectivity is not swallowed up by the ship itself. Rather, the ship, its crew, black subjects, the ocean and ports, make geography what it is, a location through which a moving technology can create differential and contextual histories. To return to Equiano, the slave ship is not simply a container hiding his displacement. It is a location through which he articulates hardship and human cruelty, in part mapping and giving new meaning to the vessel itself.

The connections, across the seeable and unseeable, the geographic and the seemingly ungeographic, and the struggles that indicate that the material world is assessed and produced by subaltern communities, these shape my discussions. Geographic domination is a powerful process. However, if we pursue the links between practices of domination and black women's experiences in place, we see that black women's geographies are lived, possible, and imaginable. Black women's geographies open up a meaningful way to approach both the power and possibilities of geographic inquiry. I am not suggesting that the connections between black women and geography are anything new—indeed, I assume a legacy of black women's geographies and geographic knowledges. Rather, I am suggesting that the relationship between black women and geography opens up a conceptual arena through which more humanly workable geographies can be and are imagined. I am therefore interested in the kinds of historical and contemporary geographies that interest and impact upon black women and how, for some, existing arrangements do not work at all, "easy as that."[3]

## GEOGRAPHIES OF DOMINATION, TRANSATLANTIC SLAVERY, DIASPORA

Black matters are spatial matters. And while we all produce, know, and negotiate space—albeit on different terms—geographies in the diaspora are accentuated by racist paradigms of the past and their ongoing hierarchical patterns. I have turned to geography and black geographic subjects not to provide a corrective story, nor to "find" and "discover" lost geographies.

Rather, I want to suggest that space and place give black lives meaning in a world that has, for the most part, incorrectly deemed black populations and their attendant geographies as "ungeographic" and/or philosophically undeveloped. That black lives are necessarily geographic, but also struggle with discourses that erase and despatialize their sense of place, is where I begin to conceptualize geography. I therefore follow the insights of Kathleen Kirby, noting that the language and concreteness of geography—with its overlapping physical, metaphorical, theoretical, and experiential contours—must be conceptualized as always bringing into view material referents, external, three-dimensional spaces, and the actions taking place in space, as they overlap with subjectivities, imaginations, and stories.[4] I want to suggest that we take the language *and* the physicality of geography seriously, that is, as an "*imbrication* of material and metaphorical space,"[5] so that black lives and black histories can be conceptualized and talked about in new ways. And part of the work involved in thinking about black geographies is to recognize that the overlaps between materiality and language are long-standing in the diaspora, and that the legacy of racial displacement, or erasure, is in contradistinction to and therefore evidence of, an ongoing critique of both geography and the "ungeographic." Consequently, if there is a push to forge a conceptual connection between material or concrete spaces, language, and subjectivity, openings are made possible for envisioning an interpretive alterable world, rather than a transparent and knowable world.

Geography, then, materially and discursively extends to cover three-dimensional spaces and places, the physical landscape and infrastructures, geographic imaginations, the practice of mapping, exploring, and seeing, and social relations in and across space. Geography is also Geography, an academic discipline and a set of theoretical concerns developed by human geographers, such as the importance of the ways in which material spaces and places underpin shifting and uneven (racial, sexual, economic) social relations. In order to examine black women's relationship to these diverse geographic conceptualizations, I have employed the term "traditional geography," which points to formulations that assume we can view, assess, and ethically organize the world from a stable (white, patriarchal, Eurocentric, heterosexual, classed) vantage point. While these formulations— cartographic, positivist, imperialist—have been retained and resisted within and beyond the discipline of human geography, they also clarify that black women are negotiating a geographic landscape that is upheld by a legacy of exploitation, exploration, and conquest.[6] If we imagine that traditional geographies are upheld by their three-dimensionality, as well as a corresponding language of insides and outsides, borders and belongings, and inclusions and exclusions, we can expose domination as a visible spatial project that organizes, names, and sees social differences (such as black femininity) and determines *where* social order happens.

The history of black subjects in the diaspora is a geographic story that is, at least in part, a story of material and conceptual placements and displacements, segregations and integrations, margins and centers, and migrations and settlements. These spatial binaries, while certainly not complete or fully accurate, also underscore the classificatory *where* of race. Practices and locations of racial domination (for example, slave ships, racial-sexual violences) and practices of resistance (for example, ship coups, escape routes, imaginary and real respatializations) also importantly locate what Saidya Hartman calls "a striking contradiction," wherein objectification is coupled with black humanity/personhood.[7] In terms of geography, this contradiction maps the ties and tensions between material and ideological dominations and oppositional spatial practices. Black geographies and black women's geographies, then, signal alternative patterns that work alongside and across traditional geographies.

Indeed, black matters are spatial matters. The displacement of difference, geographic domination, transatlantic slavery, and the black Atlantic Ocean differently contribute to mapping out the real and imaginative geographies of black women; they are understood here as social processes that *make* geography a racial-sexual terrain. Hence, black women's lives and experiences become especially visible through these concepts and moments because they clarify that blackness is integral to the production of space.[8] To put it another way, social practices create landscapes and contribute to how we organize, build, and imagine our surroundings. Black subjects are not indifferent to these practices and landscapes; rather, they are connected to them due to crude racial-sexual hierarchies *and* due to their (often unacknowledged) status as geographic beings who have a stake in the production of space. Black women's histories, lives, and spaces must be understood as enmeshing with traditional geographic arrangements in order to identify a different way of knowing and writing the social world and to expand how the production of space is achieved across terrains of domination.

The production of space is caught up in, but does not guarantee, long-standing geographic frameworks that materially and philosophically arrange the planet according to a seemingly stable white, heterosexual, classed vantage point. If prevailing geographic distributions and interactions are racially, sexually and economically hierarchical, these hierarchies are naturalized by repetitively spatializing "difference." That is, "*plac[ing]* the world within an ideological order," unevenly.[9] Practices of domination, sustained by a unitary vantage point, naturalize both identity and place, repetitively spatializing where nondominant groups "naturally" belong. This is, for the most part, accomplished through economic, ideological, social, and political processes that see and position the racial-sexual body within what seem like predetermined, or appropriate, places and assume that this arrangement is commonsensical. This naturalization of "difference" is, in part, bolstered by the ideological weight of transparent space, the idea that space "just is," and the illusion that the external world is readily knowable and not in need of evaluation, and that what we see is true. If *who* we see is tied up with *where* we see through truthful, commonsensical narratives, then the placement of subaltern bodies deceptively hardens spatial binaries, in turn suggesting that some bodies belong, some bodies do not belong, and some bodies are out of place. For black women, then, geographic domination is worked out through reading and managing their specific racial-sexual bodies. This management effectively, but not completely, displaces black geographic knowledge by assuming that black femininity is altogether knowable, unknowing, and expendable: she is seemingly in place by being out of place.

The simultaneous naturalization of bodies and places must be disclosed, and therefore called into question, if we want to think about alternative spatial practices and more humanly workable geographies. Borrowing from Ruth Wilson Gilmore, I want to suggest that geographies of domination be understood as "the displacement of difference," wherein "particular kinds of bodies, one by one, are materially (if not always visibly) configured by racism into a hierarchy of human and inhuman persons that in sum form the category of 'human being.'"[10] Gilmore highlights the ways in which human and spatial differentiations are connected to the process of making place. The displacement of difference does not *describe* human hierarchies but rather demonstrates the ways in which these hierarchies are critical categories of social and spatial struggle. Thus, practices of domination are necessarily caught up in a different way of knowing and writing the social world, which foregrounds the "geographical imperatives," that lie "at the heart of every struggle for social justice."[11] This material spatialization of "difference"—for my purposes, the spatialization of the racial-sexual black subject—in various times and locations in turn makes visible new, or unacknowledged, strategies of social struggle. Geographic domination, then, is conceptually and materially bound up with racial-sexual displacement and the knowledge-power of a unitary vantage point. It is not a finished or immovable act, but it does signal unjust spatial practices; it is not a natural system, but rather a working system that manages the social world. It is meant to recognize the hierarchies of human and inhuman persons and reveal how this social categorization is also a contested geographic project.

I draw on the history of transatlantic slavery to illustrate that black women are both shaped by, and challenge, traditional geographic arrangements. My discussions are underwritten by transatlantic slavery because this history heightens the meanings of traditional arrangements, which rest on a crucial geographic paradigm, human captivity. Transatlantic slavery profited from black enslavement by exacting material and philosophical black subordinations. A vast project, the practice of slavery differently impacted upon black diaspora populations in Africa, the Caribbean, South America, Canada, the United States, and various parts of Europe, between the seventeenth and nineteenth centuries. Slavery differed markedly in different locations. For example, periods of institution and abolishment, the scale of the trade, and uses of slave labor all produce unique time-space differentiations. At the same time, the particularity of slaves' lives and selves—gender, age, labor tasks, phenotype, ethnicity, language, time, place—fracture the meanings of slavery even further. As histories, recollections, and narratives of slavery clearly demonstrate, different slaves negotiated bondage in very different ways.[12] While it is not within the scope of this introduction or project to particularize and spatialize all geographies of transatlantic slavery, I sketch out below the central ideas that have shaped my analysis.

What I feel is important to outline in terms of the geographies of transatlantic slavery and my larger discussion on black women's geographies is not so much the vast and differential processes of captivity. Instead, I turn to slavery, through memories, writings, theories, and geographies, to address the idea that locations of captivity initiate a different sense of place through which black women can manipulate the categories and sites that constrain them. Of course the technologies and violences of slavery, as they are spatialized, do not disappear when black women assert their sense of place. But black women also *inhabited* what Jenny Sharpe calls "the crevices of power" necessary to enslavement, and from this location some were able to manipulate and recast the meanings of slavery's geographic terrain.[13] Their different practices of spatial manipulation make possible a way to analyze four interrelated processes that identify the social production of space: the naturalization of identity and place, discussed above; the ways in which geographic enslavement is developed through the constructs of black womanhood and femininity; the spatial practices black women employ across and beyond domination; and the ways in which geography, although seemingly static, is an alterable terrain.

I have drawn on the legacy of transatlantic slavery to advance a discussion of black women's geographic options as they are, often crudely, aligned with historically present racial-sexual categorizations. More specifically, transatlantic slavery incited meaningful geographic processes that were interconnected with the category of "black woman": this category not only visually and socially represented a particular kind of gendered servitude, it was embedded in the landscape. Geographically, the category of "black woman" evidenced human/inhuman and masculine/feminine racial organization. The classification of black femininity was therefore also a process of *placing* her within the broader system of servitude—as an inhuman racial-sexual worker, as an objectified body, as a site through which sex, violence, and reproduction can be imagined and enacted, and as a captive human. Her classificatory racial-sexual body, then, determined her whereabouts in relation to her humanity.

As some black feminists have suggested, the category of "black woman" during transatlantic slavery affects—but does not necessarily twin—our contemporary understandings of human normalcy.[14] Further, our present landscape is both haunted *and* developed by old and new hierarchies of humanness. If past human categorization was spatialized, in ships and on plantations, in homes, communities, nations, islands, and regions, it also evidences the ways in which some of the impressions of transatlantic slavery leak into the future, in essence recycling the displacement of difference. Of course, much has changed in the natural and social environment, but our historical geographies, and the ways in which we make and know space now, are connected; they are held together by what Carole Boyce Davies and Monica Jardine describe as "a series of remapping exercises in which various land spaces are located within an orbit of control."[15] I am not suggesting that the violence of transatlantic slavery is an ongoing, unchanging, unopposed practice, but rather that it is a legacy that carries with it—for black and nonblack peoples—"living effects, seething and lingering, of what *seems* over and done with."[16]

I want to suggest that the category of black woman is intimately connected with past and present spatial organization and that black femininity and black women's humanness are bound up in an ongoing geographic struggle. While black womanhood is not static and ahistoric, the continuities, contexts, and ruptures that contribute to the construction of black femininity shed light on how black women have situated themselves in a world that profits from their specific displacements of difference. Identifying black women as viable contributors to an ongoing geographic struggle, rather than, for example, solely through the constructs of "race" or race/class/gender/sexuality is critical to my argument: I want to emphasize that contextual spatial analyses do not relegate black women to the margins or insist that the spatialization of black femininity "just was" and "just is." While I have suggested that geography—through and beyond practices of domination—is an alterable terrain through which black women can assert their sense of place, questions of "race," or race/class/gender/sexuality, are contributors to the where of blackness, rather than the sole indicators of identity/experience.

So, what philosophical work can geography actually do for us, as readers and occupiers of space and place, if it is recognizably alterable? What is at stake in the legacy of exploration, conquest, and stable vantage points if we insist that past and present geographies are connective sites of struggle, which have *always* called into question the very *appearance* of safely secure and unwavering locations? And what do black women's geographies make possible if they are not conceptualized as simply subordinate, or buried, or lost, but rather are indicative of an unresolved story?

I am emphasizing here that racism and sexism are not simply bodily or identity based; racism and sexism are also spatial acts and illustrate black women's geographic experiences and knowledges as they are made possible through domination. Thus, black women's geographies push up against the seemingly natural spaces and places of subjugation, disclosing, sometimes radically, how geography is socially produced and therefore an available site through which various forms of blackness can be understood and asserted. I do not seek to devalue the ongoing unjustness of racism and sexism by privileging geography; rather I want to stress that if practices of subjugation are also spatial acts, then the ways in which black women think, write, and negotiate their surroundings are intermingled with place-based critiques, or, respatializations. I suggest, then, that one way to contend with unjust and uneven human/inhuman categorizations is to think about, and perhaps employ, the alternative geographic formulations that subaltern communities advance. Geographies of domination, from transatlantic slavery and beyond, hold in them both the marking and the contestation of old and new social hierarchies. If these hierarchies are spatial expressions of racism and sexism, the interrogations and remappings provided by black diaspora populations can incite new, or different, and perhaps more just, geographic stories. That is, the sites/citations of struggle indicate that traditional geographies, and their attendant hierarchical categories of humanness, cannot do the emancipatory work some subjects demand. And part of this work, in our historical present, is linked up with recognizing both "the where" of alterity *and* the geographical imperatives in the struggle for social justice.

Spatial acts can take on many forms and can be identified through expressions, resistances, and naturalizations. Importantly, these acts take place and have a place. One of the underlying geographic themes and "places" in this work is the black diaspora and the black Atlantic. Discussions draw on the work, ideas, and experiences advanced by theorists, writers, and poets from Canada, the United States, the United Kingdom, and the Caribbean. I have not drawn on these diasporic locations to reify a monolithic "black space," but rather to examine how practices of and resistances to racial domination across different borders bring into focus black women's complex relationship with geography. I cite/site several diasporic texts in order to consider where geopolitical strategies take place in the face of racial dominations. This conceptual framing of black diaspora geographies is in part inspired by Paul Gilroy's *The Black Atlantic: Modernity and Double Consciousness*.

Gilroy's *The Black Atlantic* has allowed me to think about black populations as part, but not completely, of geography. The text focuses on alternative geographies, countercultural positions, which are simultaneously deemed ungeographic yet hold in them long-standing spatial negotiations.

And this positionality—in Canada, the United States, the United Kingdom, the Caribbean—is inextricably linked to a discourse of modernity wherein questions of progress are underwritten by the terrors of slavery, the living memories of slavery, and diasporic migrations. Further, the idea of "belonging" in and to place—whether it be a particular nation, a specific community, real/imagined Africa, homelands—is incomplete, premised on a struggle toward some kind of sociospatial liberation. Importantly, this struggle can go several ways at once: it might be developed through the language of nation-purity, or desired reconciled belongings that reiterate hetero-patriarchal norms; it might be formulated as Pan-Africanism, or through "outernational" musical exchanges and cultural borrowings; it might draw on European thought, Afrocentric philosophies, or both; it might foresee black nations, in Liberia, Ethiopia; it might involve crossing borders or enforced, chosen, temporary, or permanent, exiles. Black Atlantic populations, then, inhabit place in a unique way, which is, in part, upheld by geographic yearnings and movements that demonstrate "various struggles toward emancipation, autonomy, and citizenship" and a reexamination of "the problems of nationality, location, identity and historical memory."[17] *The Black Atlantic* works to loosen the naturalization of (black) identities and place, arguing for the ways in which a different sense of place, and different geographic landmarks, might fit into our historically present spatial organization. And while his critique of transparent space is not explicit, Gilroy does provide some tools through which we might reconsider the terms of place, belonging, and unfulfilled liberties. That is, he sites black geographies through a terrain of struggle.

What I continue to like about Gilroy's text is the way he develops these ideas alongside geographic materialities. His work is not often examined for his invocation of three-dimensionalities, which correspond with how we can understand the space of the black subject.[18] Of course, *The Black Atlantic* is not a forthright spatial investigation; indeed, criticism includes Joan Dayan's discussion of what she describes as Gilroy's slave ship and middle passage metaphors, symbols which, she argues, produce a deterritorialized "cartography of celebratory journeys."[19] But I want to read *The Black Atlantic,* and the black Atlantic, differently: as an "imbrication of material and metaphorical space,"[20] in part because the text is so noticeably underscored by a very important black geography, the Atlantic Ocean, through which the production of space can be imagined on diasporic terms. In fact, I would suggest that it is precisely because Gilroy draws on real, imagined, historical, and contemporary *geographies,* that Dayan can imagine and document the materialities, the landscapes, he elides in this work. That is, metaphors of the middle passage or the Atlantic Ocean are never simply symbolic renditions of placelessness and vanishing histories—this is too easy and, in my view, reinforces the idea that black scholars and writers are ungeographic, trapped in metaphors that seemingly have no physical resonance. Coupling Gilroy's insights into modernity and intellectual histories with his decision to position black cultures in relation to the Atlantic Ocean and other physical geographies helps to explicate where the terrain of political struggle fits into black cultural lives. I suggest that if *The Black Atlantic* is also read through the material sites that hold together and anchor the text—the middle passage, the Atlantic Ocean, black travelers in Europe, Canada, and elsewhere, the slave ship, the plantation, shared outernational musics, fictional and autobiographical geographies, nationalisms—it clarifies that there are genealogical connections between dispossession, transparent space, and black subjectivities. Historical and contemporary black geographies surface and centralize the notion that black diaspora populations have told and are telling how their surroundings have shaped their lives. These connections flag, for example, the middle passage, expressive cultures, and the plantation on historio-experiential terms, spatializing black histories and lives, which are underwritten by the displacement of difference. It is important, then, to recognize that black Atlantic cultures have always had an intimate relationship with geography, which arises out of diasporic populations existing "partly inside and not always against the grand narrative of Enlightenment and its organizing principles";[21] principles that include the naturalization of identity and place, the spatialization of racial hierarchies, the displacement of difference, ghettos, prisons, crossed borders, and sites of resistance and community.

## THE POETICS OF LANDSCAPE

Édouard Glissant's "poetics of landscape" brings attention to geographic expression, specifically, saying, theorizing, feeling, knowing, writing, and imagining space and place. For Glissant, poetics are both written and unwritten, and neither process can be claimed as superior or more legitimate than the other. The poetics of landscape, in Glissant's terms, "awakens" language, offering intelligible and visible black struggles. The spatial undertones are obvious, found both in Glissant's choice of terminology and in his deeper concerns with his immediate environment, the landscapes and topography of Martinique and the Caribbean: the Other America, perpetual conceal-ment, somber greens, which the roads still do not penetrate, mahogany trees supported by blue beaches on a human scale, the salt of the sea, beaches up for grabs, "our landscape is our only monument: its meaning can only be traced on the underside."[22] Glissant's complex sense of place, his poetics of landscape, creates a way to enter into, and challenge, tradi-tional geographic formulations without the familiar tools of maps, charts, official records, and figures; he enters, through his voice-language, a poetic-politics, and conceptualizes his surroundings as "uncharted," and inextri-cably connected to his selfhood and a local community history. The poetics of landscape discloses the underside, unapparent histories and stories that name the world and black personhood. Sylvia Wynter, in discussing Glis-sant specifically, describes his poetics as a "counterconcept," which contests, as she puts it, "Man," purveyor of *universal généralisant*: unquestionable reason, value, and authority.[23]

I work with this counterconcept because it gives emphasis to the oppo-sitional speaker/community vis-à-vis their inevitable—although sometimes vexed—connection to the outer world and, to continue with Wynter's termi-nology, "Man's" geographies. Poetics of landscape constitute narrative acts, delineating a "relationship with the land, one that is even more threat-ened because the community is alienated from the land. . . . Describing the landscape is not enough. The individual, the community, the land are inextricable in the process of creating history."[24] In discussing written and oral histories, Glissant remarks that the relationship between the writer/speaker and the landscape in fact makes history and brings the subject into being. In a way, Glissant reconciles the black subject to geog-raphy, arguing that expressive acts, particularly the naming of place—regardless of expressive method and technique—is also a process of self-assertion and humanization, a naming of inevitable black geographic pres-ence. To put it another way, naming place is also an act of naming the self and self-histories. Insisting that different kinds of expression are multi-fariously even, that is, not hierarchically constituted as, for example, "written" over "oral," and that the landscape does not simply function as a decorative background, opens up the possibility for thinking about the production of space as unfinished, a poetics of questioning.[25]

What is striking here, and very useful in terms of black women's geographies, is that the poetics of landscape are not derived from the desire for socioeconomic possession. Nor are they derived from a unitary vantage point. Indeed, Glissant suggests that there are different sets of geographic tools available, which are anchored, primarily, in nonlinearity, contradictory histories, dispossession, and an "infinite variety" of landscapes.[26] The claim to place should not be naturally followed by material ownership and black repossession but rather by a grammar of liberation, through which ethical *human*-geographies can be recognized and expressed. Arguably, then, while the displacement of difference outlines processes of human and inhuman classification, it also draws attention to subaltern spatial practices, which are written into and expressed through the poetics of landscape.

The combination of material and imagined geographies is intended to unfix black women's geographies from their "natural" places and spaces by bringing into focus the "sayability" of geography. Acts of expressing and saying place are central to understanding what kinds of geographies are available to black women. Because black women's geographies are bound up with practices of spatial domination, saying space and place is understood as one of the more crucial ways geography can work for black women. The poetics of landscape, then, comprises theories, poems, dramatic plays, and historical narratives that disclose black women's spaces and places. They comprise an interdisciplinary and diasporic analytical opening, which advances creative acts that influence and undermine existing spatial arrangements. I take this inextricable combination of real-imagined geographies seriously throughout the project in order to argue that the poetics of landscape, whether expressed through theoretical, fictional, poetic, musical, or dramatic texts, can also be understood as real responses to real spatial inequalities. The poetics of landscape allow black women to critique the boundaries of transatlantic slavery, rewrite national narratives, respatialize feminism, and develop new pathways across traditional geographic arrangements; they also offer several reconceptualizations of space and place, positioning black women as geographic subjects who provide spatial clues as to how more humanly workable geographies might be imagined.

Produced alongside and through practices of domination, black women's expressive acts spatialize the imperative of a perspective of struggle. Within this work, I attempt to locate black women's geographies in space without situating these geographies firmly inside an official story or history. Rather than attempting to complete black women's geographies by "finding" them or "discovering" them, I am emphasizing that geography and black women have *always* functioned together and that this interrelated process is a new way to "enter" into space (conceptually and materially), one that uncovers a geographic story predicated on an ongoing struggle (to assert humanness and more humanly workable geographies). In this way, the displacement of difference, geographies of domination, transatlantic slavery, the black diaspora, and the poetics of landscape, throughout the study, are used to indicate the ways in which unofficial or oppositional geographies—which are so often displaced, disguised, or relocated by practices of domination—are socially produced indicators of the imaginative and real work geography can do.

## READING THE DEMONIC

Etymologically, demonic is defined as spirits—most likely the devil, demons, or deities—capable of possessing a human being. It is attributed to the human or the object through which the spirit makes itself known, rather than the demon itself, thus identifying unusual, frenzied, fierce, cruel human behaviors. While demons, devils, and deities, and the behavioral energies they pass on to others, are unquestionably wrapped up in religious hierarchies and the supernatural, the demonic has also been understood in terms that are less ecclesiastical. In mathematics, physics, and computer science, the demonic connotes a working system that cannot have a determined, or knowable, outcome. The demonic, then, is a nondeterministic schema; it is a process that is hinged on uncertainty and nonlinearity because the organizing principle cannot predict the future. This schema, this way of producing or desiring an outcome, calls into question "the always non-arbitrary pre-prescribed" parameters of sequential and classificatory linearity.[27] With this in mind, the demonic invites a slightly different conceptual pathway—while retaining its supernatural etymology—and acts to identify a system (social, geographic, technological) that can only unfold and produce an outcome if uncertainty, or (dis)organization, or something supernaturally demonic, is integral to the methodology.

In her essay, "Beyond Miranda's Meanings: Un/Silencing the 'Demonic Ground' of Caliban's 'Woman'," Sylvia Wynter develops the demonic in two ways. First, she works with the schema outlined above, specifically drawing on the theories forwarded by physicists, to suggest that a demonic model conceptualizes vantage points "outside the space-time orientation of the humunucular observer."[28] This vantage point makes possible her analysis of our historically present world-human organization, the "order-field" wherein "race" functions to distinguish Man from his human (black, native, female) others. Her analysis does not lead her to discuss Man verses other, however. Rather, her demonic model serves to locate what Wynter calls cognition *outside* "the always non-arbitrary pre-prescribed," which underscores the ways in which subaltern lives are not marginal/other to regulatory classificatory systems, but instead integral to them. This cognition, or demonic model, if we return to the nondeterministic schema described above, makes possible a different unfolding, one that does not *replace* or override or remain subordinate to the vantage point of "Man" but instead parallels his constitution and his master narratives of humanness. It is this conception of humanness that I read as Wynter's contribution to re-presenting the grounds from which we can imagine the world and more humanly workable geographies.

In developing a second, but related, use of demonic, Wynter describes "the grounds" as the absented presence of black womanhood. "Beyond Miranda's Meanings" is one of Wynter's more thorough and explicit analyses of black feminism.[29] For those familiar with William Shakespeare's *The Tempest,* the demonic here connotes a geographical, ontological, and historical lack, the missing racial-sexual character in the play: Caliban's potential mate through whom the reproduction of his race might occur, who Wynter suggests is absent, and demonic, precisely because she is outside the bounds of reason, "too alien to comprehend," as Audre Lorde wrote.[30] Wynter asks, then, what would happen to our understanding and conception of race and humanness if black women legitimately inhabited our world and made their needs known? And how does her silence, absence, and missing desired and desirable body, figure into the production of selfhood? What does her nondeterministic impossibility add to our conceptualization of humanness? Demonic grounds, then, is a very different geography; one which is genealogically wrapped up in the historical spatial unrepresentability of black femininity and, to return to the demonic model above, one that thinks about the ways in which black women necessarily contribute to a re-presentation of human geography.[31]

I want to encourage reading *Demonic Grounds* in the spirit of Sylvia Wynter's writings because her philosophies aim to identify a transition *toward* a new epistemology. That is, the grounds of Wynter's project contribute to what David Scott describes as a "revisioned humanism," which is fashioned as a "direction, a *telos*."[32] Of course this present work, *Demonic Grounds*, does not pretend to twin Wynter's extraordinary and intricate contributions to metaphysics and humanism! However, I use her work to clarify what the tenets of geography make possible, not just in the areas of mapping domination and subordination, but also in the areas of working toward more just conceptualizations of space and place. Importantly, then, the demonic grounds outlined by Wynter in "Beyond Miranda's Meanings" are not simply identifying categories of difference, absence, and the places and voices of black women and/or black feminism; they also outline the ways in which this place is an unfinished and therefore transformative human geography story; thus, Wynter works toward "a new science of human discourse."[33]

I think, then, Wynter gives us a new place to go, a "direction," as David Scott puts it, in human geographic inquiry. In terms of reading *Demonic Grounds*, I hope that my discussions cite and site at least a small part, or "a piece of the way," in this debate.[34] My argument is not intended to be a corrective discussion—or a new map—but a contribution to the connections between justness and place, difference and geography, and new spatial possibilities. The chapters that follow are intended to raise questions about the ground beneath our feet, how we are all implicated in the production of space, and how geography—in its various formations—is integral to social struggles. *Demonic Grounds* is not meant to be read as a text that finds, discovers, and surveys the places black women inhabit; rather, it begins what I hope will be a discussion about what black women's historical-contextual locations bring to bear on our present geographic organization. *Demonic Grounds* seeks to consider the ways in which practices of domination are in close contact with alternative geographic perspectives and spatial matters that may not necessarily replicate what we think we know, or have been taught, about our surroundings. So the conceptual work of my discussions is quite simple: how do geography and blackness work together to advance a different way of knowing and imagining the world?

Can these different knowledges and imaginations perhaps call into question the limits of existing spatial paradigms and put forth more humanly workable geographies?

I use these questions as a thematic through which my discussions can be read. I begin with what I consider to be the key debates and problems in geographic inquiry. However, rather than building my argument around questions of absences (for example, who, what is missing from the discipline of human geography?), I consider what happens, conceptually and materially, when black studies encounters the discipline of geography, and blackness is imagined through specific geographic inquiries. I note that while there is a wide disciplinary gap between human geography, black experiences, and black studies, it is not indicative of a black sense of place. In chapter 1, then, I argue for what black geographies have always made possible—materially, theoretically, imaginatively. The geographic relationship between the past and the present and racial geographies is crucial here, as it works to examine the ways in which understanding blackness has been twinned by the practice of *placing* blackness *and* rendering body-space integral to the production of space. Equally important are the ways in which the material and conceptual possibilities geography offers also raise a new set of concerns for black subjects, beyond and through what is considered the given, knowable, and profitable perimeters of space and place. This paradox underscores my interdisciplinary methodological approach, which is to combine different conceptualizations of space and place and demonstrate that while traditional spatial formulations are powerful, geography is also a terrain through which blackness makes itself known. Drawing on Toni Morrison, W. E. B. Du Bois, Neil Smith, Édouard Glissant, Frantz Fanon, and Dionne Brand, I explore traditional geographies, bodily-spatial struggles, and a "different sense of place." I argue that a close examination of black geographies simultaneously points to cycles of racial-sexual domination and oppositional geographic practices, which in turn offer what Marlene Nourbese Philip calls "a *public* genealogy of resistance": histories, names and places of black pain, language, and opposition, which are "spoken with the whole body" and present to the world, to our geography, other rhythms, other times, other spaces.[35]

What kind of philosophical and spatial work can a public genealogy of resistance do if it sites blackness, black femininity, and the body as speaking to and across the world? In chapter 2 I think about this question in relation to bodily captivity, enslavement, and emancipation, which I believe heighten the paradox of black women's geographies. Specifically, as noted above, I am interested in the ways in which black women inhabited "the crevices of power" necessary to enslavement, and through which some were able to manipulate and recast the meanings of slavery's geographic terrain. I therefore read a moment in Harriet Jacobs's slave narrative, *Incidents in the Life of a Slave Girl,* in order to examine the ways in which a black sense of place communicates the terms of captivity. In her narrative, Jacobs (as Linda Brent) describes the seven years she spent in her grandmother's tiny garret, a retreat she was forced to take in order to save her life and her children's lives. The garret highlights how geography is transformed by Jacobs/Brent into a usable and paradoxical space. More than this, the garret is situated in and amongst the violent geographies of slavery; Jacobs's/Brent's position in the garret allows her to witness and say these geographies "from the last place they thought of," not on the margins, or from a publicly subordinated position, but from the disabling confines of a different slave space, what she describes as her "loophole of retreat."

What interests me, in addition to geographic possibilities of the garret that Jacobs/Brent discloses, are the ways in which her racial-sexual body, and the naming of her (unprotected) body, underwrite other diasporic feminisms. That is, Jacobs/Brent names the body as a location of struggle. Throughout the narrative, skin, hair, arms, legs, feet, eyes, hands, muscles, corporeal sexual differences—these physical attributes, of Jacobs/Brent, her family, and her lovers, contribute to the possibilities and limitations of space. I follow my discussion of *Incidents in the Life of a Slave Girl* by analyzing the conceptual threads between black women's enslaved bodies, the garret, and Marlene Nourbese Philip's poetics. I make these connections not to present an ahistorical reading of black femininity, but rather to address the ways in which the contributions of second-wave black feminism are diasporic precisely because the body, and the legacy of racial-sexual discrimination, have forced a respatialization of white Euro-American feminisms. I then discuss the geographic underpinnings of black feminism because this politics can also be understood as a struggle over space and place, within the academy, in theory and activism, and across women's literatures. In what ways are these body-identity politics showing the alterability of space and black women's long-standing geographic contributions, but also perhaps reifying the margin and "garreting" black femininity? Is the garret a continuous assertion of black politics, conceptually and experientially reframed as the margin? What kinds of metaphoric and material demands does the margin make on how we politicize difference? Or, can the margin be recast in less geographically constrictive terms, perhaps evidencing a part of an enlarged story field?

I add to these queries through a different study when I consider the slave auction block. In a sense, the slave auction block reorients how space and place are communicated through the category of black femininity. This historical-contextual site not only adds to the complexities of paradoxical space, but also delineates how intimate physical attributes—skin, hair, arms, legs, feet, eyes, hands, muscles, corporeal sexual differences—can also shape external geographies, those scales that exist outside the body proper. By focusing on "the moment of sale," a concept borrowed from historian Walter Johnson, chapter 3 looks at three interconnected ways the slave auction block simultaneously marks the unfree body and the spaces outside of it: through displaying and exhibiting difference and the seeable body in terms of human/inhuman; through marking the differences between *kinds* of places (such as the body, the auction block, the plantation, the region, the nation); and through demonstrating how differences between kinds of places are not enclosed but rather entwined, and arguably sustained, by the moment of sale (the body for sale on the auction block, for example, bolsters the local economy and expresses racial differences in place).

These connections and differences suggest, however, that the slave auction block is not an unalterable materiality. Instead, the slave auction block is part of a social process that situates and localizes the moment of human sale, and in turn enables the objectification of black women and the repetitive naturalization of race-sex. But because the slave auction block is wrapped up in the "striking contradiction" of black objectification-humanity, it follows that it is necessarily a location of unresolved struggle. Building on the displacement of difference, I also suggest that the auction block opens up the possibility of human and bodily contestation: it creates a space through which black women can sometimes radically disrupt an otherwise rigid site of racialization and sexualization. I then read an excerpt from Robbie McCauley's play *Sally's Rape* as evidence of the historically present meaning of the auction block. Through the poetics of landscape, McCauley considers the auction block as a viable site of dramatic re-visitation and re-presentation: in *Sally's Rape,* the auction block is evidence of our pasts, and of a historically specific geography that exacted subordinations; but it is also a way for McCauley to question how this legacy puts demands on our contemporary geographic arrangements.

An important aspect of my argument is the illumination of the seeable and unseeable—black subjects hidden and on display. Black Canada offers a different way to think through the seeable and the unseeable. In chapter 4, I study the ways in which the absented presences of black peoples in the nation assert a different, less familiar national story. I introduce the concepts of "surprise" and "wonder" in order to conceptualize Canada as a feasible site of blackness. That is, while existing debates in Black Canadian Studies about the past and present places of black Canadians focus on absences, absented presences, and black Canadian marginality, they also embed these subjects within the nation-space. Specifically, these debates are also a way to insist that black Canadian populations are bound up in how we understand Canada-nation. It is suggested, then, that blackness is an unexpected but long-standing presence within Canada. I then position Canadian slave Marie-Joseph Angélique as a historical figure whose contestable presence makes black Canada believable. Angélique was accused of and executed for burning down most of Montreal, New France, in 1734. I suggest that Angélique's geographies—the difference she made to the nation and Montreal spatially and philosophically—have created other spaces through which black Canada can be articulated. That is, her alleged arson is a geographic opposition that needs to be (but is not necessarily) believable in order to help verify the presence of black Canada.

*Incidents in the Life of a Slave Girl,* the garret, Marlene Nourbese Philip's poetics, the slave auction block, *Sally's Rape,* Marie-Joseph Angélique, absented presences and black Canada, differently challenge how we have come to know geography; these texts, memories, women, and locations are just some of the ways to imagine and talk about black geographic struggles in the material, theoretical, and imaginative landscapes we occupy and express. Chapter 5 develops ways to present these spatialities through the work of Sylvia Wynter. I present Sylvia Wynter's ideas in relation to black geographies, showing that her unique understanding of space and place can perhaps direct us toward more humanly workable geographies. This chapter speaks to earlier chapters, arguing for a less descriptive presentation of black geographies and a turn to an interhuman reading of the production of space. Wynter makes possible a different approach to geography, one that is not marginal or subordinate or even developed across existing spatial patterns; her enlarged understanding of race, racism, geography, and displacement tells the story of interhuman geographies as evidence of struggles that put new demands on our historically present planet.

*Demonic Grounds* is a study of connections. It connects black studies, human geography, and black feminism. The textual sources connect literature, theory, poetry, drama, remembrances, images, and maps. These connections and expressions are not intended to name what/who is missing—from black studies, human geography, black feminism, or our historically present geographic landscapes. They are, instead, intended to illustrate the ways in which human geographies are, as a result of connections, made alterable. The combination of diverse theories, literatures, and material geographies works to displace "disciplinary" motives and demonstrate that the varying places of black women are connected to multiple material and textual landscapes and ways of knowing. These discussions are also about geographic stories. Places and spaces of blackness and black femininity are employed to uncover otherwise concealed or expendable human geographies. Because these geographic stories are predicated on struggle, and examine the interplay between geographies of domination and black women's geographies, they are not conclusive or finished. I hope to make clear that the ongoing geographic struggle of and by black women is not simply indicative of the adverse effects of geographic domination, but that geography is entwined with strategic and meaningful languages, acts, expressions, and experiences. What I am trying to illustrate are the powerful connections among race, sex, gender, and displacement, and the oppositional implications of saying, thinking, living, and writing black geographies. These connections, I think, make clear how the livability of the world is bound up with a human geography story that is not presently just, yet geography discloses a workable terrain through which respatialization can be and is imagined and achieved.

# I Lost an Arm on My Last Trip Home: Black Geographies

And suddenly, there was an avalanche of pain, red impossible agony! And I screamed and screamed.

—OCTAVIA E. BUTLER

But a scream is an act of excessiveness. Our land is excessive.

—ÉDOUARD GLISSANT

In the final moments of Octavia Butler's *Kindred,* the protagonist, Dana Franklin, returns from the past. Dismembered, bloody, screaming, Dana has violently come through a wall into the present, having endured repeated supernatural returns to antebellum Maryland. Octavia Butler's novel offers an interesting introduction to black geographies: Dana's predicament, as a contemporary subject forced into a time-space compression and a time-space reversal, allows her to confront and produce several landscapes. Present and past geographies, while distinguishable and particular, are also enmeshed vis-à-vis Dana's bodily and psychic experiences. Her supernatural status, as a time-traveling present-past subject, fractures rational time-space progression by allowing her to be experientially tied to urban California in 1976 and a Maryland slave plantation roughly 200 years earlier. By stacking time and place on top of one another, and allowing a black woman to ensure that the connections between past and present are, at once, contextually specific and bound, Butler effectively deepens black geographies. Dana, by stepping into what might be considered unknown or inaccessible spaces and places (the past, underacknowledged black geographies, time-space reversal), respatializes the potential of black femininity and black subjectivity in general. Blackness becomes a site of radical possibility, supernatural travels, and difficult epistemological returns to the past and the present. Butler presents us with landscapes shaped by selves and experiences that are extraordinary in that they are not comfortably situated in the past, present, or future. The landscape is neither complete nor fully intelligible. Physical geographies—the walls and rooms of Dana's 1976 apartment and the perimeters and buildings of an antebellum plantation—are not static. Instead, they are permeable and material indications of the uncertainty of place. Rational, linear, and knowable spatial patterns are not possible in Butler's narrative, and this leads us to consider that our engagement with place, and three-dimensionality, can inspire a different spatial story, one that is unresolved but also caught up in the flexible, sometimes disturbing, demands of geography, which some people "wouldn't think was so sane."[1]

Octavia Butler's hooking together of past and present locations, through time-travel, memory, knowledge, and literary production, allows us to imagine that black geographies, while certainly material and contextual, can be lived in unusual, unexpected, ways. Being materially situated *in place* is an inconclusive process; being materially situated *in place* holds in it possibilities that do not neatly replicate or privilege traditional geographic patterns of geometry, progress, cartography, and conquest. Indeed, the geographies of *Kindred* indicate the ways in which the built environment and the material landscape are sites that are intensely experiential and uneven, and deeply dependant on psychic, imaginary work. These spaces are entered and exited on terms that require an engagement with "something lost, or barely visible, or seemingly not there to our supposedly well-trained eyes."[2] Octavia Butler's novel and characters suggest that material geographies are sites of possibility, which are discerned and unraveled by what Kathleen Kirby calls "the space of the subject."[3] That is, the racialized, gendered, sexed, classed, and imaginative body-self necessarily interprets space and place—in its limitations and its possibilities. Dana's production of, and interaction with, topographical, geopolitical, corporeal, psychic, and discursive spaces matter, greatly, because she and her geographies reveal the uncertainty of traditional spatial patterns.

Édouard Glissant suggests that geographies produced in conjunction with, and often because of, white European practices of domination expose "various kinds of madness."[4] These forms of sociogeographic madness are, for Glissant, tied to transatlantic slavery and colonialism: the landless black subject is, importantly, anchored to a new world grid that is economically, racially, and sexually normative, or, seemingly nonblack; this grid suppresses the possibility of black geographies by invalidating the subject's cartographic needs, expressions, and knowledges. Toni Morrison, additionally, explains that racialized geographies are pathologies, indications of the ways in which space and place contribute to the dehumanization, fragmentation, and madness of both free and unfree peoples and their lands.[5]

What kinds of spatial restraints, values, and possibilities would incite these three divergent black theorists and authors to claim that the land, and land experiences, provoke various kinds of madness and fantastic time-travels? What is it about space, place, and blackness—the uneven sites of physical and experiential "difference"—that derange the landscape and its inhabitants? In order to begin thinking about these questions, it is important to highlight first the understanding that racial domination and human injustices are spatially propped up by racial-sexual codes, particularly bodily codes, such as phenotype and sex. That is, racism and sexism produce attendant geographies that are bound up in human disempowerment and dispossession. This can be seen, most disturbingly, in locations of racial and sexual violence—dragged bodies, historical and contemporary lynchings, rape—wherein the body is not only marked as different, but this difference, precisely because it is entwined with domination, inscribes the multiple scales outside of the punished body itself. Bodily violence spatializes other locations of dehumanization and restraint, rendering bodily self-possession and other forms of spatial ownership virtually unavailable to the violated subject. One of the many ways violence operates across gender, sexuality, and race is through multiscalar discourses of ownership: having "things," owning lands, invading territories, possessing someone, are, in part, narratives of displacement that reward and value particular forms of conquest.[6] And, at least for my purposes, this reward system repetitively returns us to the body, black subjecthood, and the where of blackness, not just as it is owned, but as black subjects participate in ownership. Black diasporic struggles can also be read, then, as geographic contests over discourses of ownership. Ownership of the body, individual and community voices, bus seats, women, "Africa," feminism, history, homes, record labels, money, cars, these are recurring positionalities, written and articulated through protest, musics, feminist theory, fiction, the everyday.[7] These positionalities and struggles over the meaning of place add a geographic dimension to practices of black reclamation. Yet they also illustrate the ways in which the legacy of racial dispossession underwrites how we have come to know space and place, and that the connections between what are considered "real" or valuable forms of ownership are buttressed through racial codes that mark the black body as ungeographic.

Often, but not always, the only recognized geographic relevancy permitted to black subjects in the diaspora is that of dispossession and social segregation. Recall the essays in Toni Morrison's edited collection *Race-ing Justice, En-Gendering Power,* wherein black men and women—including, but not limited to Clarence Thomas and Anita Hill—are continually read vis-à-vis a historical-racial landscape that expresses the impossibility of black self-possession. Black self-possession and self-entitlement cannot quite be read as feasible geographic processes in the terms laid out by traditional geographies because the close ties between the body and the landscape around these bodies (the traces of history) refuse such a reading, and arguably translate black geographies as homogenous sites of dispossession. And here, affluence, professionalism, class, dress, and education sometimes slip away: stereotype, often racial-bodily stereotype, becomes the primary medium of exchange.[8] This exchange is displayed, misconstruing and spatializing our imaginations because it is so tightly bound to the idea that dispossessed black bodies are naturally in place.

It is telling, then, that Morrison begins her introduction to the collection by reading another important geographic story, Daniel Defoe's *Robinson Crusoe,* a tale of a shipwreck and Crusoe's colonial relationship with "barbarous" Friday.[9] Friday's geographies are so intimately tied to his perceptible savage body that he must *willingly* give up on his understanding of land in order to fulfill Defoe's representational narrative of subaltern subjugation. That is, due to his complex relationship with Crusoe, Friday is positioned as a subject whose *own* geographies, whose *own* sense of place, are unrecognizable and valueless. And Morrison suggests that Friday's predicament is an ongoing dilemma, writ large in contemporary U.S. lives. I add the dimension of geography to her example in order to call attention to the ways in which the black body often determines the ways in which the landscape around the black body is read.[10] This is not meant to suggest that black people do not own land, that stereotypes do not have lived repercussions, that geographic reclamations are irrelevant, or that blackness easily corresponds with poverty. Instead, it reveals that the question of ownership is often wrapped up in a legacy of race/racism bolstered by compelling hierarchical categories, stereotypes of dispossession (captivity, lost homelands, evictions, joblessness, criminality, incarceration, welfare queens). So, the ways in which blackness has been translated as ungeographic is my central interest here, because it cites/sites how dispossession is an important racial narrative, which socially and economically rates ownership, domination, and human/life value. This also, particularly if we keep in mind Friday's ongoing spatial dilemma, allows us to consider that the ungeographic is a colonial fiction, sometimes cast in real life, thus functioning to determine how we only seem to see black geographies in hierarchical, stereotypical, human/inhuman terms, and therefore as ostensible impossibilities.

Yet those without formal, or sanctioned, land-possession point to the limitations of existing geographic patterns and, consequently, reveal alternative spatial strategies and desires. Butler, Glissant, and Morrison each bring into focus geographic patterns that are underwritten by black alienation from the land, but their analyses do not end here. Instead, they ask what this alienation brings to bear on processes of marginalization and how we might imagine black geographies in new ways. The material landscape itself, as it is produced by the black subject and mapped as unimaginably black, must be rewritten into black, and arguably human, existence on different terms. The various kinds of madness, the pathological geographies, the dismembered and displaced bodies, the impossible black places, the present-past time-space cartographers, and topographies of "something lost, or barely visible, or seemingly not there"—these material and metaphoric places begin to take us there. First, by recognizing the ways in which the social production of space is inextricably tied up with the differential placement of racial bodies. And second, through signaling a different sense of place, one which does not exactly duplicate the traditional features of geographic ownership that we seem to value so much.

The writings of Butler, Glissant, and Morrison are critical of, and therefore also an indication of, the discursive and material power of transparent space. Transparent space assumes that geography—specifically, physical and material geographies—is readily knowable, bound up with ideologies and activities that work to maintain a safe socioeconomic clarity: the walls of Dana's apartment are not permeable, Friday's lack of a sense of place is natural rather than enforced and socially produced, the landscape is not open to various kinds of madness. This transparency "goes hand in hand with a view of space as innocent, as free of traps or secret places."[11] While transparent space is a view, or perspective (what we *see* is knowable, readily decipherable), governing social desires continually bolster its seemingly self-evident characteristics: particular local and global mappings, infrastructures, regional boundaries, and transportation routes are examples of how transparent space, seemingly innocent, is materialized in the geographic environment.[12] Prevailing spatial organization gives a coherency and rationality to uneven geographic processes and arrangements: a city plan, for example, can (and often does) reiterate social class distinctions, race and gender segregation, and (in)accessibility to and from specific districts; the flows of money, spaces, infrastructure, and people are uneven, in that the built environment privileges, and therefore mirrors, white, heterosexual, capitalist, and patriarchal geopolitical needs.[13] This upholds processes of naturalization where "inequality [is] blazoned into the geographical landscape . . . for certain socially determined ends."[14] Such conceptions of natural, transparent geographies, are discursively and materially built up and mapped; the outer-world is organized according to systems of power-domination, systems that have a stake in the continued objectification of social spaces, social beings, and social systems.

The linkages between transparent space and the space of the subject begin to clarify the ways in which black geographies can be conceptualized. While the power of transparent space works to hierarchically position individuals, communities, regions, and nations, it is also contestable—the subject interprets, and ruptures, the knowability of our surroundings. What this contestation makes possible are "black geographies," which I want to identify as "*the terrain* of political struggle itself," or, *where* the imperative of a perspective of struggle takes place.[15] Here, the locations of black history, selfhood, imagination, and resistance are not only attached to the production of space through their marginality, but also through the ways in which they bring into focus responses to geographic domination. That is, black geographies cannot be fully understood if they are primarily conceptualized through utterances such as "invisible" or "peripheral." Indeed, following Neil Smith and Cindi Katz, this language can take away from the grounded everyday meanings metaphors impart by emptying out the material contours implicit in spatial articulations.[16] It is important to also think about the ways in which black geographies demonstrate both the limitations and possibilities of traditional spatial arrangements through the ways the black subject is produced by, and is producing, geographic knowledges. That is, invisible geographies, marginality, indicate a struggle, and ways of knowing the world, which can also illustrate wider conceptual and material spaces for consideration: real, lived dispossessions and reclamations, for example. The margins and invisibility, then, are also lived and right in the middle of our historically present landscape.

Black geographies comprise philosophical, material, imaginary, and representational trajectories; each of these trajectories, while interlocking, is also indicative of multiscalar processes, which impact upon and organize the everyday. Black geographies are located within and outside the boundaries of traditional spaces and places; they expose the limitations of transparent space through black social particularities and knowledges; they locate and speak back to the geographies of modernity, transatlantic slavery, and colonialism; they illustrate the ways in which the raced, classed, gendered, and sexual body is often an indicator of spatial options and the ways in which geography can indicate racialized habitation patterns; they are places and spaces of social, economic, and political denial and resistance; they are fragmented, subjective, connective, invisible, visible, unacknowledged, and conspicuously positioned; they have been described as, among other things, rhizomorphic, a piece of the way, diasporic, blues terrains, spiritual, and Manichaean.[17] The complexity of these geographies is found in the ways they reveal how ideas—black and nonblack—get turned into lived and imaginary spaces that are tied to geographic organization.

These tensions, between black and nonblack, transparent space and particular knowledges, real and imagined geographies, put forward some initial ideas about black geographies. I explore these tensions in order to propose how we might integrate a rich and complex geographic story into our present geographic imaginations and lives. I discuss black studies and human geography together, integrating some key points that help disclose the complexities of black geographies. Drawing on literature, literary criticism, geographic studies, geographic theories, and black social theories, I illustrate that interdisciplinary investigations make possible the category of "black geographies": subaltern or alternative geographic patterns that work alongside and beyond traditional geographies and site a terrain of struggle.

For the remainder of this discussion, I draw on black studies and human geography to outline how the production of space is bound up with racial ideologies and experiences. Specifically, I address the theoretical and geographic possibilities that are opened up when certain instances and ideas relevant to black studies encounter or come into conversation with human geography theories. While my discussion does not explore all of the debates, tenets, and possibilities within black studies and geography, I do hope this framework illustrates where further investigations might go. This interdisciplinary approach has allowed me to think about how black geographies are produced in an environment that rewards transparent space and practitioners of social and geographic domination and eschews black spatial struggles. I outline some of the ways the production of space, particularly within the discipline of geography and traditional spatial conceptualizations, fosters discourses that equate blackness with subordination, the ungeographic, and metaphor. And I suggest that, while this discursive marginalization is certainly powerful, it does not prevent the making of black geographies if we seek out other interdisciplinary analytical tools to enlarge how we understand uneven social processes. I follow this with a discussion of the work of Neil Smith and Édouard Glissant to begin to "fill in the conceptual abyss between metaphorical and material space," but also to take seriously the ways in which Glissant's poetics-politics put forward new geographic demands.[18] There is some urgency here, if we want to make sense of, and recognize, the ways in which black struggles—evident in language, poetics, politics, musics, and the built environment—are real responses to real inequalities. Black geographies are often unimaginable because we assume they do not really have any valuable material referents, that they are words rather than places, or that their materiality is always already fraught with discourses of dispossession. So, what happens if these places, spaces, words, and experiences are imaginable and complex geographies, which have always existed before our very eyes? Can they lead to a different spatialized politics?

## EN ROUTE TO DEEP SPACE AND A POETICS OF LANDSCAPE

Finding and recognizing black geographies is difficult, not only because sociospatial denial, objectification, and capitalist value systems render them invisible, but also because the places and spaces of blackness are adversely shaped by the basic rules of traditional geographies. Prevailing geographic rules have a stake in the ghettoization of difference and/or the systemic concealment of physical locations that map this difference. Transatlantic slavery, which will be expanded upon in the following chapters, provides a striking example of how the physical landscape and geographic knowledges, together, suppressed, imprisoned, and spatialized the black population. Thus, the production of black spaces in the diaspora is tied to locations that were and are explicitly produced in conjunction with race, racism, captivity, and economic profit. Traditional geographies did, and arguably still do, *require* black displacement, black placelessness, black labor, and a black population that submissively stays "in place."[19] Enforcing black placelessness/captivity was central to processes of enslavement and the physical geographies of the slave system. Slavery concealed a black sense of place and the possibility of "black geographers" through punishment, dehumanization, and racist discourses, which undermined (but did not prevent) black knowledges. This means, of course, that while black people certainly occupied, experienced, and constructed place, black geographies were (and sometimes still are) rendered unintelligible: racial captivity assumes geographic confinement; geographic confinement assumes a despatialized sense of place; a despatialized sense of place assumes geographic inferiority; geographic inferiority warrants racial captivity. Or, unruly deviant bodies do not have the capacity to produce space and effectively participate in geographic progress; unruly deviant bodies should be kept "in place." Black geographies, ostensibly, do not make sense in a world that validates spatial processes and progress through domination and social disavowal. I therefore think it is important to begin to address some of the key ways black geographies can be recognized, and are produced, in landscapes of domination. This will demonstrate, consequently, that black imaginations and mappings are evidence of the struggle over social space.

I am interested in working across black studies and human geography because these philosophical, conceptual, and empirical approaches to race and geography remain somewhat oppositional: these knowledges are rarely described as overlapping, despite the axiomatic connections between traditional geopolitical objectives of inclusion, exclusion, land-possession, and imperialism. The black subject and black communities are rarely given any formal academic geographic relevancy, whether in terms of a black way of interpreting the world, analyses of black places, a black politics of location, or black senses of place as *mutual to* other forms of understanding, politicizing, and mapping the world. The disciplinary distances between black studies and human geography often crudely repeat archaic geographic aims, valuing white, patriarchal, and European understandings of space over the work of nonwhite geographers and geographies. Connecting black studies and human geography opens up three meaningful points: first, as mentioned, are the ways in which disciplinary and epistemological desires privilege traditional geographic options; second, are the ways in which traditional geographic aims in fact illustrate how blackness and black subjectivity are implicit to the production of space; and finally, are the ways in which alternative imaginary and real formulations of space and place disrupt and augment existing geographic narratives and maps.

It has been argued that the reasons for the disconnection between black studies/black lives and academic geographic investigations are located within the discipline of human geography. In the special issue of *The Professional Geographer,* which is subtitled "Race, Racism and Geography," several authors explicitly or implicitly suggest that race is "marginalized and fragmented within geography."[20] What each of the essays makes clear is that race is not completely absent from geographic investigations—in recent years in particular, "race" has been a critical analytical category for some geographers. Rather, the critique these human geography theorists impart is that race is not integrated into wide-ranging understandings of spatial power and geographers' commitment to social justice: "no aspect of the discipline, and no spatiality, has escaped racialization" yet racist practices, discourses, colonialist heritages, and whiteness "permeate the epistemological foundations of geography and the institutional structures and practices that shape [its] work environment."[21] And while several of the authors contributing to "Race, Racism and Geography" do not focus on black lives specifically, they do outline how race/racism is segregated or underacknowledged due to disciplinary practices. In this way, they provide a glimpse into where black geographies fit, or do not fit, within spatial analyses: the long commitment of geography and its practitioners to patriarchal and imperialist projects, such as mapping, exploration, conquest, and domination; the ease with which nonwhite women, men, and children are excluded from canonical geographic investigations and/or limited to *objects* of study (oddities in the seamless white landscape), rather than relevant geographic *subjects* (producing, critiquing, and writing human geographies); the paucity of nonwhite women and men within geography departments; sexual and racial epistemological and physical segregations; and, the lingering positivism implicit in geographic investigations, which tends to document racial inequality without analyzing other genealogical and heterogeneous processes of racialization, race, and difference.[22]

What is both troubling and telling about the disconnection between human geography and black studies are the ways in which this gap perceptibly augments traditional spatial patterns that strategically arrange and define the planet from a unitary vantage point: if black people and communities are left out of, or are simply objects in, geographic studies, they are inevitably cast as unavailable or unreliable geographers and geographic subjects; black knowledges, experiences, and maps remain subordinate to and outside other traditional geographic investigations. Thus, the few critical geographers who are committed to analyzing and dismantling the geographies of race and racism suggest that while the world is fundamentally racialized, "race" is rarely incorporated into research projects, the classroom, institutions, or the everyday conceptualizations (and consequently the real production) of space and place.[23] This omission produces a cycle in which knowledges seem to bifurcate: traditional geographic patterns and practitioners organize the outer world and subordinate difference and non-dominant communities; knowledges and experiences are spatialized accordingly, as present-white/absent-black or dominant-white/subordinate-black; blackness is perceived as inevitably, or naturally, ungeographic and/or ghettoized. The "natural" center (of knowledge, of place, of ethical geographies, for example) is reified as "naturally" *central to* geographic explorations, while difference/blackness is either absent, or only understood as outside of, rather than mutual to, the production of space.[24]

Geographic needs—patriarchal, economic, imperial, academic, and sexual needs—therefore repetitively enact racism (not simply "race") and other discriminatory practices, enforcing what Ruth Wilson Gilmore describes as "a death-dealing displacement of difference into hierarchies that organize relations within and between the planet's sovereign political territories."[25] Gilmore's call to racialize geographic patterns is useful in that she clarifies that race and racism are *serious* geographic projects and processes—despite the disciplinary disconnection. The philosophical and analytical disconnection between "black" and "geography" undermines the very real, and very meaningful, ways in which the world is organized. This is crucial because the ways in which geographic knowledges are produced and materialized in the built environment in fact synthesizes the ostensibly bifurcated geographic paths. Gilmore, then, offers one way to reframe race, racism, geography, and the discipline of human geography by illustrating how academic, ontological, representational, and material locations are meaningfully connective because blackness "is a spatially and temporally differentiated produced, and *real*, condition of existence and category of analysis."[26]

The connection between geography and blackness is crucial to identifying some of the conditions under which race/racism are necessary to the production of space. The interplay between black experiences in the diaspora, past and present, and spatial organization, are tightly bound in two interconnected ways: black historical and contemporary subjects have not only contributed to the strenuous physical production of space and place in the diaspora (through slave labor, indentured labor, and racially and sexually differentiated labor economies), they also have an investment in the meanings and makings of place due to racial displacement, forced exile, homelessness, rented and owned dwellings, poverty, integration, segregation, political sites, professionalization, community gatherings and locales, nationalism(s), activism, and globalization.

The material physicality of the diaspora—I am thinking of plantations, houses, churches, streets, fields, factories, shops, museums, offices, and so forth—and the negotiation of racialized spaces within the diaspora advance the key ways black subjects have contributed to physical and imaginary geographic projects. Black women, men, and children have been, forcefully and not, implicated in the uneven development of space because overarching traditional geographic projects require that they be placed and displaced. That is, black subjects have to "go" and inhabit somewhere. Empirical analyses in particular illuminate the ways in which racial differences are reflected through material conditions and the impact of this upon geographic opportunities in Canada, the United Kingdom, and the United States.[27] Empirical studies, while differing in subject matter and method, show how patterns of racial domination are fundamentally geographic. Race becomes attached to place in detrimental ways because local conditions reify and naturalize identity-difference: black women live in "bad"/black neighborhoods, have unhealthy children, restricted employment opportunities and resources, longer work days, and so on. Or: polluted + inexpensive regions = unhealthy/black dwellings = sub-human/sub-woman/bad-mother.[28] Indeed, some (not all) empirical geographic studies tend to environmentally determine particular "races" in particular "places." As critical geographer Don Mitchell notes, environmental determinism was one of the key ways some European and U.S. human geographers "scientifically" documented human differences and justified imperialist ambitions in the late-nineteenth and early-twentieth centuries.[29] And some current empirical studies, at least to me, evince and endorse this ongoing imperial project—albeit on subtler, sometimes less obvious "imperial" terms—by nodding to and reifying the overwhelming power of the naturalization of identity and place, the knowability of "different" bodies and their "different" attendant geographies.

Importantly, how we know, write, and document space and place can contribute to processes of discriminatory, class-based racialization—again, ideas are turned into spaces: phenotype *can* reflect place and place *can* reflect phenotype. Or, why *are* all the black people living in that particular neighborhood? The socioeconomic mapping of blackness, the unjust and economically driven naturalization of difference, shows the material base of race/racism, the conditions under which many subaltern populations live and have lived, and the spatial constitution of socially produced categories. As mentioned, this mapping of blackness is also limiting and deterministic, in that it de-emphasizes other spatial experiences and imaginations that intersect with geographic materiality, affordability, and geometry. Black geographic togetherness and community ties also identify, for example, the sociocultural pull *away from* what bell hooks describes as terrifying and deathly representations of whiteness, or, the sociocultural pull *into* black spaces, such as familial-based migrations, cultural commitments, safe spaces, and the locations of churches, entertainment venues, and community and political organizations.[30] But where "they" are, as indicative of who "they" are, continues to be powerfully connected to practices of subjugation.

If systems of domination keep transparency operative and conceal other nontransparent activities (such as sites of resistance, geographies of human pain or love, locations of subversion, the place of the black everyday, or diasporic geographies), black subjects are bound up in the patterns that relegate and naturalize difference. The racialized and gendered subject—particularly those who occupy what Sylvia Wynter calls "poverty archipelagos" (the underdeveloped, the jobless, the homeless, the throwaways), those who laboriously build, work, maintain, clean, protect, re-imagine, and resist landscapes of racial differentiation and denial—are also those who are at stake in the production of space and who have paradoxically been missing from several geographic analyses.[31] A strong disciplinary synthesis asks that we think across and beyond the mapping of "man's inhumanity to man" by noting the geographic outcome of expressing, living, and representing, together, "black geographies"—as they are intimately tied to geographic domination and as they are re-presenting space.[32]

## DEEP SPACE AND THE POETICS OF LANDSCAPE

Recognizing that black subjects and communities are openly and complexly geographic, but distanced from sanctioned geographic knowledges, problematizes how we know the world and organize our knowing. Black geographies produce unsettling questions about how knowledge and ideas about race and difference are incorporated into social, political, and economic patterns. I have so far suggested that some geographic analyses tend to conceal the meaningful relationship black subjects have had with space and place and that this has resulted in reifying the ideological assumption that blackness is equated with the ungeographic and a legacy of dispossession. Even important empirical discussions that map black populations, dwellings, and representations, such as those mentioned above, often fail to attend to the ways in which black subjects articulate their positionality through selfhood. That is, those few studies which do show an interest in black geographies do not really emphasize that space is socially produced and alterable, but rather that racial difference is measurable, knowable, and indicative of dispossession. In noting these two analytical traditions within geographic investigations—overlooking and measuring blackness— it is important to return to my earlier assertion: that while these analyses are limiting, they also suggest that geographic knowledge is racialized and can tell us something about the ways in which black geographies are a response to existing spatial paradigms. Traditional geographic practices have suggested to me that we might look elsewhere, within and beyond the discipline of geography, in order to illuminate new spatial practices. That is, overlooking and measuring blackness in fact begins to reveal that there are other ways race makes itself known in the landscape. But we first

have to enter into the material landscape from a different location, perhaps using varied conceptual tools, and trust not only that all knowledges
are partial, but that all knowledges are geographic.

I want to turn to Neil Smith's discussion of deep space in order to open
up some of these concerns, specifically with reference to black studies and
the poetics of landscape, but also as a way to think about how geography,
as a discipline and a means of social organization, might be reoriented
toward more humanly workable frameworks. In the afterword to the 1990
edition of *Uneven Development: Nature, Capital and the Production of Space,*
Smith conceptualizes deep space in two interconnected ways. First, he
notes that social, economic, and political shifts of the 1980s created a series
of multiscalar respatializations. The stock market crash of 1987 and the
democratization of Eastern Europe/reunification of Germany (symbolized
by the destruction of the Berlin Wall in 1989) are geographic moments
that underline "the relativity of terrestrial space, the space of everyday life
in all its scales from the global to the local and the architectural in which,
to use Doreen Massey's metaphor, different layers of life and social landscape are sedimented onto and into each other."[33] Deep space is the *production* of space intensified and writ large, ideological and political shifts
that impact upon and organize the everyday in multiple contexts and
scales—within and across homes, factories, streets, local and world banks,
social services, military invasions, developing and overdeveloped nations,
resistance tactics, gentrification projects. In this sense, deep space identifies the immediacy, materiality, and power of Smith's larger concerns, specifically, uneven geographic development as it is perpetuated by, and lived
according to, unjust social systems. Deep space and its production, he
writes, are "crushingly real."[34]

Second, and related, deep space is imbued with sociospatial theories
produced outside the discipline of geography. The writings of Frederick
Jameson and Michel Foucault, for example, are underwritten by geographic concerns: the epoch of space, cognitive mappings, and so forth.
And Smith goes on to suggest that these geographic concerns—which are
of great interest to some within the discipline of geography—connect the
materiality of deep space with a struggle over theorizing its crushing realness. That is, the late-twentieth century "speeding up" of time-space, the
simultaneity of an expanding and shrinking world, the lives which were
lost and the lives which profited, created new analytical and political

spaces. Deep space, in its crushing realness, has also led to "subject positions," "conceptual space," "theoretical space," "contested spaces," "spaces
of negotiation," [and] "spaces of signification."[35] This reassertion of space
in social theory—Smith gives the excellent example of how "mapping
seems to cover virtually every kind of plausible translation from one text
to another"—has in part rendered the material contours of deep space
metaphoric. Yet Smith's critique of social theory is not simply a condem-
nation. Rather, he suggests that we seek out the connections between
material and metaphoric space:

> . . . it makes sense to conceive of deep spaces as combining the inherently
> social processes and produced structures of space together with the most
> superficial refractions from space in any given fixed form. Metaphorical and
> material are this inseparable in deep space yet remain distinct. To the extent
> that metaphor dominates our conceptions of space it is the latter refraction
> of fixed form that informs us; metaphorical appropriations of space are
> "real" enough but they conceal the life of deep space . . .[36]

What kind of theoretical work can deep space do for black geographies?
Before I turn to how material space, metaphoric space, and social theory
might be reimagined through black studies and human geography, I want
to suggest that investigations of deep space might also examine the political,
ideological, and economic ruptures pertinent to historical and contemporary subaltern lives. Specifically, if we trust that the important economic
and political occurrences in the 1980s intensified and corresponded with
important shifts, on the ground and in social theory, we can also look to
key geographic moments played out across the black diaspora as bringing
into focus the material workings of deep space. I am thinking specifically
about the importance of 1492 and new world expansion but also about the
civil and human rights movements of the 1960s.[37] The former, which ush-
ered in exploration, conquest, and transatlantic slavery, and the latter, which
sought to desegregate, decolonize, and liberate, exposed the limits of transparent space and reoriented the meaning of human social theories. And
these moments were markedly geographic: new maps were developed; big-
ger, better, slave ships were produced; European subjects expanded into,
exploited, and made cartographically intelligible, "newer" worlds; lands
and resources were lost and claimed; aboriginal communities were destroyed

and colonized; escapes were plotted and charted; slave labor built roads, plantations, houses; material places were boycotted; marches were organized; nationalisms were heightened; women and men were incarcerated; women and men demanded new forms of citizenship; colonial political systems were challenged. I am suggesting, then, that it is important to consider the ways in which deep space is also recognizable in these diasporic ruptures. Here, the contestations over space, place, and race are heightened, worked out across the soil and within and across nations and communities.

With these sociogeographic shifts in mind, Smith's concerns also provide a useful entry point into how black geographies might be differently theorized—inside and outside the discipline of geography. Space cannot be simply metaphorical, cognitive, or imaginary, as this risks undermining those underlying experiences that are unrealized, very real, and critical of real spatial inequalities. Deep space, then, offers black geographies exciting spatial possibilities—possibilities that parallel Édouard Glissant's poetics and politicization of landscape discussed in my introductory remarks: a serious engagement with the ways in which the production of space is connected to expression and difficult material conditions and the development of a spatial grammar that unhinges space from the limiting demands of colonialism, practices of domination, and human objectification.[38] Glissant's poetics of landscape attaches the imaginative to the social; it demands a gathering of sociospatial processes that reposition the black subject in and amongst that which has been "wiped out" and signs "in the everyday world."[39] Glissant's poetics engage a geographic struggle that brings together the everyday, the invisible, and the discursive/metaphorical—a political articulation of three-dimensionality and expressive cultures.

Deep space and a poetics of landscape *reposition* black geographies through taking notice of the ways in which space and place are fundamentally tied to the material landscape and daily social processes. Black geographies, imaginative and material, are critical of spatial inequalities, evidence of geopolitical struggles, and demonstrative of real and possible geographic alternatives. Here we can note ideas, places, and concepts such as: "the middle passage," "the underground," Ralph Ellison's "invisible man," Houstan A. Baker Jr. and Marlene Nourbese Philip's black (w)hole(s), the slave ship, Dionne Brand's "a map to the door of no return," bell hooks's "margin" and "homeplace," Carole Boyce Davies's "politics of location," and Paul Gilroy's "the black Atlantic."[40] These black geographies, while often cited as conceptual tools, are also political and material in that they draw on, and require an engagement with, everyday spaces of blackness. The interconnections between the metaphorical and the material (for example real and symbolic underground[s]) bring into focus the terrain of struggle inside and outside social theory.

Let me discuss some examples. A key historical example of the complexities black geographies illuminate is the Underground Railroad. Both a material and psychic map, the Underground Railroad contained and signified secret knowledge and secret knowledge sharing. These black geographies and travels remained secreted because disclosing the routes to the public would "close the slightest avenue" to black freedoms.[41] The Underground Railroad was an emancipatory lifeline if untold/unwritten, and site of violence/death if told/written. A covert operation, which was developed through human networks rather than scientific/cartographic writings, the Underground Railroad illustrates how historical black geographies are developed alongside clandestine geographic-knowledge practices. These practices signaled that spaces of black liberation were invisibly mapped across the United States and Canada and that this invisibility is, in fact, a real and meaningful geography. The life and death of black subjects was dependent on the unmapped knowledges, while the routes gave fugitives, Frederick Douglass wrote, "invisible agency."[42] Continuing in a different direction, the middle passage is, obviously, not simply a theoretical concept: it is a body of water and time on a body of water, which is interconnected to black imaginative work and different forms of black politics and black travels and exiles. The meanings of the middle passage are simultaneously multiscalar and contextual. It is a geography that matters because it carries with it (and on it) all sorts of historically painful social encounters and all sorts of contemporary social negotiations.[43]

Additionally, what is considered the invisibility of black spaces and places is spatialized through deep space and a poetics of landscape. That is, the politics of black geographies expose racial disavowal on spatial terms: what is seemingly not there, is; what is geographically missing for some is geographically relevant to others. Invisibility, alone, will not do the work of black geographies. Ralph Ellison's invisible man is *not really* invisible; rather he is an "imperceptible" social, political, and geographic subject who is rendered invisible due to his highly visible bodily context as a black U.S. man: he is "*un*visible," inside and outside the novel.[44] His geographies are both impossible (because he is invisible, an incomplete citizen, black) and possible (because he is an invisibly present subject). This unvisiblity became markedly apparent, a lived geography, during the sanitation strike in Memphis, Tennessee, in 1968, when the workers— under armed police surveillance—carried and wore signs that read "I *AM* A MAN."[45] The workers spatially constituted the meaning of black masculinity, and labor, on terms that articulated possession, repossession, and dispossession. Racial disavowal is seeable, recognizable, and ontological. The invisible, the unspoken, the unremembered, the impossible, to be sure, spatially evidence blackness.

Deep space and the poetics of landscape are also relevant to understanding the places of blackness because these geographies are all too often positioned as an invisible, metaphorical, and/or conceptual tool that relationally advances academic geographic analyses. For example, several geographic engagements with identity/difference, in responding to recurring racial and sexual crises within the discipline of human geography, position the black subject, and her/his politics of location, as symbolic (rather than real) interruptions in the landscape. Black social theorists such as Stuart Hall, Paul Gilroy, bell hooks, and Frantz Fanon advance several investigations into the production of racialized and gendered social spaces, especially vis-à-vis the scale of the nonwhite body/subject. The discussion of the margin, homeplace, whiteness, and oppositional politics by hooks is particularly popular, as is hooks herself (as geography and as a body scale). And I have argued elsewhere that several of these geographic investigations of blackness and black culture stop at bell hooks: this conceptual endgame is detrimental to geographic investigations in that it reduces black geographies, black feminist geographies, and arguably hooks herself, to a transparent visual illusion—the black female body, knowable and knowing, and unaccompanied, answers the question to difference while allowing theorists to disregard heterogeneous ways of being black.[46]

Through symbolic-conceptual positioning, the black subject (often, but not always, a black woman) is theorized as a concept (rather than a human or geographic subject) and is consequently cast as momentary evidence of the violence of abstract space, an interruption in transparent space, a different (all-body) answer to otherwise undifferentiated geographies. Spatially and conceptually, the black female subject is briefly granted one or two sentences to support "arguments about difference and diversity" and raise some "painful questions" about traditional geographic patterns.[47] This, of course, points to broader feminist debates around social differences and politics and the ways in which women of color are included to bolster arguments (and therefore fulfill a particular inclusive antiracist agenda) but remain, in the end, "too alien to comprehend."[48] Black subjects are rarely, then, critically analyzed for the ways in which they are mapped and cited in order to "flesh out" specific disciplinary, and interdisciplinary, knowledges. These practices, which locate and say race, for example, without thinking about black geographic subjects who are committed to dismantling geographies of privilege and pain, evidence intellectual practices of conceptual ghettoization. Indeed, the margin becomes a real, and really conceptual, place. That this work, of locating/citing blackness, is not also identified as territoriality—adding a bit of blackness, raising some momentary painful questions, saying and marking gender alongside race and class—is simultaneously problematic and unsurprising.

Although the academic engagement with blackness (and social differences in general) in human geography is relatively new and potentially progressive, the resistance to a serious engagement with black histories, black subjectivities, black conditions of existence, and black geographies on, inside, *and* outside of the body, continues. The displacement of difference is perpetuated because when and if blackness and black people are taken up, they are employed as metaphorical annexes—often a unitary black body that is detached from the legacy of sexism and racism and other diasporic conditions. Michael Keith and Steve Pile thus write that the work of Paul Gilroy in *There Ain't No Black in the Union Jack*, is, most *usefully*, imaginative work; the black diaspora is a third space, which is produced vis-à-vis discursive geographies. While they are certainly correct in identifying Gilroy's supranational mappings as "cultural fusions" and black dialogue connections, their *phrasing* gives way to a reading of black geographies that insists that a black sense of place, and a black theory of space, is not only devoid of an intellectual history, but that the very materiality of black political geographies are only representable vis-à-vis "expressive cultures" (musics, literatures, poetry, etc.). Of course black political geographies are expressive, but the authors fail to see (or cite) expressive cultures and fail to imagine how expressive cultures might also connect to the material landscape. What is troubling is not that Keith and Pile misread

Gilroy—I do not think they do—but that they spatialize his intellectual work as unaccompanied by other black theorists and suggest that black geographies are primarily *un*representable in the everyday; they cannot seem to imagine black imaginations or expressions as spatially represent-able. The "imagined spatiality of diaspora politics," in their reading, takes precedence over daily forms of black existence that connect the material and the imaginary and the past and the present.[49] This reading, I suggest, de-spatializes black expressive cultures, because it refuses to see or site where this expression is taking place and how it comes to take place/space. In *There Ain't No Black in the Union Jack,* in fact, Gilroy places and spaces out black geopolitics through the site of London: in courtrooms, in news-papers, in family units, in political parties, on football teams, in dance halls and music contests, in music-making, in protests.[50] The Union Jack is real and discursive; its meanings and materiality, together, intersect with black sociogeographic patterns. Importantly, Gilroy considers the ways in which the spaces and places of London are reconfigured, and therefore point to significant political concerns, because the city—its soil, its buildings, its institutions and transportation routes—is inhabited by black subjects.

I suggest that the spatial strengths and the spatial imaginary in black narratives and theory return the reader to important questions about the production of space: why are space and place so significant to black theo-rists and authors? And in what ways do black subjects critically respond to spatial constraints and ideologies? Geographies of the everyday that are normally undermined or prohibited by transparent space and traditional racial and sexual geographic inequalities are re-expressed in a medium that can bear to take on difference: black fiction, black theory, black musics, black geographies, black imaginations. The writing up of black geogra-phies presents new, and old, patterns, which shed light on real social con-ditions and identities that are otherwise deemed irrelevant to traditional human geographies: the site of memory, exodus, highway chile, going to the territory, submarine unity, migrations of the subject, tough geography, rhythm nation, fear of a black planet, the wretched of the earth, a very small place, paradise, daughters of the dust, dust tracks on the road, the color-line.[51] So what might be thought of as merely the black-symbolic or black-talk is in fact unmistakably geographic, and imaginatively real, in multiple ways. These black geographies are deep spaces and poetic land-scapes, which not only gesture to the difficulties of existing geographies and analyses, but also reveal the kinds of tools that are frequently useful to black social critics: books, ideas, maps, places, musics, and geographic ideas, spaces and places that can mark and release the self from what Dorothy Allison calls processes of "public silence and private terror."[52] These alternative geographic analyses are evident, most obviously, in geographically rigorous texts such as the fictional and theoretical work of Dionne Brand and Toni Morrison, but also in spatially driven analyses, such as C. L. R. James's *Beyond a Boundary,* Melvin Dixon's *Ride Out the Wilderness,* and Audre Lorde's "master's tools–master's house" black feminist critique.[53]

Deep space and a poetics of landscape reframes a conceptual space, such as W. E. B. Du Bois's influential "color-line," as produced (and therefore lived) with and beyond metaphor. This color-line is, among other things, material evidence of double consciousness, a black sociological interruption in U.S. sociological imaginations, a study on black positionality and white-black contact (including Du Bois's *own* politics of location), a commentary on the spatial and economic legacy of slavery and North-South U.S. regionalism, a geographic tool with which several black critics continue to engage in order to open, and reevaluate, philosophical debates.[54] The color-line is material, philosophical, and an analysis of what it means to know and re-imagine "place": it draws lines, separates, criminalizes, wavers, and disappears.[55] In *The Souls of Black Folk,* Du Bois continually reminds us that the color-line is also manifested by and produced in relation to the physical environment, particular and thematic racial materialities. Buried things, spiritual worlds, the Veil (which separates and racializes), wooden schoolhouses, great fireplaces, Africa, America, universities, plantations, slave-quarters, are documented in the text as the materiality of the color-line and social divisions.[56] The text is a journey through different regions of the United States, wherein the author makes a series of "stops" in order to map his surroundings, account for his conceptual concerns through the landscape, and extend the immediate geography beyond transparency. Du Bois therefore provides a kind of geographic genealogy, which couples black geographies with black knowledges in order to expose how U.S. democracy was laboriously built up, and the ways in which the production of this particular nation-space is uneven. The color-line is an intellectual and material geography, a line that separates, yet connects, what Du Bois calls "two worlds," in the United States:

Four and six bob-tailed thoroughbreds rolled [the plantation owner's] coaches to town . . . parks and groves were laid out, rich with flower and vine, and in the midst stood the low wide-halled "big-house," with its porch and columns and great fire-places. And yet with all this there was something sordid . . . for was not all this show and tinsel built upon a groan? "This land was a little Hell," said a ragged, brown, and grave-faced man to me. We were seated near a roadside blacksmith-shop, and behind was the bare ruin of some master's home. "I've seen niggers drop dead in the furrow, but they were kicked aside, and the plough never stopped. And down in the guard-house, there's where the blood ran."[57]

Here two worlds—the big house and the guard house—are understood together. They were both built upon "groan," spatially produced by black slave labor. And they are inflected with black blood and death. The color-line is sordid; it delineates a land of hell, where social and racial divisions are marked in the landscape. If, as Du Bois noted, "the problem of the Twentieth Century is the problem of the color-line," was he not also suggesting that the problem of the twentieth century is necessarily connected to geography?[58] Is the color-line an urgent geographic expression of the displacement of difference, a poetics-politics which sites/sights "physical extent fused through with social intent"?[59]

## TERRAINS OF STRUGGLE: FANON, MORRISON, HALL, AND BRAND

The writings of W. E. B. Du Bois demonstrate how ideas—specifically ideas about racial-sexual difference—get turned into space. Importantly, *The Souls of Black Folk* combines classificatory racial geographies with Du Bois's philosophical commentary. He therefore provides a response to the ungeographic, invisibility, and marginality, but links them to ways in which race and dispossession are inevitably part of early-twentieth-century U.S. landscapes. Deep space and the poetics of landscape add new contours to geographic inquiries such as this, asking us to take seriously the ways in which spatial expressions are wrapped up in everyday struggles and critiques. I want to delve a little deeper into the interdisciplinary philosophical openings Smith, Glissant, and others make possible by turning to the work of Frantz Fanon, Stuart Hall, Dionne Brand, and Toni Morrison.

I turn to these writers not because they are the only way to develop deep space and the poetics of landscape, but because they have inspired my own understanding of black geographies. And I hope they motivate other geographic stories through the ways in which they show how alterable, and vexed, geography is. These thinkers insist on an alternative vantage point and therefore a different sense of how geography is, and might be, lived out. While the self-evident workings of transparent space have normalized uneven geographies, it is important to remember that they are also experienced, and mapped, vis-à-vis different (in this case black) vantage points. It follows, then, that new or different geographic demands are always *taking place*. These demands not only document how displacement is differently lived out by black subjects on the ground, they also reify how the production of space, and the project of geographic exclusion, while unjust, can inspire a different kind of spatial politics.

Before I turn to a discussion of Frantz Fanon, it is important to recall that his relationship with and understanding of colonial spaces—particularly in *The Wretched of the Earth* and *Black Skin, White Masks*—are underwritten by colonial attempts to "fix the geography of social power . . . and constricting the compass of human self-knowledge."[60] That is, geography for Fanon is not simply bodily, or "black skin"; geography is unquestionably human geography. And in Fanon's work the crushingly real intensities of deep space are evident. He is concerned with national black liberation movements and anticolonial strategies of the mid-twentieth century— the diasporic ruptures I mentioned earlier—and the ways in which these political contestations are also structured by psychic and physical geographies. That is, soil, nation, and race matter greatly to Fanon; human liberation is understood in tandem with a radical remaking of human geographies. The racial geographies in Fanon's texts—the oppositional, segregated, white/black, uneven, absolutely *different* spatialities—are, as Ato Sekyi-Otu notes, palpitating "with life, human, all-too-human life."[61] I signal this geographic humanism and Sekyi-Otu because below I only touch on a small section of Fanon's discussion, specifically what the Fanonian black body brings to bear on sociospatial organization. However, I keep in mind that the body is necessarily part of a human struggle, identifiable unattained liberties, and therefore signals that black geographies are human geographies, not simply skin. To put it another way, nonwhite

phenotype imparts traditional geographic organization; it is a seeable justification for apartheid and unfreedom, which is underscored by humanness and ontological knowledge.

Of central importance to black geographies are what Frantz Fanon describes as the historio-racial schema and the bodily (or corporeal) schema.
These two concepts advance how space, place, identification, and history
collapse to inscribe the black body as racial Other; they also illustrate
Fanon's human desires—for and beyond his body. The bodily schema
identifies a "composition of [the] *self* as a body in the middle of the spatial and temporal world."[62] The bodily schema is not, according to Fanon,
imposed on the subject; "it is, rather, a definitive structuring of the self
and of the world—definitive because it creates a real dialectic between
[the] body and the world."[63] This ontology is described by Sylvia Wynter
as an implicit knowledge, a pre-given schema, one "specific to what it is
like *physically* to be human."[64] What Fanon offers to black geographies
through his introduction of the bodily schema is the mutuality of identity,
self, and place. This mutuality brings into focus the alterability of space
and place from the *perspective* of a terrain of struggle because the black
body, as Fanon reminds us, repeatedly encounters the white world—his
bodily schema is threatened, his physically human sense of place is reoriented on strikingly racial terms.

The historio-racial schema is described by Fanon as the ideologies and
forces of racism that "imprison" his body. He writes that his blackness and
his ethnic characteristics dislocate his humanity, forcing him to recognize
his black "place" in the world.[65] The deep spaces of black geographies,
cited by Fanon as sites of his potentiality and existence, are recast by dominant culture as transparently invisible, or unvisible, through the racial
and racist cultural texts that attach themselves to black bodies and psy-
ches. Fanon writes, then: "I was told to stay within bounds, to go back
where I belonged."[66] Identity, place, and existence thus risk being violently produced by a historio-racial schema. When he is seen and named,
his body and his skin impart an intelligible, racialized, subjugated history:
"Look," "Mama, see the Negro!," "I was battered down by tom-toms, can-
nibalism, intellectual deficiency," and so forth.[67] His body is consequently
"sprawled out, distorted, recolored."[68] The idea of a black place and a black
sense of place are reduced to distortion, hypervisibility, and placelessness;

race signs, metaphors for blackness, absolutely define his location; Fanon becomes visibly ungeographic. The self—and therefore black human geographies—are defined by an unwelcoming white world determined to imprison and objectify. More specifically, the sprawled out and distorted body, and the Fanonian self, is "hemmed in . . . learns to stay in his place, and not to go beyond certain limits."[69] At the same time, the colonial body-self continually encounters the material landscape itself: "a world divided into compartments, a motionless Manicheistic world, a world of statues: the statue of the general who carried out the conquest, the statue of the engineer who built the bridge; a world which is sure of itself, which crushes with its stones the backs flayed out by whips: this is the colonial world."[70] To return to Sekyi-Otu, "the body is at once sequestered and forcefully given space."[71]

These dual schemas, working simultaneously to mark/imprison and undo black human geographies, shape how Fanon comes to describe the physical world. Importantly, black geographies become principally apparent through the historio-racial schema: the captive, the dispossessed, the ungeographic; segregation, death, dehumanization, public punishment; lynching, Negroes whipped in the streets, strikers cut down by machine guns.[72] Geographically, the "multiplicity of the spaces assigned to the black body is at once belied by, and yet is a function of, the "totalitarian character" of colonial coercion and racial segregation."[73] What do we do with the repetitive colonial reassertion of absolute—historio-racial—space? How do we reinvent and imagine black geographies as real physical human geographies? If we, and Fanon, have come to know, understand, and map the world according to disavowal and violence, *where* does this take us? How do we spatialize Fanon's perspective of struggle and his experiential (racial-geographic) knowledges?

There are several ways to begin answering these big questions. But I want to focus on one specific possibility: by noting the ways in which Fanon presents the mutuality of place, identity, and humanness. To begin, Fanon's attention to the material landscape is telling as he identifies sites of subjugation and loss, dispossession, and violence as implicit, rather than marginal, to sociospatial order. That is, the three-dimensional, racialized world is named, mapped, and peopled, not solely for its profitable imperialist reach and transparency, but for what these discourses communicate to the body, the soul, and the world: whippings, machine guns, nausea, corporeal malediction, the train, blood, Africa, industrialized big buildings, the shadow of your native country, "he is afraid of the fear that the world would feel if the world knew."[74] Fanon inhabits and populates the world on new terms, drawing on his immediate experiences and the poetic and dramatic writings of his colleagues; he discloses the violence of the human land-scape. As I have argued elsewhere, Fanon's geographies are particularly meaningful in *The Wretched of the Earth,* as he describes in explicit detail the ways in which inhabiting colonial spaces—and ethically understand-ing place—can and cannot correspond with politicized emancipatory strategies.[75] Indeed, Fanon gives us an important clue to moving toward a new humanism in *The Wretched of the Earth,* which is dependent on rethinking the material landscape through what Neil Smith calls "the abro-gation of boundaries."[76]

In *Black Skin, White Masks,* each site Fanon encounters gives rise to a different sense of identity, a different kind of self, and a different sense of place.[77] His positionality and status shift from moment to moment, com-prising some, or all, of his identities and identifications as a black man, an intellectual, a writer, a psychiatrist, a black object, a black subject, an activist, a poet: "In the world through which I travel I am endlessly creat-ing myself."[78] The flexibility of identity, self, and place returns us to the dialectic between Fanon's physical body and his world(s). The dialectic, while flexible, also reveals how the imprisoning workings of colonialism and race are detrimental to the "relation of coexistence" between the self, the body, and the world.[79]

This mutual construction of identity, self, and place is crucial because for Fanon it requires not only that black subjects be recognized as already human (my black consciousness is not a lack, it *is*), but that their sense of place is different due to the ways this humanity is required, under racism, to be lived as objectification.[80] This invites respatialization because he argues that "black" is not simply bodily or object, but that the black body comprises a self who desires equality on several geographic scales, from the body and beyond. To return to Édouard Glissant, forging a relationship with and writing geography, in part, brings the subject into being; body liberation coincides with dismantling how and where specific bodies are hemmed in. Fanon thus writes a future poetics-politics, his soul "as im-mense as the world . . . deep as the deepest rivers."[81] A black sense of place, then, is produced by and through long processes of racialization; it is not necessarily a bound or unintelligible place for the black subject, but a condition of "all-too-human" existence, which is understood through the displacement of difference and future possibilities.

I have spent some time outlining the tensions between Frantz Fanon's two schemas because I think that his intellectual work poses two important geographic questions: What happens to the cartography and understanding of the world when it is continually re-imagined through and beyond the legacy of race and racism? What are the implications of acknowledging this different (black human) worldview, and how do black subjects contribute to its meaning(s)? These questions add another layer to a poetics of landscape by respatializing and recoding what is considered the natural order of social space and the natural order of human hierarchy. More specifically, the ideas Fanon is concerned with not only locate black geographies in and amongst a tight racial grid (historio-racial schemas, landscapes of whiteness), they also depend on the flexibility of identity and place. These ideas, coupled with Fanon's assertion of his humanity, rupture traditional geographies by insinuating a different geographic language into the landscape, a language not always predicated on ownership and conquest. This re-ordering of geographic knowledges, peoples, and landscapes opens up new and radical spaces for discovery and different sites of being. Thus, geographic struggles transform—philosophically and materially—blackness and black humanity in the world; they map subaltern subjects with and through existing spaces and also call into question obligatory geographic rules that perpetuate injustice.

Stuart Hall's discussion of "new ethnicities" adds to Fanon's discussion by emphasizing more recent shifts in cultural studies and cultural politics. Indeed, Hall's discussion of black identities hints at the incompleteness of the historio-racial schema, exposing it as a changing discursive fiction that is called into question by black writers, filmmakers, and theorists.[82] The essay "New Ethnicities," which takes up black identity and representation, signals what Hall describes as "the struggle around positionalities": "the end of the essential black subject . . . a recognition that the central issues of race always appear historically in articulation, in a formation, with other categories and divisions and are constantly crossed and re-crossed by the categories of class, of gender and ethnicity."[83] Hall's attention to positionality is important in that it is not only gesturing to ongoing debates in critical social theory (within feminism, cultural studies, black studies,

queer studies) but also because he insists that selfhood and biography create and politicize this positionality. The historio-racial schema is relocated
by Hall, undone and respatialized when there is

> a recognition that we all speak from a particular place, out of a particular
> history, out of a particular culture, without being contained by that posi-
> tion as "ethnic artists" or film-makers. We are all, in that sense, ethnically
> located and our ethnic identities are crucial to our subjective sense of who
> we are. But this is also a recognition that this is not an ethnicity that is
> doomed to survive . . . only by marginalizing, displacing and forgetting
> other ethnicities.[84]

Hall's "the end of the essential black subject" underscores the complexities
of black subjectivities, or more specifically their particularities. The politicization and representation of "difference" involves a complication of the
category of "race" and the category of "black." For Hall, new ethnicities
are produced in conjunction with location—historical, geographic, cultural,
economic, and so on—as this location is understood vis-à-vis an alternative *sense* of place, one predicated on difference and diversity. That is, a
decoupling of ethnicity "as it functions in the dominant discourse, from
its equivalence with nationalism, imperialism, racism and the state."[85]
Detaching the category of "black" from natural or essentialist ideologies
and places reveals the nuances of sociospatial processes; it puts categories
such as place, ethnicity, difference, and blackness in motion rather than
repeating colonial displacements, historio-racial schemas, crude social classifications, and geographic stasis.

Hall's argument pivots on black representational politics, which I would
suggest are also underwritten by the poetics of landscape: how black communities represent themselves, how black cinema represents black social
differences, how political representation is connected to those static mis-
representations Frantz Fanon finds so restrictive. I would add to these forms
of representation: how black people represent the world around them,
how they represent "place" in a world that has profited from black displacement, and how black geographic representation is recast through a
struggle, rather than a complacency, with space and place. New ethnicities
bring into play a different sense of place not only through exposing how
axes of difference—race, sex, sexuality, age, gender, ability, class—inform

and reorder transparent space but also through denaturalizing space and place. New ethnicities negotiate existing geographic patterns and also undo the seemingly natural connections between blackness and class-based spatialization: for example, the (black) workplace, as transparently knowable, will not do as a geopolitical site; the workplace and the workers are not only shifting, sexual, gendered, classed, and raced, they are critical sites through which the black self is both racially and experientially produced and called into question.

Note the denaturalization of space and place, as well as the ways in which a different sense of place advances Dionne Brand's geographic concerns in her essay "Job":

> It was that tiny office in the back of a building on Keele Street. I had called the morning before, looking for a job, and the man answering remarked on that strong Scottish name of my putative father and told me to come right in and the job would be mine. Yes, it was that tiny office in the back of a building on Keele when I was turning eighteen, and I dressed up in my best suit outfit with high heels and lipstick and ninety-seven pounds of trying hard desperate feminine heterosexuality, wanting to look like the man on the phone's imagination so I could get the job. When I went to the tiny office and saw the smile of the man on the phone fade and disappear because all of a sudden it needed experience or was just given to somebody else . . . Yes, it was that man on the phone, that office on Keele Street, the man's imagination for a Scottish girl he could molest as she filed papers in the tiny office, it was that wanting to cry in my best suit and high heels I could barely walk in and the lipstick my sister helped me to put on straight and plucked my eyebrows and made me wear foundation cream in order, I suppose, to dull the impact of my blackness so that man in the tiny office would give me that job. . . . That I could ever think of getting such a job, even so small and mean a job, that some white man could forget himself and at least see me as someone he could exploit . . . My sister worked in the kitchens of hospitals and that is where I did find a job the next week, and that is where we waited out the ebb and flow of favour and need in this white place.[86]

I have quoted Brand's concerns at length because, like most of her work, "Job" maps a critique and reversal of transparent space. If we begin reading the quotation vis-à-vis Stuart Hall's "new ethnicities," that is, with Brand/ the speaker as a complex black subject who is *in articulation with* essentialist modern categories, black geographies take shape according to her position-particularities: she is named and historicized; she is on the telephone as a presumed white/Scottish girl; she is performing lipsticked, high-heeled heteronormativity; she is imagining white desire; she is exploitable; she is eighteen; she has a working sister; she is, upon entering the office, no longer racially and sexually desirable; she is reflecting on north Toronto, Ontario, marking Keele Street; she charts the size and meaning of the office; she gains "proper" black employment in a "proper" black place. These position-particularities inform "that tiny office" and "this white place," by citing/sighting the violence of transparent space and unearthing what might be considered the hidden spaces of blackness: the office/ Canada/Keele Street is undemocratic, sexually violent, and maintained by sociogeographic conformity; that tiny office is, explicitly, a materialization of seeming spatial transparency, which requires that the body, identity, and place neatly replicate white, heterosexual, patriarchal expectations.

But what happens to this transparent "tiny office"? It is wrapped up with a legacy of racism and sexism, marked with a mean, hurtful, confining, tiny-ness, and unraveled by the speaker. A different sense of place is employed as both critique and geographic disgust. The correspondences between black femininity, the tiny office, and "this white place" are not, according to Brand, natural correspondences: she must "put on" her (hetero)sexuality, she must dull her blackness, and she must follow the rules of capitalism and the displacement of difference, only to be thrown out of place and put back in place. Moreover, "Job" is, at least to me, a terrifying and instructive political geography of race. The rules of transparent space and traditional geographic patterns are interrupted by a sense of place that distorts and bends these very rules and patterns. The production of space is not only denaturalized because a "new ethnicity" is legitimately occupying space, but also because Brand is impacting upon how we know traditional and alternative geographic paradigms. She is both complicit to and critical of the production of space; the text marks and questions the ways in which race, sexuality, gender, class, and identity are mutually constructed.

"Job" is suffocating. It is a reminder of how powerful Fanonian historioracial schemas are. But clearly something else is going on in Brand's work— the schema has changed. The schema has a new place, different historical

markers, a different body through which race makes itself known. How do
we commingle this new place with a different set of historical questions?
How do new ethnicities grapple with historical geographies in new ways?
"Job" *is* suffocating, but is the history of the tiny office simply Manichaean, wrapped up in ahistorical Fanonian struggles? Are Fanon's geographies not also alterable? What else do diasporic subjects bring to the past,
now? Can the geographic disgust, the moment of rupture when Brand
legitimately occupies and writes place, also turn us toward a different past?
If Stuart Hall was right—that positionality invites particularity, and a particularized history—then Dionne Brand's different sense of place is also
inscribed with what Toni Morrison calls "the site of memory." Morrison's
question for black geographies, as I see it, asks how places and spaces of
blackness can be recovered when they were formerly identified as irrelevant and/or nonexistent. Her question for the tiny office might be, in what
ways does Brand's use of the "man's imagination" and the geographies of
black Canada reinvent the past?

Toni Morrison's important essay "The Site of Memory" discusses the
representation of black subjects in a world that has dehumanized and
erased the possibility of black interior lives. Her work seeks to reconstruct
these interior lives through the "remains" she is given: geographic narratives and images, such as the outer world, sounds, musics, colors, behaviors, dialects, fragrances, stories.[87] This is imaginative work that provides
a "route to the reconstruction of the world," through the exploration of
"two worlds—the actual and the possible."[88] The site of memory thus
works in tandem with deep space and a poetics of landscape: two worlds,
the actual and the possible, chart a way into the imagination, the past, and
a different sense of place. The site of memory begins to re-imagine a different worldview, wherein black lives are validated through black intellectual
histories and the physical landscape. Morrison calls upon, for example,
Frederick Douglass's childhood home, the dark caverns of the hell of slavery, the Middle Passage, Zora Neale Hurston's dead-seeming old rocks with
memories within, that veil, James Baldwin's empty bottles waiting to hold
meaning, the collards, the okra, the Mississippi River flooding and "remembering where it used to be."[89] The site of memory has to be real, and
it has to be trusted as real, in order to recast the ways in which remembering and writing three-dimensionality—the physicality of the office, the bodies hemmed in, the problem of the twentieth century, ethnic locations—

is underscored by political reimaginations. Indeed, I am suggesting that the site of memory be used to rethink historical geographies, including interior lives, but also as a way to reaffirm contemporary geopolitical possibilities of black poetics. That is, there are new histories, and new memories, and new historical geographies we can engage with, now.

But this geographic work—acknowledging the real and the possible, mapping the deep poetics of black landscapes—is also painful work. The site of memory is also the *sight* of memory—imagination requires a return to and engagement with painful places, worlds where black people were and are denied humanity, belonging, and formal citizenship; this means a writing of where and how black people occupy space through different forms of violence and disavowal. Geographically, the site/sight of memory illustrates the ways in which Morrison contributes to the physical land-scapes of the United States, and therefore the physical landscapes of black domination. Reconstructing what has been erased, or what is being erased, requires confronting the rationalization of human and spatial domination; reconstruction requires "seeing" and "sighting" that which is both expunged and "rightfully" erasable. What you cannot see, and cannot remember, is part of a broader geographic project that thrives on forgetting and displac-ing blackness.

The spatial dilemma—between memory and forgetfulness—produces what has been called a black absented presence. Absented presence is evi-dent in several black and black feminist narratives that outline how pro-cesses of displacement erase histories and geographies, which are, in fact, present, legitimate, and experiential. [90] The site of memory, then, suggests that erasure is lived and livable through the past and the present. The site of memory displays and utters new sites of being, and a different sense of place, as they are embedded with forgetfulness. Morrison's *Beloved,* Dionne Brand's *At the Full and Change of Moon,* Octavia Butler's *Kindred,* black Canadian engagements with the demolition and remembering of Africville in Nova Scotia, artist Kara Walker's cut paper and adhesive recollections of slavery, the development and debate over "black studies," "black femi-nism," and the black Atlantic: these sites/sights of memory populate the landscape with new ethnicities; we are inhabiting new places and new his-tories. And when reading black diaspora fiction, theory, film, and art, this spatialization of displacement, the placing of placelessness, is difficult—because we know that black writers and artists are re-placing that which was/is too subhuman, or too irrelevant, or too terrible, to be formally geographic or charted in any way.

The site of memory is a powerful black geography because employing it assumes that the story of blackness in the diaspora is actual and possible, and that the discursive erasure of black peoples does not eliminate how they have been implicated in the production of space. Reconstructing past interior lives of black people in the diaspora is an important geographic act, which brings to life new ethnicities and different senses of place; by humanizing black subjects who are otherwise bound to the historio-racial schema, it situates the geographies of the black diaspora in a time when this was considered impossible; it allows past and present black geographies to be believable. In addition to this, though, are the ways in which memory and forgetfulness are advanced by Morrison as she sites, sights, and cites memory: her reliance on geographic signals—images that construct the worlds black people *inhabit*—harnesses the erased and forgotten to "memories within," now, thus delivering that which is too terrible, or beyond recollection, or unintelligible, into the everyday black existences.

This is the work involved in Smith's deep space and Glissant's poetics of landscape, and black geographies in general: retellings that *place* the dilemma of black placelessness as it is contingent to, but expressing beyond, traditional geographies. Dislocation and displacement, the historio-racial schema and the mapping of man's inhumanity to man have all "placed" and bound blackness through the discourses of race, racism, and essentialism. Many black responses to this spatialization of difference radically oppose geographies that objectify their sense of self and humanity. A different sense of place, then, is mapped—materially and imaginatively— through heterogeneous representational texts and geographies. The spatial terms of new ethnicities, as I see them, require that identity and place be understood as mutually constructed and changeable; this reveals a different sense of place, which "crosses those frontiers between gender, race, ethnicity, sexuality, and class."[91] With this—these new places, new ethnicities, and new historical geographies—the very logic of geographic exclusion, as it is spatialized through practices of racial, economic, and sexual subordination, is called into question. Geographic solutions to difference and political crises (such as segregation, imprisonment, ghettoization, genocide, the sexual-racial division of labor, surveillance, as well as social theories that "add on" a subaltern body) are undermined when difference is taken seriously, when a sense of place does not neatly correspond with traditional geographies, when transparent, stable political categories are disrupted by places unbound, and all sorts of humans open up different, less familiar, alterable geographic stories.

## WHERE IS DANA'S ARM?

The first line in Octavia Butler's *Kindred*, "I lost an arm on my last trip home. My left arm," is also the end of the protagonist's narrative.[92] Dana has lost her arm as a result of unnatural time-space physics. Her painful supernatural returns to the Maryland plantation tore her apart. Her body is partly elsewhere, historically and geographically. The moment Butler offers is both fantastic and horrific: Dana's arm, Dana's body, and Dana's memory are past-elsewhere and present-incomplete. Her arm, also no longer visible in her immediate present, is both hauntingly reminiscent of Sojourner Truth's working arms, through which Truth claimed her black femininity to white slave abolitionists and Toni Morrison's Baby Suggs, preaching on the top of a huge flat-sided rock, insisting, "they do not love your hands. Those they only use, tie, bind, chop off, and leave empty. Love your hands! Love them."[93] But Dana's present dismembered body also invokes a new sense of place, and a new kind of historical present, which others "wouldn't think was so sane"; it highlights her complex relationship with history, black femininity, place, and her dismembered body.[94] The geographies of *Kindred* inspire a spatial story that is unresolved and caught up in the uncertain, sometimes disturbing, demands of geography. I am going to follow alongside this story with a discussion of garrets, bodies, auction blocks, fires, and demonic grounds.

*chapter 2*

# The Last Place They Thought Of:
# Black Women's Geographies

A small shed had been added to my grandmother's house years ago. Some boards were laid across the joists at the top, and between these boards and the roof was a very small garret, never occupied by any thing but rats and mice. It was a pent roof, covered with nothing but shingles, according to the southern custom for such buildings. The garret was only nine feet long and seven feet wide. The highest part was three feet high, and sloped down abruptly to the loose board floor. There was no admission for either light or air.

—HARRIET A. JACOBS

I begin this discussion of black women's geographies with the hiding place Harriet Jacobs [Linda Brent] describes in her slave narrative, *Incidents in the Life of a Slave Girl: Written by Herself*, her grandmother's garret. Learning from her slave owner, Dr. Flint, that her children would soon be "broken in" and that his abuses of her would escalate, Linda Brent devised a plan to flee his plantation in Edenton, North Carolina, with the purpose of saving herself and her children.[1] After concealing herself in neighbors' homes and a local swamp, Brent fled to the small 9′ x 7′ x 3′ attic above her grandmother's house (see Figure 1). She describes the garret as her "loophole of retreat," a hideaway that set in motion her escape to the North and the emancipation of her children.[2] After she hid for two years in the garret, her children were sold to their white father, Mr. Sands, and permitted to stay with Brent's grandmother; they were later taken north with Sands's family. After seven years in the garret, and unsuccessful searches by Dr. Flint, Brent escaped to New York—her body and soul still suffering from the long imprisonment in the attic.[3]

The life story of Linda Brent has been described as an antecedent black feminist narrative.[4] The central themes in the slave narrative—family, sexual

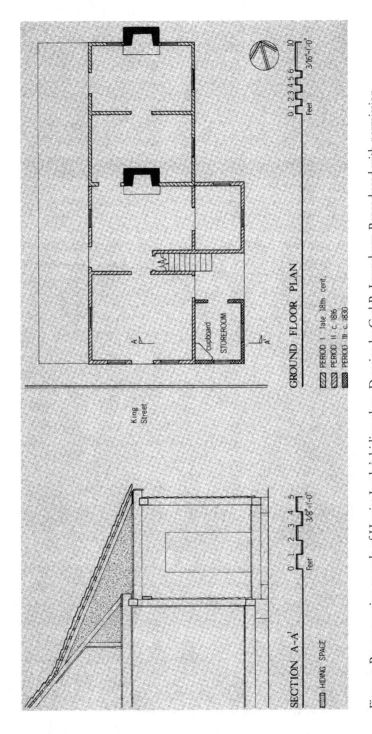

GROUND FLOOR PLAN

King
Street

A ↗
A ↙

cupboard
STOREROOM

0 1 2 3 4 5 6      10
Feet        3/16"=1'-0"

PERIOD I   late 18th cent.
PERIOD II   c. 1816
PERIOD III   c. 1830

SECTION A-A¹

HIDING SPACE

0  1  2  3  4  5
Feet        3/8"=1'-0"

Figure 1. Reconstruction to scale of Harriet Jacobs's hiding place. Drawing by Carl R. Lounsbury. Reproduced with permission.

violence, mothering, love, emancipation, community, womanhood—and Linda Brent's resistances to racial-sexual domination are some of the fundamental issues black women experienced during transatlantic slavery. Several theorists, such as Hortense Spillers, Saidiya Hartman, Valerie Smith, and Hazel Carby, have taken up the issues Jacobs describes in her narrative.[5] What *Incidents in the Life of a Slave Girl* has offered these and other theorists includes: models of early black U.S. women's literary devices and genres; evidence of black women's unique gendered relationship to slavery; patterns of racist-sexist domination and gendered resistance, which can be traced into the present; and a critical engagement with the project of slavery, including Brent's critique of femininity, motherhood, selfhood, and whiteness. Jacobs's narrative thus makes possible an examination of the ways in which some black women write and express their existence through and beyond slavery.

Additionally, the story Linda Brent tells is extremely complex. Theorist Jenny Sharpe suggests Brent's actions in the narrative are a conundrum because her resistances to slavery and Dr. Flint are necessarily bound up in the legalities of bondage.[6] The ideological and legal validation of rape, punishment, and racial-sexual subordination, and the terrifying threats made by her owner, Dr. Flint, shroud Brent's resistant choices—such as her retreat to the garret—in processes of subjugation. This does not mean that Brent is simply a victim, but rather that her story and her actions blend black female oppression and captivity with glimpses of individual control and agency.[7] This blending of oppression, captivity, control, and agency underscores what Brent describes as "the shape of mystery":[8] the racial-sexual captivity she experiences (enforced by Dr. Flint and the legalities of slavery), the life-threatening strategies she must execute while in bondage (to avoid and undermine slavery), and the irrational workings of slavery, which operate to delimit and disclose Brent's humanity and self-liberation. Underpinning the shape of mystery, then, is a commentary on "how the realm of freedom is conceptualized by those who have never been free."[9] Geographically, the shape of mystery can be identified as a mapping of the terror and transparency of slave spaces that incorporates Brent's unique spaces of self-confinement (particularly in the attic), strategy, and critique.

The shape of mystery is also the space of pain Brent avoids and experiences in the garret: she remembers Dr. Flint's aggressive sexual advances;

she witnesses slave suicides and punishments; her limbs are benumbed by inaction; she loses the power of speech; she remains unconscious for sixteen hours; she questions her spiritual beliefs and the seeming indifference of God; she becomes delirious; and dark thoughts fill her mind.[10] Linda Brent's experiences in her grandmother's garret exact, geographically, what she describes as the shape of mystery: Brent must suffer to avoid self and familial sufferings. The question of geographic freedom is wrapped up in the racial, sexual, and bodily constraints before and during her retreat to the attic. That which is outside the garret—human bondage and racial-sexual hierarchies, imminent and actual rape, the links between property, ownership, and racist-sexist punishments—are, for seven years, connected to the physically disabling perimeters of the 9′ x 7′ x 3′ cell.

Brent's spatial experiences and strategies illustrate how the geographic workings of slavery simultaneously produce spatial boundaries and subject-knowledges that can subvert the perimeters of bondage. That which is used to geographically displace and regulate black women during slavery, specifically patriarchal ways of seeing and white colonial desires for lands, free labor, and racial-sexual domination, rest on a tight hierarchy of racial power and knowledge that is spatially organized. This organization assumes white masculine knowledge and the logic of visualization, which both work to objectify Brent and her community and negate their unique sense of place.[11] For a black women such as Linda Brent, the logic of visualization and patriarchal knowledge means that her place and body are seen to be, and understood as, naturally subordinate to whiteness and masculinity; it also means that her seeable presence is crucial to Dr. Flint's sense of place. Race, sex, and gender—her seeable body-scale—inscribe Brent as worthy of captivity, violence, punishment, and objectification; her bodily codes produce her slave master's surroundings. If the geographies of slavery are primarily about racial captivities and boundaries, and the garret is both a site of self-captivity and a loophole of retreat, it becomes increasingly clear that it is Brent's different sense of place that allows her to explore the possibilities in the existing landscape. This is especially relevant given the lack of authority black women's geographic knowledges and experiences are given during (and after) transatlantic slavery. The spaces Brent discloses, both in the landscape of slavery and through her sense of place, demonstrate an unresolved, but workable, opposition to geographic domination.

Under slavery, geographic options such as escape, concealment, and racial-sexual safety can be, as Brent explains, bound up with troubling spatial strategies. Of the garret she writes, "[t]he continued darkness was oppressive. It seemed horrible to sit or lie in a cramped position day after day, without one gleam of light. Yet I would have chosen this, rather than my lot as a slave . . ."[12] Brent's spatial options are painful; the garret serves as a disturbing, but meaningful, response to slavery. Disabling, oppressive, dark, and cramped surroundings are more liberatory than moving about under the gaze of Dr. Flint who threatens her "at every turn."[13] Importantly, she claims that in the garret she is *not* enslaved and that her loophole of retreat is a retreat to emancipation. For Brent to declare that her emancipation begins in the garret—which she also repeatedly refers to as her dismal cell, her prison, and this dark hole—is evidence of how she uses the existing landscape and architecture to name the complicated geographies of black womanhood in/and slavery.

The garret makes available a place for Brent to articulate her lived experiences and emancipatory desires, without losing sight of the dehumanizing forces of slavery. She bores holes in the garret with a gimlet, in order to allow air in and observe her surroundings and her children's activities; this, along with her location within her grandmother's house, allows her to partially listen, see, and feel her immediate surroundings without formally participating in the daily activities of the town. While in the garret, Brent accentuates what Gillian Rose calls "paradoxical space." Brent's self-captive location in the garret is far from a passive space. In fact, her position in and outlook from the garret evidence several material, experiential, and representational spaces "that would be mutually exclusive if charted on a two dimensional map . . . [but are] occupied simultaneously."[14] The garret is transformed into a paradoxical space because Brent creates its meaning, and its geographic work, through her memories, experiences, and observations:

> Through my peeping-hole I could watch the children, and when they were near enough I could hear their talk . . . O, those long, gloomy [winter] days, with no object for my eye to rest upon, and no thoughts to occupy my mind, except the dreary past and the uncertain future! I was thankful when there came a day sufficiently mild for me to wrap myself up and sit at the loophole to watch passers by . . . I heard many conversations not intended for my ears. I heard slave-hunters planning how to catch some poor fugitive.

Several times I heard allusions to Dr. Flint, myself, and the history of my
children . . . The opinion was expressed that I was in the Free States. Very
rarely did any one suggest that I was in the vicinity . . . [my grandmother's
attic] was the last place they thought of. Yet there was no place, where slavery existed, that could have afforded me so good a place of concealment.[15]

The 9′ x 7′ x 3′ space discloses different, often contradictory, forms of captivity, concealment, and resistance. Brent hears of slave escapes (including
her brother's flight), slave captures, and the reward for her capture; she
marks the place-meaning of the Free States; she listens as her grandmother
and children are questioned by her slave holder; through the peeping-hole
she views punished bodies, running slaves, her children's play, and Dr.
Flint; she recalls the dreary past and anticipates the uncertain future; she
listens to family Christmas festivities and hears of Dr. Flint's repeated ex-
cursions north, in search of her; she witnesses her grandmother's illness,
her Aunt Nancy's slow murder, and her children's move north. Indeed, the
paradoxical space of the garret is advanced even further when Brent arranges
to have several letters posted to Dr. Flint from New York and Boston.
When the letters from the north arrive in Edenton, Dr. Flint is thrown off
by Brent's geographic trick and continues to pursue her where she does
not exist, in New York and Boston.[16] Brent is everywhere and nowhere,
north and south, unvisibly present across the landscape, in the last place
they thought of.

For seven years Brent holds her body captive while observing and hearing activities not always meant for her eyes or ears. There is both a separation from and connection to the world outside the attic; she is both
inside and outside, captive and free. The garret can be conceptualized as
usable paradoxical space, which opens up a different way to observe slavery and underscores the geographic shape of mystery. That is, Brent is a
black woman who is positioned across (rather than inside or outside, or
inevitably bound to) slavery while in the garret. The garret locates her in
and amongst the irrational workings of slavery as a witness, participant,
and fugitive. These multiple subject positions—formulated in "the last
place they thought of"—gesture to several different geographic possibilities and experiences, such as places seen, remembered, hoped for, and
avoided by Brent. At the same time, there is the constant reminder that
"the last place they thought of" is also spatializing one realm of freedom

through witnessing the terrible lives of other slaves, enforced family separation, and bodily pain. Her "freedom" is arranged according to: the outer geographies of slavery, which remain life-threatening and violent; the tight and disabling garret; and necessary child abandonment.

Yet Brent's position in the garret—above ground level, unseen while being able to see within and across the plantation—quietly critiques and undoes traditional geographies. While she is in the garret, Brent undermines the patriarchal logic of visualization by erasing herself from the immediate landscape and *knowing* what she terms "a different story."[17] The combination of seeing and knowing the self and the irrational workings of bondage from "the last place they thought of," in part, privileges Brent's geographic perspective. While she is attending to the painful contradictoriness of slave geographies, she is also not unlike a disembodied master-eye, seeing from nowhere.[18] Paradoxical space is therefore highlighted once again, through Brent's concealed, elevated positioning: she provides the primary geographic knowledge through which the reader, or more significantly Dr. Flint, engages with her enslavement; her concealed sense of place looks outward, offering a different perspective through which slavery can be mapped.

In the garret, in the last place they thought of, Linda Brent articulates—to return to those themes which began chapter 1—the hidden spaces that are antagonistic to transparent space. The combination of perspective, disabling bodily pain, emancipation, and the racial-sexual violence outside the garret allow Brent to tell a different story, which is in the shape of mystery, a conundrum, a sense of place that explores alternative geographic options within and through racial-sexual oppressions. That black women's geographies are not easily resolvable for Brent is not surprising. The ways in which the paradoxical space of the garret and her individual spatial predicaments are presented in *Incidents in the Life of a Slave Girl* mark the tensions of geography rather than a simple solution to geographic domination. While Brent is concealed, looking outward into the landscape of terror and transparency, it is also very clear that her oppositional place in the garret remains punishable. What her geographies tell us—about the shape of mystery, spatial conundrums, a different sense of place, and racial-sexual particularities—are relevant, in part, because the question of geographic freedom is tied to the dismal perimeters of the garret and the threat of actions that would be taken by Flint *if* Brent were to be found and recaptured. Brent's desired place cannot be fully resolved on the existing geographic terms laid out for her; she rightly notes that, where slavery exists, there is no place that is wholly liberatory.[19] Thus, while the geographic organization of blackness and black femininity are not dramatically shifted in Brent's narrative, her sense of place is useful in introducing the workings of racial-sexual displacement because her story is not only multifaceted, her geographic accounts from the garret illustrate what can and is manifested in "the last place they thought of," particularly when her oppositional geographies are caught up in violent geographic arrangements.

The last place they thought of hides Jacobs's/Brent's body, but the garret does not foreclose her geographic strategies and critiques. Indeed, this story presents a new kind of spatial positioning, through which her body is painfully protected deep within the crevices of power. A critical geographic reconfiguration is exposed—a terrain of struggle, which spans seven years and centralizes the terms under which Jacobs/Brent can bring her self into being across uneven geographies.

## HOW BODILY GEOGRAPHY CAN BE

The history of the black diaspora converges with bodily schemas and racial codes. Most obviously, the geographies of transatlantic slavery were geographies of black dispossession and white supremacy, which assumed racial inferiority and justified enslavement. Geographies such as the slave ship, the slave auction block, slave coffles, and the plantation, are just some of the sites that spatialized domination under bondage. In particular, the ties between ownership and blackness rendered the black body a commodity, a site of embodied property, through ideological and economic exchanges. For black women, this legacy of captivity and ownership illustrates how bodily geography can be. Ownership of black women during transatlantic slavery was a spatialized, gendered, often public, violence; the black female body was viewed as a naturally submissive, sexually available, public, reproductive technology. The owned and captive body was thus most profitable if it was considered to be a healthy, working, licentious, reproductive body. These characteristics were considered measurable and quantifiable, seeable sites of wealth, sexuality, and punishment. Geographically, in the most crude sense, the body is territorialized—it is publicly and financially claimed, owned, and controlled by an outsider. Territorialization marks and names the scale of the body, turning ideas that justify bondage into corporeal evidence of racial difference.

Once the racial-sexual body is territorialized, it is marked as decipherable and knowable—as subordinate, inhuman, rape-able, deviant, procreative, placeless; or, to borrow from Dionne Brand, "the exposed, betrayed, valiant, and violated female self, the vulnerable and fearful, the woman waiting for the probable invasion" is made known through her bodily markings.[20] Challenging these knowable bodily markers—asserting, for example that blackness does not warrant rape-ability—was/is punishable. Objectified black female sexualities represent the logical outcome of a spatial process that is bound up in geographic discourses, such as territory, body/land possession, and public property. Geographic conquest and expansion is extended to the reproductive and sexually available body. Black women's own experiential and material geographies, consequently, indicate a very complex and difficult relationship with space, place, and dispossession.

Narratives such as *Incidents in the Life of a Slave Girl*, as alluded to, make inextricable the links between black feminine bodies, ownership, and geography. The unresolved spaces Harriet Jacobs/Linda Brent presents—on the Flint plantation, in the garret, with and among her family—are complexly linked to her unprotected, public, and unfree body as a black woman. Jacobs's/Brent's retreat to the garret is a geographic tactic designed to protect her body and her children's future bodies—from rape, violence, auctions, coffles, and labor that is analogous to "a slow murder."[21] What is made clear—by Jacobs's/Brent's "garreted" body and the legacy of racism and sexism—is that the stories of black women contain in them meaningful geographic tenets, but these are often reduced to the seeable flesh and unseeable geographic knowledges. However, Jacobs's/Brent's retreat to the garret gets in between the seeable and the unseeable. In doing this, she creates a way to think about the histories of black women as they are wrapped up in a legacy of unprotected public bodies situated across the logic of traditional spatial arrangements—on slave ships and auction blocks, in garrets, under a white supremacist gaze, in white and nonwhite places. The very close ties among and between geography, race, gender, class, and sexuality become apparent through this history, and consequently develop new questions for our present social organization.

I am interested in thinking about the "close ties" between black women and geography because the connection reveals, as mentioned, how bodily geography can be. While the geographies of black women are certainly not always about flesh, or embodiment, the legacy of racism and sexism demonstrates how social systems organize seeable or public bodily differences. The creative work of poet and theorist Marlene Nourbese Philip illustrates how black femininity, as a seeable body-scale, comes to be understood through uneven geographies and resistances. Specifically, Philip's work illustrates the ways that racial-sexual difference is produced vis-à-vis an ongoing bodily history, which is both entrenched and alterable. Her important essay "Dis Place—The Space Between" reveals the kinds and types of geographies black women disclose and reinvent.[22] Asserting that the black female body and black female subjects are unquestionably geographic, and that a black sense of place is linked to what she calls "body-memory," Philip uses real and poetic geographies to map a world that is necessarily infused with racial-sexual discourses. Philip uses the legacy of captivity and dispossession to write a historical present that cannot exist without black femininity and flexible geographies. She connects material geographies, such as the plantation, the nation, public streets, and legal borders, to a poetic geography of black femininity in order to show that the scale of the body, for black women, is both illustrative of public racial-sexual disavowal and a location of politicization. That is, the body is understood by Philip as a historically produced terrain through which a different story is told—a geographic story produced from the last place they thought of, from the "place in between" the legs: the seemingly silenced and expendable black feminine body/parts and selves.

Marlene Nourbese Philip's figuring of black women's geographies moves between two important bodily processes: the social construction of "the space between the legs" and the racial-patriarchal uses of the space between the legs. Because female slave bodies are transformed into profitable sexual and reproductive technologies, they come to represent "New World" inventions and are consequently rendered axiomatic public objects. Black women are *the* mechanics of slavery:

> Between. The legs. The Black woman comes to the New World with only the body. And the space between. The European buys her not only for her strength, but also to service the Black man sexually—to keep him calm. And to produce new chattels—units of production—for the plantation

machine. The Black woman. And the space between her legs. Is intended to
help repopulate the outer space.[23]

By centralizing black women's reproductive organs, capacities, and sexualities—units of production—Philip locates where, and how, black women
are situated in the creation of New World spaces. The spatialization of
black femininity as "only the body" and "service" shows how black
women's sense of place *and* those who see/consume the black body can be
ensnared by the racial workings of sex and sexuality. She positions black
women firmly in a body space that not only repeats Western Enlightenment binaries of sexual difference (female = passive, all body) but also
one that emphasizes the strong working body purchased for arduous physical and reproductive labor. Philip's analysis of the black body and the
space between the legs shows how the logic of visualization, or the seeable
black female body, naturalizes sexual difference and distinguishes black
women from white women and men and black men. But the construction and uses of the space between the legs also disrupts normalized gender categories (male-aggressive, female-passive, male-public, female-private),
which are predicated on whiteness. Specifically, the kind of black femininity
Philip describes moves "between" white and nonwhite patriarchal gender
categories. Not an innocent site of private passivity and respectability nor a
wholly public and/or rational self, but rather a collection of ideological
scripts that assert objecthood: useable, public, psychically empty, working-
technology.[24] This puts forth a complicated bodily geography, which troubles discussions outlined by some feminists and feminist geographers
because it cannot easily reside within white gendered dichotomies.[25] Importantly, Philip denaturalizes and subverts sites of white femininity and
masculinity by outlining the complexities of naturalized and resistant black
selves. She identifies the space between the legs as a real and an analytical
geography, one which can name and/or alter body hierarchies. Philip
places "displacement" and the "in between" by giving it flesh, violence, a
history, and a voice.

The links Marlene Nourbese Philip makes between racist ideologies
and embodiment, or social constructions and lived experiences, are also
crucial. She emphasizes the different ways gender is lived via the experiential scale of the body in order to further denaturalize essentialist black
places and spaces. While black women are positioned as objectified sexual

technologies, they also continually make, remake, and articulate geography across practices of domination:

> . . . bodydeadbodiesmurderedbodiesimportedbredmutilatedbodiessoldbodi esboughttheEuropeantrafficinbodiesthattellingsomuchaboutthemanandw hichhelpingfueltheindustrializationofthemetropolisesbodiesbodiescreating wealththecapitalfeedingtheindustrialrevolutionsmanytimesoverandovera ndoverthebodies . . .

> Between the legs     thespace
> /within the womb    thespace
> colonized like place and space

> thesilenceof
> thespacebetween
>       the legs

> thesilenceof
> thespacewithin
>       the womb . . .[26]

The "silence of the space between the legs" is not only written out and made available through Philip's poetic framework, it is also deeply connected to the physical landscape and the actual movement of bodies: real bodies are mutilated, bought, sold, trafficked; they also metropolize, industrialize, and create wealth. The enforced movement and placement of the space between the legs contributes to the built environment and colonization. The space between the legs therefore genders both the black diaspora and European geographic patterns. This accomplishes two important conceptual advances: it sets blackness and black femininity *between* socially constructed categories and material realities by situating the paradoxical outcomes of the displacement of difference (creating wealth and capital, colonized like space and place, silence); and, it moves the sexed body through time/place (bought, trafficked bodies, creating wealth, over and over).

Philip repositions and scatters the sexed body through time and place in order to delineate how black femininity carries with it, on the body, traces of the past—the historio-racial schema at work. She achieves this by considering how race/gender informs the white and patriarchal logic of visualization: the black body is seen and inscribed under the rubric of privileged visual ideology; the black woman is seen, rather than heard, and her position in the New World, as *knowable* racial-sexual object invokes "[b]ody memory bodymemory."[27] Bodymemory and body silence, Philip argues, are:

> inscribed with the texts of events of the New World. Body becoming text. In turn the Body African—dis place—place and s/place of exploitation inscribes itself permanently on the European text. *Not* on the margins. But within the very body of the text where silence exists.[28]

Bodymemory is passed down and reinterpreted through generational remembrances, teachings, forewarnings, and advice: "The body must re/member to/re/member the forgotten/the not-known yet known . . ."[29] Bodymemory is a corporeal continuity, which moves through time and recognizes where "permanent" racial-sexual time-spaces appear in dominant texts. Philip allows silence and invisible body histories to be seeable, spatial, and ontological. She spatializes the New World differently; she identifies the paradox of the space between the legs through a poetics that calls into question, but holds steady, racism-sexism. That is, she produces new spaces, and New World spaces, by showing where black femininity actually *takes place*.

The space in between the legs symbolically, materially and physically goes several directions at once: it moves *out* of the body and reinscribes the invention of the black woman/woman-slave as knowable reproductive machine; it re-enters her body and shapes her captivity and other geographic material conditions; it subverts inner/outer and active/passive dichotomies by speaking through time/place/histories; it reproduces New World children; and, it signifies threat, reclamation and violation. So while the feminine black body is seemingly kept in place via "the space in between her legs" (inner space, oppressive definitions of the racial-sexual body), the space between the legs constructs contextual and subjective outsides. Gender position is rewritten and contested; the speaking body is unsilenced through the invention of S/Place:

S/Place. Where the inner space is defined into passivity by, and harnessed to, the needs and functions of the outer space—the place of oppression. Run it down even further into Caribbean English: s/place mutates into "dis place." *"Dis place"*: the outer space—the plantation, the New World. *"Dis Place"*: the result of the linking of the inner space between the legs with the outer space leading to "dis placement." *"Dis Place"*—the space between. The legs. For the Black woman "dis placed" to and in the New World, the inner space between the legs would also mutate into *"dis place"*—the fulcrum of the New World.[30]

S/Place, dis place, this place, is the body and mind coalescing to represent the places of black women in the New World. The geography of the body touches elsewhere—it moves between the local (the inner space between the legs), the outside (the place of oppression, the plantation), the New World, and circles back again to reinvent black (female/New World) diaspora histories. Philip negotiates her way out of transparent or knowable flesh by mobilizing bodily histories that demonstrate how identity and place are mutually constructed. While she notes the ways in which identity, space, and place are flexible and socially produced, geography remains a struggle for black women because racist-sexist schemas are also recyclable, lasting, and spatially rigorous. Philip's historicization, sites of bodily memory, and linguistic reinventions break the silence of black femininity and make seeable, and sometimes fleshy, black women's complex geographies.

The history of silence and racist-sexist disavowal is renamed and respatialized as a "permanent" geographic body on the terrain of the New World:

body as text
body inscribed
      on text
      on body

to interrupt
    disrupt
    erupt
the text of the new world

is a text of

a history of

Inter/uptions

Of bodies . . . [31]

Body disruptions, texts, histories, and inter/uptions demonstrate that the space between the legs is an analytically, historically, and socially produced category. Understood this way, terrains *outside* black women's bodies and produced by and through black femininity are also analytical, historical, socially produced—and therefore alterable. This alterability is clarified through Philip's excerpts from her play *The Streets. The Streets* illustrates how different black women understand geography and use their bodies to refashion and reclaim the material landscape.[32] Briefly, *The Streets* takes place in 1865 in a lower-class area of Port of Spain. The play traces the experiences of two gangs of Jamettes/stick-fighters (women "hanging about" the street, in public). After a public battle between the two groups of women, and police attempts to control the fight, Boadicea, the leader of one of the gangs, reveals her naked body to the authorities/men. The stick-fighters, from both gangs, follow her lead.

The women, momentarily, reclaim the streets and their bodies ("the streets is we own . . . de space between the legs is we own and we not frighten of these streets") and fearlessly dismiss the police, men, and the geographic meaning of Port of Spain. Soon after, Boadicea is disgraced—deemed an inappropriate un-colonized woman by the community—and arrested. Her trial is interrupted by the Jamettes who forcefully liberate and release Boadicea from the barristers and judge.[33] Although this refashioning, or reclamation of body/space by the Jamettes is policed, the characters and their bodies are reinvented by Philip during the play's process: black women *and* their sense of place, dis place, de space, indicates their struggle with the legal, social, economic, and political structures imposed on them. The women, Jamettes, whores, disposable, expendable, inappropriate, un-colonizable, do not necessarily transform the space between the legs into a site of absolute resistance; rather they show how the history of the body is connected to a way of being, and therefore a viable site through which black femininity can sometimes transform bodily and non-bodily geographies of domination.

"Dis Place—The Space Between" is, for this reader, a radical geographic text. Philip's re-presentation of the history of geography and its connections to black femininity and bodymemory are developed through a poetics of landscape that is unforgettable, in part because she is so attentive to the ways in which the public black body documents where erasure and dispossession takes place; the connection with the public refuses a private, quiet, undocumented geography. Philip therefore insists that black women have always engaged in a struggle, which can be seen in dis place, this place. The ways in which Philip re-languages space maps an intimate and conspicuous geography; she considers that historic formulations of black public space disclose embedded political concerns, right before our eyes, between the legs, across and beyond classificatory racial-sexual schemas.

## THE MARGIN: BLACK FEMINISM AND GEOGRAPHY

The linkages between black feminism and human geography are not forthrightly clear in social theory.[34] I have been trying, however, to present a frame through which the complex (paradoxical, bodily, poetic, "in the last place they thought of," mysterious, "in between") locations of black women might be analyzed. While the work, ideas, and geographies I have presented thus far are to some degree limited (bodies, garrets, legs, memories, seeable-public-unvisible women, in and across the black diaspora) and do not exemplify the breadth and particularities of black women's geographies in the diaspora, identifying some of the spatial themes black women draw attention to indicates how traditional geographies continually arrange uneven spatial practices. This unevenness, which is predicated on the logic of visualization and seeable body-flesh, is underlined by continuities and ruptures: black femininities that continually call into question the possibilities and limitations of space and place. To put it another way, the spatial and bodily remnants of transatlantic slavery are unresolved. Yet that which is unresolved is recast as a geographic struggle, which points to the tensions and gaps in existing landscapes. This can be seen on, through, and outside black women's body-spaces, throughout the innovative poetics of bodymemories and "in betweens," in the last place they thought of, and through the shape of mystery—the critical attic-space

Harriet Jacobs/Linda Brent hides in. Furthermore, if the body clarifies the "close ties" between black women and geography, what deep space and poetics of landscape open up—as Marlene Nourbese Philip puts forward—is a way to express and politicize otherwise absent, or "garreted," histories and lives. Bodily geographies are not only unfinished and incomplete, they must have a place. Recognizing black women's knowledgeable positions as integral to physical, cartographic, and experiential geographies within and through dominant spatial models also creates an analytical space for black feminist geographies: black women's political, feminist, imaginary, and creative concerns that respatialize the geographic legacy of racism-sexism.

In the introduction to *The Black Feminist Reader,* editors Joy James and T. Denean Sharpley-Whiting provide a brief genealogy of black feminist thought. Beginning with the antislavery activism of Sojourner Truth and Harriet Tubman, and concluding with heterogeneous political perspectives of black women in the late twentieth century, James and Sharpley-Whiting argue that black feminism is an important site of inquiry, which has created a space for a more "viable democracy."[35] The preliminary points James and Sharpley-Whiting outline in their introductory remarks trace the ways in which U.S. black feminist thought has developed during and after transatlantic slavery.[36] Within and through structural and ideological racism-sexism, black feminists have provided texts, theories, activist work, and political agendas that specify the resistances and accomplishments of black women. Rebellions, slave narratives, fiction, political work, feminist/womanist criticism, and academic endeavors, are just some of the ways in which black feminists have responded to and analyzed unequal sociopolitical relations. Black feminism and black women, the editors argue, have critically and creatively intervened in how liberty has been, and is, perceived: the unique perspective of black women, what bell hooks calls a "special vantage point," indicates a long-standing critique of racial-sexual marginalization.[37] This critique is important because it discloses the multiple realities of racial, economic, and sexual oppressions and advances a progressive politics that conceptualizes "difference" beyond domination.

*The Black Feminist Reader* collects several black feminist analyses— what some might call "classic" or "canonical" texts, such as the work of Angela Davis, Toni Morrison, bell hooks, Barbara Christian, Hortense Spillers, Patricia Hill Collins—which were written in the United States during the 1970s, 1980s, and 1990s. While the reader privileges U.S. thought, the ideas compiled by Joy James and T. Denean Sharpley-Whiting in their introduction point to the ways in which black feminist thought—manifested in the margins, or, in the last place they thought of—is implicitly underpinned by a spatial politics. If black geographies and black women's geographies are imaginable, through recognizing the displacement of difference, a different sense of place, and the powerful connections between landscape, body, and imagination, what kinds of geographic strategies are asserted by black feminists and black feminism? I suggest that black feminism can, and in many cases has, contributed to geography through meaningful political practices and agendas. What I mean by this is that black women have an investment in space, and spatial politics, precisely because they have been relegated to the margins of knowledge and have therefore been *imagined* as outside of the production of space. But as Marlene Nourbese Philip reminds us, this position outside is just that, imagined and socially produced. As mentioned, symbolic and material captivity during and after transatlantic slavery, the social regulation of black femininity, and the regulatory terms of economic injustices have implied that black women's relationship to geography is negligible. And, in relation, like other black geographies, black women's geographies are rendered absent in broader geographic debates.

The political trajectories of black feminist thought, particularly those that are underpinned by spatial language and processes (such as the margin, erasure, the body) but also those that are not, are critically engaged with the outcome of uneven geographies: domestic violence; homelessness; racial-environmental injustices; prisons; racism in the media; legal, medical, political, and economic restrictions; academic inequalities and knowledge marginalizations; resistances, activisms, reclamations.[38] If social displacements and reclamations help clarify the materiality of black lives, it follows that black feminism is also a spatial project that works to rethink and respatialize structural inequalities. Further, imagining the margins and other black feminist concerns as manifested in a "permanent" place— although sometimes from the last place they thought of—reorients the geographic work of black feminism. I am therefore not as interested in detailing the contents of *The Black Feminist Reader* as I am in thinking about the kinds of possibilities black feminism opens up in terms of geography. I want to look fairly closely at the ways in which the margin (or periphery) underpins a political agenda that gives authority to self-body perspectives but, due to its racially inhabitable materiality, simultaneously denies deep geographic inquiries. The geography of black feminism holds in it the possibility of thinking about how margin-politics are, in fact, underacknowledged geographies bound up in embodiment, metaphor, knowledge, and ownership.

Explained at length in bell hooks's *Feminist Theory from Margin to Center* but also evident in other black feminist texts, such as Patricia Hill Collins's *Black Feminist Thought* and the 1982 reader *All the Women Are White, All the Blacks Are Men, But Some of Us Are Brave,* marginalization is an experiential geography that highlights ideological confinement and the peripheral place of black gendered bodies. The Combahee River Collective writes, for example, that black women's experiences on the periphery have been a "life-and-death struggle for survival and liberation"[39] and that peripheral and marginal lives incite a political stance that is adversarial, oppositional, resistant, experiential, valuable, and hard-working. The identity-location of particular black women, fostered by a legacy of racism and sexism, is thus refashioned as a politics that is underpinned by geographic metaphors, lived experiences, and different worldviews.[40]

The margin, then, is not straightforwardly metaphoric; it is, Iris Marion Young reminds us, about processes of *marginalization* and the exclusion of particular groups from various arenas of social justice.[41] If we read bell hooks closely, we can unpack how she uses the language of the margin to spatialize U.S. feminist debates around positionality, power, race, and equality. She writes, for example, that "[a]ttempts by white feminists to silence black women are rarely written about. All too often they have taken place in conference rooms, classrooms, or the privacy of cozy living room settings, where one lone black woman faces the racist hostility of a group of white women."[42] Thus, the margin is a descriptor for women's politics that simultaneously marks place and takes place. Indeed, for hooks, the margin is also about living black femininity and black feminism and disrupting the geographic tenets of white Euro-American feminism. The margin is thus indicative of and produced in relation to: the place of the classroom, the theoretical and activist space(s) of feminism, neighborhoods, nation-spaces, political venues, bodies, the psyche, and so forth.

Periphery and margin positions locate the ways in which identity and subjectivity can politicize absences, erasures, and oppressions. This politicization, while often cast as "talking back" or metaphoric, occurs in place, within and through dominant discourses and social systems:

> . . . marginality [is] much more than a site of deprivation . . . it is also the site of radical possibility, a space of resistance. It was this marginality that I was naming [in *From Margin to Center*] as a central location for the production of counter-hegemonic discourse that is not just found in works but in habits of being and the way one lives. As such, I was not speaking of a marginality which one wants to lose—to give up or surrender as part of moving to the center—but rather a site one stays in . . . It offers to one the possibility of radical perspective from which to see and create, to imagine alternatives, new worlds.[43]

The work of hooks and some other second-wave black feminists—while certainly developing very different political agendas—calls attention to the ways in which the subaltern self attends to and creates workable material and imaginary geographies. Ways of being, real lives, seeing, creating, oppositional discourses, resistances—these are indicative of black women's everyday struggles.

As a descriptive and analytical tool, "the margin" and other places "outside" the dominant discourse, allow black feminists and other subaltern communities to locate the complexities of their unique relationship to patriarchy, whiteness and white femininity, struggles for liberation, and feminism. By insisting that black femininity is a location, their geographic politics reveal how racial-sexual displacements are experiential, historical, and specific to and among diverse black women. And hooks, importantly, stakes a claim to the margins, and in doing so—because it is a location of selfhood—speaks back to processes of bodily territorialization, ultimately reclaiming the body through the self and self-knowledge. The self-body perspectives—the outcome of marginal places and placements—implicitly suggest that black feminist politics are *where* one speaks from and that the "where" of black femininity disrupts a variety of metanarratives (feminist, black, national, academic, bodily, and so forth). The "where" of black femininity locates and demands all sorts of political positions and connections without distorting the theoretical possibilities and material realities of spaces unheard, silenced, and erased.

But is the margin too marginal? Is hooks's terminology too Manichaean, too reminiscent of black women being hemmed in on the outside? Or is the margin, as Patricia Hill Collins argues, "a flattened theoretical space" which fails to divulge real structural differentation?[44] Or is it both—a hemmed in, empty, black body/theory? While black feminist theory, and black women's struggles in general, are underwritten by a radical disruption of white patriarchal space, it should be emphasized that we think of this disruption not simply through the *language* of space. And I say this because, as mentioned, all too often black women, or their experiences, or their ideas, are momentarily called on to raise some painful questions, or complicate an otherwise white space. Indeed, metaphors like the margin are repetitively and sporadically called on to name difference: the margin is emptied out, placeless, just theory, just language, and seemingly the *only* black feminist geography available in wider social theories. Collins importantly traces margin/center debates and argues that these theoretical/political positions have effectively decentered all sorts of hegemonic knowledge claims. However, she also makes the important observation that because "the margin" is fundamentally understood as a metaphor, it is "recast as yet another ahistorical, 'universal,' construct applied to all sorts of power relations." With this, she continues, "[c]onceptions of power shifted—talk of tops and bottoms, long associated with hierarchy, was recast as flattened geographies of centers and margins."[45]

Collins's plea to rethink the "flat" geographies of black feminism and other radical social theories is interesting. And it becomes clear that Collins imagines the margins as flat precisely because she is frustrated with the theoretical inattentiveness to actual geographic displacements, those lived and living bodies that were/are fundamentally entwined with unequal multiscalar political and economic systems. I would add to her discussion that the trouble with the margin is also connected to its geo-conceptual spatial stasis; theoretically, the margin is always already marginal, peripheral, because it also carries with it—in its metaphorical utterance—the materiality of real margins and real centers. The margin is the edge or border of a surface, the ignored or unimportant sections of a group, the blank border on each side of a page, adjacent to or in opposition to the center. This language, the where of the margin, shapes it as an exclusively oppositional, unalterable site that cannot be easily woven into the ongoing production of space because the bifurcating geographies—margins are *not* centers—prohibits integrative processes. This is demonstrated often, as I mentioned in chapter 1, through the body and ideas of bell hooks. The margin hems in bell hooks; her claim to this space is radically disconnected from the new worlds she intends to imagine and create. Her body is a margin, which is an empty metaphor for "difference."

I think Collins and I have similar concerns, but I would like to push her geographic imagination even further to suggest that one additional reason the margin is so consistently cast as metaphor is precisely because it is actually inhabited by subaltern communities—and within feminism, black and other nonwhite women's bodies occupy this space. The margin is therefore not a legitimate area of deep social or geographic inquiry—it is a site of dispossession, it is an ungeographic space, it is all too often a fleeting academic utterance and therefore easy to empty out, ignore, and add on in times of multicultural crises. Like hooks herself, it is an additive, metaphoric, inhuman stand-in for "difference." In terms of geographic theory in particular, I ask, what difference has the margin actually made to the political and theoretical concerns of geographers? Or is there no geographic difference made at all, just a margin on the margins? We need to pay attention to the ways in which the margin stays on the intellectual, disciplinary, and geographic borders because it is simultaneously empty and nonwhite. And we need to think about the theoretical spaces of the margin simultaneously "hemming in" and flattening out black women's geographies.

Indeed, Barbara Christian's discussion of peripheral theory demonstrates my concerns, as her ideas are deeply connected to the soil and the placement of ideas:

> "Periphery" too is a word I heard throughout my childhood, for if anything was seen as being at the periphery, it was those small Caribbean islands which had neither land mass nor military power. Still I noted how intensely important this periphery was, for U.S. troops were continually invading one island or another if any change in political control even seemed to be occurring. As I lived among folk for whom language was an absolutely necessary way of validating our existence, I was told that the minds of the world lived only in the small continent of Europe. The metaphysical language of the New Philosophy, then, I must admit, is repulsive to me and is one reason I ran from philosophy to literature, since the latter seemed to me to have the possibilities of rendering the world as large and as complicated as I experienced it, as sensual as I knew it was.[46]

For Christian, three important issues arise and bring together poetics, geography, and politics. First, the periphery is a sociospatial and intellectual struggle, which cannot be understood outside military conquests and Eurocentric geographic determinism. Second, she importantly suggests that we be cautious about articulating "difference" without also understanding the ways in which particular geographic and historical contexts underwrite intellectual and imaginary politics. And finally, Christian brings together poetics and politics—feeling and knowing the large sensual world—to reconfigure the spatial and ontological limitations of periphery theories, geographic determinism, and feminist politics.

The periphery, she continues, reveals the "tendency to want to make the world less complex by organizing it according to one principle, to fix it through an idea which is really an ideal . . . one major element of ideologies of dominance, such as sexism and racism, is to dehumanize people by stereotyping them, by denying their variousness and pleasure."[47] Christian's attentiveness to the limitations of peripheries and margins, understood alongside small Caribbean islands, the small continent of Europe, troops invading, philosophical binaries, and feeling/knowledge, also opens up other geographic imaginations, poetic and otherwise, which might not be so tightly bound to stasis. Here we can return to Christian's useful understanding of the breadth of black women's theory and theorizing—which encompasses fiction, stories, folklore, ideas both "sensual and abstract," daily experiences—as they are entwined with lives that have always been political and geographic.

## GARRETING

Can black feminist geographies be differently conceptualized as heterogeneous, alterable political sites that are continually intervening in, rather than reinscribing, the ongoing legacy of racism-sexism? Can bodymemories refuse the simultaneity of "all-body" geographies and empty metaphoric margins? What, then, is geographically at stake in black feminism? And what do we learn if we put metaphorical margins into conversation with the poetic and experiential ways of being that black women are interested in exploring. I want to suggest that there are three intertwining processes that we should take note of. First, as mentioned, that we consider that black feminist theory, like other theories, can be erased because they are often relegated to a conceptual arena, rather than through the imbrication of material and metaphoric space; the margin can stand in for the black female body and the body itself is rendered conceptual rather than a site of humanness and struggle. It is necessary to think about our politics of citation and the margin/hooks as the only black feminist "space" seemingly available in wider social and political theories. This critique is not meant to discredit hooks or the margin but rather to notice the geographic processes that are taking place underneath and throughout black feminist politics and feminism in general. That is, regardless of what we think of hooks's margin and her politics, these issues are also spatial issues with telling spatial consequences. Second, and Harriet Jacobs helps us think about this, black women have always had a meaningful relationship with geography. In addition to important contemporary feminist theories and their interruption in white Euro-American social theories, black women's lives are underwritten by ongoing and innovative spatial practices that have always occurred, not on the margins, but right in the middle of our historically present landscape. Marlene Nourbese Philip makes this ongoing geographic relationship very clear when she sites the space between the legs as a location through which the material New World is socially and materially produced. But we can see this elsewhere. There are other maps and other "non-hooksian" geopolitical strategies. In addition to discussing feminism, and black feminist theory, several black women are talking and writing about environments, landscapes, geographies of pleasure and pain. To think about black feminist geographies, we need to return not only to those "classic" black feminist texts "housed" in the *Black Feminist Reader,* but also to art (Ellen Driscoll's 1990 camera obscura installation titled the "Loophole of Retreat" would be an interesting start), fictional geographies, activist spaces, musics, poetry.[48] These creative and theoretical spaces are not just words, images, or ideas; they locate real social struggles. Here, the work of Carole Boyce Davies is notable. Davies's theoretical and poetic concerns transgress boundaries; her interests in collective and collaborative diasporic writings, as well as multiple and interdisciplinary theoretical positionings, unsettles monolithic understandings of black femininity and black bodies. It is impossible to keep blackness statically "in place" in Davies's work, while it is equally impossible to ignore historical and geographic specificities. Carole Boyce Davies also asks us to "hear" black women, and therefore hear geography differently, suggesting that space and place are always connected to audible demands and political action.[49] That black women allow their particular surround-ings to speak, and be heard, reorients existing spatial practices, asking us to think not only about the "where" of politics but how the production of space is not a silent process. Finally, and related to both, geography, as we know, is always about knowledge. And the ways in which we know and are taught geography, now, is connected to powerful processes of colo-nialism, exploration, and conquest. So the geographies of black feminism, and the geographies of feminism in general, also need to be interrogated for the ways in which they spatialize politics. I am thinking about owner-ship here, about who can and cannot be a feminist, a black feminist, or an Afrocentric feminist, or a womanist and how this is also a geographic political project, which may be underwritten by the very ideas—specifi-cally, discursive territorialization—that we are working against.

In "Mama's Baby, Papa's Maybe: An American Grammar Book," Hor-tense Spillers writes that the life of Harriet Jacobs/Linda Brent is a story of "garreting." Spillers argues that Jacobs's slave narrative enables an explo-ration of black women's histories and lives, which are in "not-quite spaces."[50] Without casting aside Jacobs's/Brent's specific attic-confinement, Spillers addresses a geographic process that locates how captivity, racist-sexist reg-ulation, bodily objectification, and black femininity exist through and beyond the garret. Several black feminist theorists have suggested that the terrain of the racial-sexual body continues to insinuate itself onto post-slave geographies. While the terrain of the racial-sexual is garreted, or "in the last place they thought of," Spillers proposes, not unlike Marlene Nour-bese Philip, that these geographies intervene in and are already inscribed onto the (racial) cultural landscape. Black women's geographies and black feminist geographies underscore what Spillers describes as "insurgent grounds" of difference.[51]

The "not-quite" spaces of black femininity are unacknowledged spaces of sexual violence, stereotype, and sociospatial marginalization: erased, eras-able, hidden, resistant geographies and women that are, due to persistent and public forms of objectification, not readily decipherable.[52] As men-tioned above, these geographic processes and experiences are also empha-sized by the paradoxical space of the garret in Linda Brent's story. What I am more interested in here, however, is Spillers's suggestion that the "not-quite" are the projected spaces of black femininity through and beyond the garret, and how that which is "not-quite"—new and different kinds of garretings—have been transformed into a black feminist politic. The not-quite spaces of black women provide alternative paths through traditional geographies and take into account a political agenda concerned with racism-sexism, objectification, captivity, and respatialization(s).

The process of garreting begins to get at the geographic projection of black femininity by locating what black women bring to bear on geographic negotiations: racist-sexist ideologies that mark black women as "not-quite" legitimate world citizens; practices of domination that regard black women's histories and lives as expendable; unacknowledged body-geographies that are integral to the production of white and nonwhite spaces; and oppositional paradoxical spaces. What is even more interesting to me about Spillers's essay are ways in which she signals how black women's geographies (post-Jacobs) are garretings—they are still unresolved because of the impact the black female body does and does not have upon traditional geographic arrangements. Black women's geographies still rest on those "not-quite" spaces and the "different stories" of displacement—but this a workable and "insurgent" geography, which is produced in tandem with practices of domination. While "Mama's Baby, Papa's Maybe" is not a treatise on garreting per se, Spillers's grammatical decision—to transform the garret into a verb—within the context of her essay is important to address, in that it sets up the aforementioned tensions (the conundrums and antagonistic hidden geographies) as a genealogical geographic practice specific to black women. Ultimately, she identifies the meaningfulness of Jacobs's/Brent's garret and opens up the question of symbolic, imaginative, and/or political geographic work the garret can do beyond the attic. Black women's knowable sense of place is often still found "in the last place they thought of," across the logic of white and patriarchal maps. But this different sense of place has been cast as a politicized location—peripheral standpoints, special vantage points, margins—through which the violence, the bodily histories, and the limitations of traditional geographic arrangements are mapped. I have recast it as "the last place they thought of"; geographies of black femininity that are not necessarily marginal, but are *central to* how we know and understand space and place: black women's geographies are workable and lived subaltern spatialities, which tell a different geographic story.

In the following chapters I address black women's geographies that are differently connected to "the last place they thought of": the slave auction block (geographies that exact racial-sexual dehumanization and incite radical black respatializations), the places of black Canadian slave Marie-Joseph Angélique (unbelievable geographies of black Canada), and the "re-enchanted" human geographies intellectual Sylvia Wynter advances (uninhabitable, demonic, and interhuman geographies). Following, then, I discuss the different ways in which geography provides evidence of black women's historical and historically present geographies.

# chapter 3

# The Authenticity of This Story Has Not Been Documented: Auction Blocks

Why stands she near the auction stand, That girl so young and fair?
What brings her to this dismal place, Why stands she weeping there?

—WILLIAM WELLS BROWN

Stone table, approximately 3′ square and 3′ high. It is supported by four rectangular stones set upright into the ground. A bottom stone is shaped as a cross to fit between the posts, while the top stone slab rests directly upon the four posts at each corner. Top stone about 3″ thick; bottom stone about 2-½″ thick. No mortar used.

—ORVILLE W. CARROLL, *"Slave Auction Block at
'Green Hill' Plantation,"* Virginia

The slave auction block at Green Hill Plantation in Virginia (see Figure 2) is described as a stone table that was used for the auction and sale of slaves.[1] Orville W. Carroll, who mapped and surveyed the infrastructure and geography of Green Hill Plantation in 1960, has suggested that the auction block, while certainly evidence of plantation tradition, has an uncertain history. He writes that although "the stone table was used to display the best qualities of the slaves," the "authenticity of this story has not been documented."[2] *Clotel; or, The President's Daughter,* by William Wells Brown, which tells the story of President Jefferson's slave daughter, begins with her sale. On the auction block, Clotel caused a "deep sensation"— her fair skin, her wavy black hair, her graceful appearance, made her a valuable, desirable commodity. Brown writes that Clotel's bones, muscles, sinews, blood, nerves, and sexuality sold for five hundred dollars; her moral character sold for two hundred dollars; her improved intellect sold for one hundred dollars; and her chastity and virtue sold for four hundred dollars.[3] Thus, despite Carroll's hesitancy regarding the "authentic" accounts of the display and sale of slaves, the meanings attached to the auction block at Green Hill are telling—particularly if these meanings entwine with the marketable qualities of Clotel. The classification of her body, her detectable white lineage, racially "superior" character and intellect, her most valuable assets (bones, muscles, sinews, blood, nerves, sex, chastity, and virtue) establish that the auction block is a site of public racial-sexual domination and measurable documentation. Racial positionings—of the auctioneer, the buyers, the onlookers, the enslaved—hold steady this domination through the gaze, the exchange of money, and bodily evaluations.

While the authenticity of stories about the Green Hill auction block have "not been documented," seeing and engaging with geographies of captivity, human sale, and dehumanization render the auction block much more than a well-constructed stone object. Engaging with the materiality of the

Figure 2. Green Hill slave auction block. Photograph by Jack E. Boucher. From *Historic American Buildings Survey,* 1960. Courtesy of the Library of Congress.

auction block challenges what Carroll describes as undocumented: what we imagine, see, believe, disbelieve, and wonder upon encountering this auction block is what produces its meaning. I would like to engage with the auction block through various human interactions and interpretations and suggest that the function and uses of this site—human sale—contribute to its sociospatial meanings as it is humanly construed and imagined.

I begin this discussion with the auction block at Green Hill because it is, compared to other historical representations of auction blocks available, a material geography. Other archival images of auction blocks are primarily sketches and prints, which tended to be used for antislavery texts and pamphlets.[4] The representative value of the Green Hill photograph offers a different (but equally complex) reading than antislavery representations: it was produced to document and survey the land of a plantation in 1960 rather than to motivate the abolishment of slavery. The photographic image is coupled with the comments made by architect Orville W. Carroll of the auction block itself, some noted above, and a brief history of the plantation buildings and former owners.[5] However, the emptiness of the Green Hill auction block, the seeming transparency and objectivity of the "survey" and architectural data, speak to my interests in how racial-sexual continuities and ruptures are shaped by the material world and traditional geographic patterns. What is it about the survey, the data, and the empty auction block that allow Carroll to render it a location with a questionable history? And what kinds of alternative stories does this particular site invoke? Can Carroll's "objective data" and the measurable material properties of the Green Hill auction block tell a different story?

The Green Hill auction block begins a discussion of black femininity and sale slightly differently than other texts on transatlantic slavery. Several survey texts and histories use sketches and prints of occupied auction blocks from antislavery texts to visually exact the dehumanizing nature of slavery and unpack abolitionist agendas. While these antislavery representations of slavery are relevant to understanding how the auction block was/is an important signifier of bondage, I find that the Green Hill auction block provokes my imagination in a different way.[6] As an unoccupied image, it indicates the making and marketing of blackness in a way that can perhaps detract from the antislavery agenda implicit in several available images. But more than this, this particular image does not centralize the body or bodies on the auction block; instead, it represents what could have been and what was there, rather than, to borrow from Saidiya Hartman, visually displaying "injustices that are intended to shock and disrupt the [comfort of the spectator]."[7] This is not meant to suggest that the Green Hill site is not shocking, or that my discussion here is easy because it is "unoccupied" by bodies for sale. I am suggesting, rather, that the materiality of the Green Hill site is perhaps a way to think about the sale in humans through a different textual source, which does not carry with it an explicit antislavery agenda.

The Green Hill site invokes the ways in which physical geographies are enmeshed with social processes. While the Green Hill auction block is empty—unoccupied, product-less, and apparently story-less—its expressive potential demonstrates the ways in which a physical geography can be mediated by the space of the subject: the body, the self, identity, and subjectivity. Thus, what is seen here is also produced through psychic-imaginary means and, as I discuss later, the site of memory. Our imaginations can fill the empty space and recover the undocumented. We give this site its peopled history and stories. Additionally, the invocated human-occupation of the auction block at Green Hill is a social process underpinned by geographic domination; identification with the auction block carries with it, largely, a black and/or racial sense of place that is entangled with geographies of captivity, liberty, and resistance. The data, the survey, and our imaginations set forth the stories we end up telling about ourselves and each other *in relation to* the legacy of black dispossession, suffering, and human devaluation. The auction block is a site of human geography intersections, stories, and expressions; it normalizes black pain, commodifies black working-sexual bodies, and potentially motivates resistances to the naturalized place of black femininity.

In order to think about the auction block as a site of human geography intersections, I examine it as a singular location that is shaped by, and shapes, multiple spatial differentiations. The auction block signals a particular geographic moment—the moment or point of sale—and yet it also unravels to demonstrate the ways in which something extremely local, inanimate, and seemingly silent, can impact upon other kinds and types of geographies. To begin, I discuss the Green Hill auction block as a technology that "scales" the body, and then consider its placement within the larger Green Hill plantation. That is, the slave auction block also displays black bodies in relation to the wider landscape, thus linking racial ideologies to other geographic areas. Noting the connections between the auction block, the body, and the plantation reveals that black femininity intersects with other geographic processes, such as the making of the plantation/town, regional economies, and widespread essentialist ideologies about race and difference. I suggest, then, that the very local and timely moment of sale is discursively uncontained for two reasons: first, the figurative or real body on the auction block, up for sale, is connected to its surrounding geographic and social systems; and second, the geographies and bodies that are physically disconnected from the auction block—on a two-dimensional map they would be placed around it or not within the vicinity at all—are also created by and creating its meaning. Embedded in these connections and social systems is the question of what ideologies—about blackness and black femininity specifically—bring to bear on material geographies that might not be immediately equated with black bodies or slave auction blocks at all. I am therefore working through two interconnected processes: how the slave auction block creates crude and excessive sites of black subjugation; and how the geographic meanings of the slave auction block are not always inextricably bound to its local, material, and contextual properties.

I also think about the ways in which local-contextual black geographies hold in them the ability to destabilize places—and times—outside the historically dispossessed body. I add to these human geography intersections a discussion of the auction block as a site of contestation during and after transatlantic slavery. While I certainly do not want to suggest that the auction block was and is simply a location of resistance—it powerfully locates pain, regulation, and subjugation—it is important to think about the ways in which it fits into the idea that racial-sexual geographies are alterable sites of struggle. In a way, it flips and complements Harriet Jacobs's/ Linda Brent's garret, revealing that the public and bodily geographies of enslaved black women simultaneously advance ideologies of dispossession and strategies of resistance. Unfreedom and resistances demonstrate, again, the unresolved geographies of black femininity. The auction block cannot produce a definable racial-sexual object—even though its material purpose is to measure and render knowable hair, skin, muscles, blood, eyes, and the space between the legs. It is, instead, a site where the ongoing production and reproduction of difference (race, gender, sexuality, class, and so forth) takes place and moves beyond the body. It is "not quite" a know-able geography because, as mentioned above, it is continually being inter-sected by different forms of power, knowledge, imagination, contestation, and contexts. Both of these readings of the auction block—public (know-able) and unresolved (unfinished/intersected)—pivot on the moment of sale and create opportunities to think about black geographies beyond their historical, profitable, and seemingly logical functions. I end this discus-sion, then, by considering the ways playwright Robbie McCauley utilizes the auction block in her play *Sally's Rape*. McCauley further complicates black women's geographies by showing how slave auction blocks are also alterable, albeit troubling, political sites/sights of memory.

## MAPPING THE MOMENT OF SALE

In his study of slave markets in nineteenth-century New Orleans, Louisi-ana, historian Walter Johnson details the ways in which black men, women, and children were marketed and sold. Drawing on letters, slave narratives, legal documents, financial records, and newspaper advertisements, John-son shows that the slave trade bolstered the local-national economies. He also shows that the slave market in New Orleans, while unique to time and place, can clarify a broader understanding of slavery elsewhere in the United States and the diaspora, because the moment of sale is so crucial to various and varying human exchanges.[8] The moment of sale can (but does not necessarily) traverse space because, at this instant, all sorts of black bodies signify an empty vessel, a commodity, an unsuffering property; geographic context can, at least in our imaginations, also point to the con-tinuities of bondage, such as the legally sanctioned captive laboring body, which is always owned and a site of economic transaction. Multiple slave geographies, then, were underwritten by this economy of black dispos-session. Importantly, economic transactions paralleled the ways in which particular bodies are working on and through the natural landscape in order to accumulate profit. Capitalism and exchange embedded a series of divisions in labor, which were designed to alter and objectify material geographies: mental/physical, racial, sexual, and class divisions corre-sponded with capital accumulation.[9] In situating black bodies within this exchange system, it follows that slave labor and black humanity were not only differentiated according to gender roles, but were also rendered primarily physical, slave-classed, and hypersexual. The moment of sale also spatializes an economic transaction that repetitively alienated the black self not only from his/her labor accomplishments, but, at least imminently, from other social and psychic desires, such as family, love, freedom, children. In theory, then, the point of sale corresponded with the objectification of the landscape and particular humans in exchange for profit; or, the auction block and the black subject are simultaneously abstracted from humanness.

Saidiya Hartman argues, furthermore, that if the moment of sale necessarily renders the black body abstract, this reifies the buyer's/master's embodied universality and subjectivity. And this economic exchange, both Hartman and Frederick Douglass write, is "profitable as well as pleasurable" for slave buyers.[10] So the moment of sale—the instant when a human is to be purchased—affirms cross-regional racial binaries and dominant desires. In mapping the moment of sale, we can begin to understand how a local and fleeting act can disclose where and how objectification takes place in multiple contexts. And thinking about the research of Walter Johnson and Saidiya Hartman together brings into focus how the pleasurable purchasing of slaves, across geographic regions, was a series of sanctioned, repetitive, and similar acts—sometimes cast as mundane. I discuss below some of the ways in which the moment of sale was disrupted, but for now I think it is important to keep in mind the continuities this practice established. Indeed, if Douglass and Hartman are correct, the profit and the pleasure of purchasing humans, the repetitive and sometimes mundane economic exchanges, create a place for disruptions, but they do not disappear.

Auctions and auction blocks varied over time and place and occurred both privately and publicly. Human sale took place in town centers, on local plantations, at fairs, in formal auction houses, in fields, and in community buildings. Slaves could also be bartered, inherited, rented, given away, and stolen. The differing locations for the sale of slaves, as well as state and national differences, reveals that the prices of slaves varied and the reasons for sale were attached to local, community, familial, and personal interests. Increasing home or field labor, bankruptcy, sex and rape, reproducing the slave population, selling "unruly" resistant slaves, breaking apart slave allegiances—these reasons for sale, among others, show that the auction block and the point of sale were underpinned by variable interests. The sale and enslavement of humans, then, was shaped by geo-graphic contexts and individual desires.[11]

The slave auction block has been described and represented as: a table, a raised auction stage, a block (solid wood or cement), a measuring scale, a tree stump. Sketches, prints, narratives, and remembrances place the slave or slave family alone on the block, with the auctioneer to the side, and the buyers/slavers gathered around.[12] What is clear from all of these representations is that the human-commodity is put on display and the auction block serves to spatially position black men and women as objects "to be seen" and assessed. Even "private" auctions were strikingly public, requiring a seeable, measurable, black body. Regardless of the type of auction block, the enslaved woman, man, child, or family is rendered an intelligible, transparent commodity. Without a doubt, the body on the auction block is rendered an object; geographically, black men, women, and children become part of the slave trade landscape, like other objects for sale.

Drawing on Johnson's observation of the intergeographic importance of the moment of sale, I therefore feel that the auction block—rather than the auction or private sales—anchors and gives a coherency to differing black geographic experiences in the diaspora. I read the auction block, then, as a site that connects the moment of sale to black geographic experiences. Narratives about the auction block, gathered from literatures, theory, and life stories, illustrate that its materiality is intersected by human actors. That is, it becomes very clear that this structure—whether it be a tree stump, a stage, or a table—is created by those who are on, around, and even distanced from, the selling point. The processes and acts that produced the auction block demonstrate the ease with which race, ownership, and profit culminated on the auction block and continually substantiated the economic and ideological currency of blackness, whiteness, possession, and captivity. The narrative below, remembered by James Martin, outlines the ways in which the specificity of the auction block facilitates objectifications:

And we seen others sold on the auction block. They're put in stalls like pens for cattle and there's a curtain, sometimes just a sheet in front of them, so the bidders can't see the stock too soon. The overseer's standin' just outside with a big black whip and a pepper box pistol in his hand. Then they pull the curtain up and the bidders crowd around. The overseer tells the age of the slaves and what they can do. One bidder takes a pair of white gloves and rubs his fingers over a man's teeth and he says, you say this buck's 20 years old, but his teeth are worn. He's 40 years if he is a day. So they knock that buck down for 1000 dollars . . . They call men bucks and they call women wenches. Then the overseer makes him walk across the platform, he makes him hop, he makes him trot, he makes him jump.[13]

Martin's narrative indicates the control of space and spatial activities on the auction block. It reasserts how black people are named, contained, valued: the overseer's whip and the pistol, the hiding of the human product behind a curtain, the documentation of the "best qualities of the slaves," such as age, health, and labor specialty; the intimate bodily examination and demonstration; the pricing and bargaining—these activities spatialize and naturalize inequality. Additionally, the auction block staged and violently forced black performativity (hopping, jumping, trotting), rendering the body of the enslaved as seemingly naturally suited to bondage and white pleasure-gazes. The auction block, to some degree, conceals black pain and resistances through racist public expectations: a hopping, jumping, trotting body is a nonsuffering body.[14] Slaves were sometimes sold alongside livestock, furniture, land, and other forms of property; their positioning on the auction block discloses how race, sexuality, and the economy are bound up with place: the auction block *positions* excessive dehumanization and observation and obscures black humanity by violently transforming human beings into commodity objects through the act of economic exchange. The moment and point of sale documents the un-documented; it provides a framework through which imaginary and real encounters with the auction block can be articulated. This moment can, for example, show how James Martin's remembrance and the Green Hill auction block inform one another and accentuate how geography, commodification, and race—including whiteness—are publicly intertwined.

In order to broaden the geographic scope of the point of sale, I want to cast the net a little wider by turning to the ways in which this local site generates additional racial-sexual differentiations. The auction block can be understood as one of the primary sites where spatial differentiation takes place. It publicly displays different racial bodies and communicates racial hierarchies beyond the auction block. The meanings of blackness, and race in general, are reinforced, spatially and ideologically, by the process of socioeconomic exchange. Thus, the auction block works to determine and define social activity by *placing* race "up for sale." This process of placing race intersects with other human geographies, identifying how the workings of local and contextual dominations are indicative of wider socioeconomic processes and contestations. I am therefore going to turn to a discussion of scale in order to think about how placing race up for sale can impact upon geographies beyond the slave auction block.

Geographic divisions, or scales, range from the psyche to the globe. Coherently hierarchical in their implication (psyche, body, home, community, region, nation, globe), scales identify a planetary organization. While hierarchically organized, these scales are interconnected and socially produced: the body does or does not occupy the home; bodies, consciously and unconsciously, assert and define the meaning of community; regional boundaries are produced by bodily politics and home- and work-economies; the nation and nationalism produce material and ideological boundaries, which impact upon the psyche, homes, communities, bodies, regions. Additional, more nuanced, connections can be made between and among these scales; what I want to highlight, however, are the ways in which scale offers a working through of the unnaturalness of hierarchical organization and the ways in which scales are relational, socially produced "geographical totalities," which are the "contingent outcome of the tensions that exist between structural forces and the practices of human agents."[15] It is the social production of scale, the sociogeographic struggle over making boundaries, that denaturalizes its seemingly hierarchical, bound, self-evident, geographic organization.

If scale is socially produced, but implicitly profitable and materially hierarchical, then an analysis of the body-scale on and in relation to the auction block demonstrates how social processes organize the world into intelligible and different "clusters" and locations. That is, the auction block differentiates the black body by visually demarcating it and attaching discourses of dispossession and captivity to the flesh. The scale of the body, then, necessarily identifies the ways in which the historical and geographic particularities of the plantation are socially produced through powerful material technologies. In this case, the technology of slave auction block "scales" the body, differentiating it from those not on the auction block, and those areas surrounding the auction block. This is not to suggest that the scale of the body is bound, cut off from its surroundings, but rather that social processes create the idea that black flesh is distinct, radically different, captive, and not white.

The seeable display of blackness, on the auction block, creates the scale of the body and its attendant ideological discourses. Skin, blood, muscles, and hair come to be recognizable social markers that require organization. Thus, the scale of the body is not, in fact, bound, in part because it requires external social practices to communicate and justify the displacement of difference. It is necessary to link the body to wider social processes in order to distinguish it and understand its multiscalar functions. The public black body and the moment of sale suggest that something else is going on, that other scales (such as the plantation or regional economy) and social processes (such as legal bondage) are repetitively hardening, and making coherent, the intimate physiology of black subjects. So the scale of the body is a socially bound production, which intersects with regulation and classification.

I want to return to Green Hill in order to explore how practices of domination flow across the body and entwine with areas outside the black body. The auction block makes the scale of the body known and knowable through repetitively reproducing difference and legally putting blackness up for sale. However, while the scale of the body and the auction block are intimately bound, they are shaped by and shaping broader spatial processes, such as the borders of and infrastructures on plantation/town, labor, and broad racial-sexual ideologies. Through Green Hill, I want to discuss the ways in which these areas, social processes, and ideas contribute to the social production of space and set the stage for a discussion of black femininity and racial-sexual differentiation.

The Green Hill auction block is situated in and amongst other plantation geographies (see Figure 3). The plantation is often defined as a "town," with a profitable economic system and local political and legal regulations.[16] The Green Hill plantation town was divided into lower and upper areas. The upper town contains the main house, the office, the carriage house, the barn, the slave auction block, a large garden area, slave quarters, the kitchen, the mill, the stables, the cemetery; the lower town comprises woods, pasture, fields, the Staunton River, and the Virginian Railway.

If the plantation represents the scale of a town, the auction block figuratively and materially displays a smaller scale—the body or bodies—within the town. The slave auction block therefore contributes to the economic

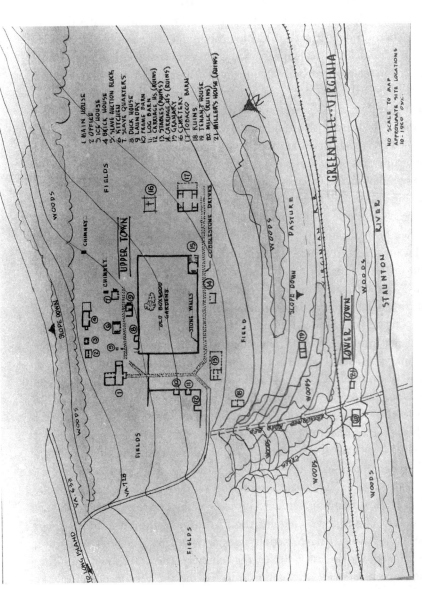

Figure 3: Map of Green Hill Plantation by Orville W. Carroll. From *Historic American Buildings Survey*, 1960. Courtesy of the Library of Congress.

and ideological borders of the area because it is necessarily implicit to the town economy. Its economic functions, while certainly bodily and visual, are also indicative of labor, leisure, and ownership. Social differences, instigated through scaled *different* bodies, therefore materially and ideologically contribute to the meaning of the plantation town. To put it another way, the auction block, like the main house or the fields, is a geo-economic site, which is also required within the plantation town to convey power, hierarchy, and social roles. This is evidenced, further, in the placement of the auction block at Green Hill: it is located in and amongst plantation town buildings, right in between the main house and the kitchen and across from the plantation office. It is a structure that geographically coupled with everyday social and economic reproduction and would be encountered by several members of the Green Hill community on a daily basis. It is also a centralized daily reminder of the trade in humans. Thus, the map of Green Hill presents a series of racialized buildings that communicate who is and who is not captive. In and amongst these buildings stands the slave auction block, an exhibit of profit, pleasure, and bodily difference. These buildings and structures are not only made intelligible by the bodies that do or do not occupy them, they show that the material geography of the plantation is structured by racial-sexual ideologies at the same time it creates them.

The production of scales beyond the body also occurs vis-à-vis the exploitation of black labor: slaves were subject to the literal and ideological production of space due to their indispensable economic roles: plantation, regional, and national economies required racialized labor and bodies to build and maintain material and discursive geographies. In terms of Green Hill—both a town and a farm—physical labor was needed to perform work tasks and attend to tobacco, livestock, laundry, food preparation, gardens, transportation, water maintenance, and so forth. Further, the buildings themselves had to be kept up, as did the tenant properties and the cemetery. Administrative labor was needed to organize work tasks and prepare outgoing and incoming products: tobacco, slaves, livestock. Slave labor, then, was implicitly tied to external economies through contributing to the production and reproduction of the plantation space.

As Clyde Woods has argued, in relation to the Mississippi Delta, the trade of humans and slave labor paralleled the rise of capitalist slavery and guaranteed the demarcation of geographic, racial, sexual, and class boundaries.[17]

Purchasing fertile slaves and fertile lands advanced several economies while also organizing who, where, and how labor was reproduced. If the economy was central to the development of broader social, political, and geographic hegemonies, the auction block figures black sexualities into this landscape: the exposure and evaluation of the black subject's healthy, working-sexual body becomes valuable to other economic processes, such as reproducing the slave population, field work, garden and agricultural labor, assembling infrastructures (including auction blocks, of course), building roadways, cooking, child care, cleaning, tending to livestock, sex-work/rape, and so on. These activities, beyond the auction block, were spatialized according to gender differentiation, as I discuss below. What is important to note, in terms of scale, are the ways in which this labor was, in part, secured by the auction block. The meticulous observations of bodies, coupled by the need for healthy working bodies, guaranteed (forced) economic advancement and progress.

If the slave auction block displays the scale of the body and/or predicts that a moment of sale is imminent within the plantation, this process implicates black subjectivity and objecthood outside the plantation landscape. These geographies position black subjects and their bodies deeply within, rather than peripheral to, the making of the plantation town and its outer regions. The landscape of the lower town is especially telling—the roads, the fields, the waterway, the railway—all represent ingoing and outgoing socioeconomic patterns, which simultaneously build up and cross the plantation borders: or, the movement of slaves in, the movement of slaves out, escape and capture.

Scale illuminates the ways in which the black subject is produced by and implicated in the making and meaning of the auction block and other slave geographies. At the same time, specific social processes demonstrate that the scale of the body, a unique subject on the auction block, can also be abstracted, transformed into a racist multiscalar ideology, which undermines heterogeneous black subjectivities. What I mean by this is that while the auction block sites and localizes human objectification and captivity, it also serves to inform other geographic patterns—which repetitively justify domination. The human-object is transformed into a recognizable sign of captivity that turns blackness into an ideological currency that moves beyond the moment of sale. If the point of sale and the auction block situate the meaning of blackness, and also show that white and nonwhite bodies are implicated in the making of other scales within and beyond the plantation, the *ideas* that make the dispossessed and captive body intelligible also cross boundaries. The point of sale marks the scale of the body as "sellable," thus abstracting human complexities and particularities and discursively naturalizing multiscalar ideologies that justify local, regional, and national violence and enslavement. That is, in scaling and mapping the black body through the moment of sale, the auction block reifies additional "essential and repressive definitions about blackness."[18] Here we can remember the ways in which Marlene Nourbese Philip's poetics map the space between the legs as a location of the "New World," and thus is also representative of the geographic landmasses of the Americas: a multiscalar bodily technology that is produced and contested under bondage. In a sense, then, the auction block produces ideologies that are upheld by the idea that all black subjects are inferior and worthy of objectification and enslavement. This is achieved through heightening the economic meaning of black flesh and is a key moment of spatial differentiation and the production of scale: flesh is marked accordingly, determining how race, class, sexuality, age, and phenotype are "placed" and made knowable in relation to and beyond the auction block. This ideological currency of dispossessed black bodies is powerful, not only consolidating and transgressing the regulatory boundaries the point of sale creates, but also pushing into future geographies and the politics of difference.

## SPATIAL DIFFERENTIATION AND BLACK FEMININITY

If the production of scale rests on relational geographic organization, the black body is one site that was, during transatlantic slavery, inscribed with, and inscribing upon, multilayered social processes. The above section outlined some of the ways in which bodies were differently implicated in the production of scale—at the level of the town and across plantation buildings and outside the plantation. I was also suggesting that the highly visual display of black bodies on the auction block, which maps the point of sale, abstracts selfhood and differences among black subjects through repetitive ideological objectifications that can cross scales. Thus, an analysis of scale shows that the working-sexual body and racial differences are at stake in the geographies of transatlantic slavery; not only does scale differentiate whiteness from blackness and corporealize sites of profitable pleasure and violence; it also demonstrates how essentialist ideas—such as racism-sexism—have multiscalar material consequences.

In addition to strengthening oppositional white and nonwhite differences, the slave auction block displays different kinds of black bodies. The slave auction block and the point of sale also map bodily scrutiny and therefore differentiate kinds, forms, and types of blackness and desirability. Black differences were refined through the sale of families together, the sale of family members apart, the sale of women with or without men, the sale of children, mixed-raced slaves, darker skinned slaves, aging slaves, disabled slaves, resistant slaves. Thus, corporeal identifiers were, to some extent, fractured by each slave buyer's particular requirements—depending on the type of work, or the type of sexual violence, desired: "brownish black," "quadroon," and "mulatto," sexually available male and female bodies, unborn bodies, healthy strong bodies, reproductive bodies, were economic issues.[19] The scaled body thus, in part, also particularized different kinds and types of blackness vis-à-vis very precise white demands, which differentially placed and differently valued black people within the bounds of captivity and sale.

Noting these differentiations, and turning specifically to black femininity and womanhood, I suggest that the racial-sexual codes produced in conjunction with the auction block distribute and redistribute uneven geographies that are particular to black women and continue, at least in part, to inform their contemporary politics. That is, while the auction block sites the objectification of black femininity through sale, the bodily consequences of this transaction invoke spatial processes that organize the places of womanhood across and beyond transatlantic slavery.

In part, the blackness "purchased" on the auction block naturalizes black women's identities as, primarily, reproductive working-sexual bodies. Significantly, public auction and the auction block displayed and scrutinized black women's sexual bodies in response to the need to reproduce the slave population. In many cases, women were put on display partially nude or fully nude; slave buyers kneaded women's stomachs; doctors publicly and privately examined their breasts, stomachs, and reproductive organs.[20] The point of sale, for a black woman, is coupled with her public racial-sexual body: her flesh, her sexed body, motherhood, family ties, her dignity, her sociosexual safety, her intelligence. Indeed, spatial differentiation was ensured by measurements, classifications, and control of black women's bodily, reproductive, and familial spaces. The feminine flesh is not just blood, muscles, hair, skin; it is also womb, breasts, the space between the legs. These physiological differences are purchased because they are not white and not masculine; they are materially and ideologically distributed in and amongst slave geographies to fulfill various violent racist-sexist demands. Violence, then, has a geography, and geographic property ownership (of black female slaves) provides the means through which violence is justified.[21]

The black female purchased on the auction block is rendered a public, rape-able, usable body-scale through which a distinct, or resistant, or human sense of place is obscured. I return later to the contested geographies contingent to the auction block. What I want to emphasize here is what is at stake if the *purchasable* and *profitable* qualities of black femininity, fundamentally, pivot around the sexed body. How does this sexual-economic exchange distribute, and redistribute, uneven geographies? Connecting two important black feminist viewpoints—that the enslaved black female body is a site of unprotected female flesh, which also reminds us of black women's essential and inalterable femaleness—I will address the linkages between geography, sexual violence, and sexual reproduction.[22] I suggest that the auction block is one site that justified multiple geographic dominations because it economized sexual domination *and* black inhumanity; differences (blackness, sexuality, class) are naturalized through white profit and violence. This naturalization depicts black *subjects,* and therefore their attendant geographies, as spatially valueless because the captive subject is both owned and rendered incapable of owning under the conditions and terms of slavery and the profitable production of space.

In several black feminist texts, it is argued that slavery, sexual violence, and sexual reproduction contributed to the social construction of black femininity. Historians and feminist theorists such as Deborah Gray White, bell hooks, Angela Davis, Kamala Kempadoo, and Hortense Spillers all suggest that the ways in which black femininity was produced during slavery was accentuated by institutionalized racism-sexism.[23] Spillers in particular uses geography—specifically the conditions of black captivity and spatial confinement—to argue that black womanhood was economically quantifiable, and therefore ideologically translatable, as unfeminine. Spillers suggests, then, that the language and stipulations of patriarchy and white-European sex-gender systems, produce a black female body "in crisis."

That is, black feminine sexuality is a site of loss under slavery: birth, parentage, heredity, motherhood, fatherhood, sexual desire, and sexual consent are produced and denied through the terms of unfreedom. The crisis is, then, the unidentifiable body, that black woman who is, both on and off the auction block, "too alien to comprehend."[24] Those who are too alien, living pieces of property, are evaluated as unprotected and unprotectable, a logical target for discursive and bodily violence. Angela Davis has a slightly different take on black femininity during slavery; for Davis, it is not her *un*identifiable sexed body that is at risk, but her identifiable and seemingly inalterable black "femaleness."[25] Thus, to borrow again from Marlene Nourbese Philip, it is "the space between the legs," up for sale and accessible, that determines the spaces through and beyond slavery.[26] Coupled, then, with sexual accessibility and justified violence are the capitalist uses of black procreation. Of primary importance is the reproduction of the slave population, the black woman's body as a fertile commodity of exchange.[27]

What Spillers and Davis offer, as mentioned above, is a reading of what the auction block lends to bodily and sociospatial differentiation: profitable public property, sites of unprotected female flesh, which are sexually/violently accessible. Spatial differentiation communicates sexually promiscuous, immoral, perpetually pregnant, inferior stereotypes; it reaffirms the places and spaces available within the racist patriarchy through the unfree body. In terms of geography, spatial differentiation is enacted through profit, objectification, and violence, and escalates beyond the body/bodily particularities. Cloaked in slave-property *rights,* other material and psychic landscapes of white supremacy, race, and sexuality have followed patterns of justifiable captivity and violence.[28] Geographies of whiteness, white femininity, white masculinity, and white corporeality are, for the most part, rendered protected and protectable. Slave quarters, plantation homes, fields, kitchens are, for black women, unprotected—it is in the material landscape, at work, in the home, and within the community, where the body is rightfully retranslated as inferior, captive, and accessible to violences.

## CONTESTING AND EXPRESSING THE BLOCK

An analysis of scale shows how the body intervenes in the oppressor-oppressed dichotomy. Here two processes should be re-emphasized. First, that scale is a way to locate how power socially produces differences between places and therefore brings into focus how a singular scale or geographic totality carries within it intricacies and connective social processes which can, and do, impact upon multiscalar areas. Second, because singular scales or totalities are relational, and not naturally hierarchical, they are materially and discursively alterable, able to be reconfigured locally and therefore within wider social contexts. Here, I am considering Neil Smith's discussion of how scale is "the technology according to which events and people are, quite literally, 'contained in space' . . . In scale, therefore, are distilled the oppressive and emancipatory possibilities of space, its deadness but also its life."[29] Smith's argument is particularly salient here because it refuses a finality in what I have mentioned above—about oppressive discursive and capitalist constructions of black womanhood—without erasing how place and identity are mutually constructed under bondage. More clearly, the scale of the body is a site of racial-sexual differentiation, which holds in it a struggle over being, making the self, and what Donna Haraway calls "situated knowledge."[30]

Black female subjects can assert political aims through redefining and refusing to fully accept traditional geographic limitations:

> When I was 15 years old, I was brought to the courthouse, put up on the auction block to be sold. Old Judge Miller from my county was there. I knew him well because he was one of the wealthiest slave owners in the county, and the meanest one. He was so cruel that all the slaves and many owners hated him because of it. He saw me on the block for sale, and he knew I was a good worker so when he bid for me, I spoke right out on the auction block and told him: 'Old Judge Miller, don't you bid for me, 'cause if you do, I would not live on your plantation, I will take a knife and cut my own throat from ear to ear before I would be owned by you.' So he stepped back and let someone else bid for me. My own father knew I was to be for sale, so he brought his owner to the sale for him to buy me, so we could be together. But when father's owner heard what I said to Judge Miller, he told my father he would not buy me, because I was sassy . . .[31]

The above remembrance by Delicia Patterson indicates that the auction block was also a site of contestation. Positioning herself as an unruly, sassy, suicidal slave-product, Patterson avoids her re-sale to the wealthiest and meanest slave owner in the county. The space of the auction and auction block allow her to display herself and her body as an unworthy, dangerous commodity. Her call for suicide simultaneously articulates her agency, the horrors of captivity, and her recognition of her valuable working-sexual body. Patterson's willingness to aim her suicidal tendencies directly at Judge Miller interrupts the expected flows of power: she prohibits *his* economic power; she, at least momentarily, controls the auction within the bounds of the auction block by redefining her body-worth. Additionally, the possibility of reunification with her father identifies the auction block as a site that can potentially bring about familial resistance. Free blacks, slaves, and slave owners repurchasing family members—and slaves purchasing themselves—recast the geographic work of the auction block. While it is clear that the auction block exudes white supremacy and limits her spatial opportunities (for example, her sassiness is consequently measured by her father's owner as (in)appropriate and it prevents their reunification), it is also evident that the auction block is not an impenetrable, transparent geography. The auction block is, instead, a site through which the conditions of captivity and sale can be contested, precisely because it is socially produced.

Patterson's distinct sense of place is informed by, and informs, the auction block. Scale is therefore called into question in that it is, as seen by her remembrance, experiential. The social activities and participants at the auction flow into the auction block, allowing Patterson to assert her situated knowledge, and her scaled body, in contradistinction to the production of slave space. The auction block is a paradoxical site of struggle, a space that articulates the tensions between and among black women, humanness, captivity, sexism-racism, profit. Firmly located within the crevices of power, the tensions are materialized by the very structures of slavery as they are critically encountered, then and now. This forces us to think about how to value the ways in which personhood is articulated within, and therefore destabilizes, socioeconomic confinement. These tensions also attend to the historical present, inviting a critical engagement with the ways in which the auction block is remembered, revisited, and reimagined in postslavery contexts.

## SALLY'S RAPE

Narratives of remembrance, antislavery representations of slave auctions, slave narratives, neo-slave narratives, and black theories differently contend with these tensions in order to recast the space of the black subject on different terms. Sherley Anne Williams's *Dessa Rose* and Robbie McCauley's *Sally's Rape* are texts that immediately come to mind. These fictional accounts pause on the sale of humans and black objectification, but reorient how one views and expresses sites of subjugation. The poetics of landscape are utilized to not only humanize the point of sale, but exploit the inherent weaknesses of scale: the metaphorical and the material coalesce to establish a usable black (feminist) geography. The creative use of landscape and black womanhood together develop the interconnections between and among scales in order to respatialize blackness. In *Dessa Rose*, for example, a black woman, a white woman, and several other slaves visit several auctions to sell/resell their blackness and escape slavery. They reinvent the scale of the auction block for black profit and freedom.[32] *Dessa Rose* also shows how the auction block can express the unresolved geographies of black femininity; the stakes of "how bodily geography can be" are used to insinuate blackness into the existing landscape for self-repossession, while the landscape paradoxically continues to displace and devalue blackness.

That the auction block is indicative of the possibility of respatialization is important. Still a site of violence and subjugation, the auction block is also a location of humanness, a place where race is made known in multiple ways. Creative texts that return to, and humanize, geographies of slavery illustrate how we are implicated in the production of space—particularly in the production of profitable, violent, transparent spaces, through reading, through knowing, through not knowing. This tension, between respatialization, transparent space, and the ways in which we are all implicated in the production of space, is thoughtfully represented vis-à-vis the auction block in Robbie McCauley's play *Sally's Rape*. *Sally's Rape* was first performed in 1989. It is described as a "work in progress."[33] The main themes of the text—feminism, slavery, womanhood, violence, and remembering—are developed through audience and actor call-and-response and actor-to-actor improvisational dialogue. The play thus changes with each performance, requiring the audience and the actors to stage a working dialogue about the central themes. A singular version of *Sally's Rape* thus gives only a partial sense of the play itself—the play changes from venue to venue and performance to performance. The play has been described as a lesson in blackface, an interracial dialogue, survival art, a social experiment, a public engagement with the undiscussable, a "plain speaking about race, between races, [which] feels practically taboo."[34]

*Sally's Rape* is a running conversation between Robbie McCauley and Jeannie Hutchins. McCauley is a black woman, Hutchins is a white woman; they are friends, they know one another's story. The audience is cited as an additional player, as "those who are there, who witness and talk back."[35] The play has ten sections or events, which address different political issues: the "proper" gendered body, family and religion, whiteness and slavery, education, language, rape, ancestors, emancipatory philosophies, social change. Both Robbie and Jeannie provide commentary that reflects "the parts of themselves that connect with the subjects of the piece."[36] Jeannie, the white actor, is also asked to play slavers, black women, white women, and herself. Robbie McCauley plays what she describes as "the people in her":[37] herself, black women, her ancestors, and different slaves. Sally, from the title of the play, is Robbie McCauley's ancestor, a slave who was repetitively raped by her master, and who bore two children by him; McCauley becomes Sally, reenacting her difficult life. At the same time, Sally is an every-woman; by this I mean that she "stands in" for other black women (including "President J's Sally"), and arguably, black men, whose pasts and presents are bound up with different forms of sexual domination, captivity, and exploitation. McCauley's past, then, is the traumatic device that she uses to anchor herself, Jeannie, and the audience. The author's intentions are clear: the casting, the content, the stage directions, the dialogue, and the characters, including the audience, all contribute to a crucial dialogue about the impact and continuity of domination. By discussing the undiscussable, by confronting the historical legacy of black women's domination and the ways in which this domination is facilitated, then and now, *Sally's Rape* asks us to learn from rather than simply learn about.[38] The play asks the reader/audience and the actors to recognize their implication in the story, how the story unfolds, and what the story teaches us as we participate in *Sally's Rape*/Sally's rape.[39]

The title of the play itself, *Sally's Rape,* immediately asks the reader or audience member to prepare for two (interconnected) kinds of violence: the symbolic and real rape of women. This violence, however, is ambivalent; it is produced and enacted through desire and disgust, love and hate, sexual pleasure and sexual displeasure. Immediately, the title of the play tells us something difficult is going to happen, or something difficult has already happened, that inequality is sexualized and that uneven sexual violence structures the play. The title asks the reader/audience to immediately engage with ambivalent participatory expectations: what is expected from a play titled *Sally's Rape,* how will sexual violence be staged, how will violence be tolerated, and what is the audience-participatory role in the rape? What does it mean to desire to see, read, and imagine Sally's rape?

I want to explore how McCauley uses the auction block in her play, as this is her most explicit re-visitation of slavery. There are two scenes in the play that return us to the auction block. I discuss the first event, in which Robbie—as Sally and herself—is on the auction block. This is how the event is described:

*Lights Change. The Auction Block. Jeannie moves bench center to be the auction block, but then improvises with Robbie, deciding to move the big table there instead. Jeannie takes the bench down left. Robbie steps onto the auction block, takes off her sack dress, drops it on the block. She is naked. Jeannie starts to chant, "Bid 'em in," coaxing the Audience, taking the time to thank them for joining in. It should be a moment of communion.*

ROBBIE: On the auction block. With my socks rolled down, I take off my sack dress. Mistress? Come on. This is what they brought us here for. On the auction block. They put their hands all down our bodies to sell you, for folks to measure you, smeltcha . . .

JEANNIE: That's what they brought us here for.

*Auction block light is blue. Jeannie circles down near Audience, leading the [bid in] chant . . .*

ROBBIE (still naked): Aunt Jessie said that's how they got their manhood on the plantations. They'd come down to the quarters and do it to us and the chickens. [Robbie continues, changing voice] A tightness between her thighs. When it lets go she screams in terror . . . Why does she keep coming to me in these nightmares? They say Sally was tough. Bought a house after slavery time. Taught her daughters to be ladies . . . She did all that and none of us ever had to be whores.

*Jeannie ends chant . . .*

ROBBIE (to Audience): I wanted to do this—stand public on the auction block. I thought somehow it could help free us from all of *this* (*refers to her naked body*) . . .

*Lights back to auction block blue. Robbie curls down onto block.* [She reenacts the rape of her ancestor Sally.][40]

This scene from *Sally's Rape* is the climax of the play. It is the moment Sally, Robbie, Jeannie, and the audience must hear, see, and participate in the sale of humans. There are several interesting representations in this particular scene. The actors' search for an auction block is especially telling. The stage directions do not prepare the audience for an auction: the lights change, and Jeannie moves a bench to center stage. Then both Robbie and Jeannie improvise, choosing to move a table to center stage instead. Both the bench and the table are written into the script as "auction blocks" but the audience is not explicitly told what the actors are doing and why they are moving what might be considered stage sets, or furniture, to the middle of the stage. I am intrigued by this moment because it sets up the capitalist geographies of slavery and reorders the black subjects' relationship to these geographies: Jeannie's initial suggestion, the bench, is deemed inappropriate. Robbie, soon to perform Sally, decides on the table. This could be for several reasons—the sturdiness of the table, the height of the table, the meaning of the table (as a place to eat, socialize, cook, write, play games); the most important, I believe, is that Robbie is required to produce her own surroundings and her own site of commodification; Jeannie, a white woman, soon to perform mistress and auctioneer, cannot fully produce/control the meaning of the auction.

The next moment, Robbie is naked, on the auction block. Jeannie is the auctioneer and asks the audience to chant "bid in." Robbie is transformed, from actor/writer/director to female slave for sale. Importantly, Jeannie is required to encourage the audience in their construction of Robbie as an object of "essential and inalterable femaleness."[41] Her position and nakedness transform the table into an auction block: the audience and Jeannie must guarantee that the transformation take place by chanting "bid in." Underlying her nakedness and the narrative, a symbolic capitalist transaction occurs; black womanhood is exposed as a public space, dehumanized, and for sale. The table and the body coalesce, and form a site of violent exchange. Not only is Robbie naked, but her nakedness seeps into the meaning of the auction block. Like her, the table is sexualized and eroticized, a site of sex and violence.

More than this, Robbie's body is held captive: her nakedness, her place on the table, and the narrative of bodily assessment—they put their hands all down our bodies, to sell you, for folks to measure you, and smell you— binds her to the auction block and implicitly gestures to the rape-ability of the black body. Both Jeannie and Robbie explain, "this is what they brought us here for": And when Robbie begins her narrative, "on the auc- tion block, with my socks rolled down . . . [they] listened while we bred," and reenacts the rape of Sally, the connections between domination, race, sex, bondage, violence, and profit are made explicitly apparent. However, Robbie's naked captivity is incomplete, because she is, in fact, human, in the present, a re-visitor of slavery; she organizes, spatializes, writes, and con- trols the significance of *Sally's Rape*/Sally's rape. What she offers is a retell- ing of auctions that explores black sexuality on new and different terms: while the auction block is a site of domination, which necessarily leads to dehumanization and sexual violence, McCauley, in the stage directions, tells us "it should be a moment of communion."[42] She is not bitterly re- counting the past and leaving us there to violate her body. Like Octavia Butler's *Kindred*, the temporal organization of the play suggests that Rob- bie and the audience must engage with a *new* "understanding of those generations forced to be nonpersons."[43]

McCauley's play sites and sights memory, staging the scale of the his- torical body in a new setting. She trusts that memory is real, and three- dimensional, and writes of a political historical present that is underscored by poetic geographies. We must, then, understand that our present con- dition informs the ways in which blackness is displayed: "we," as audience, produce, and bid on, blackness in order to, as McCauley says while refer- ring to her naked body, "help free us from this."[44] Recalling Toni Morri- son's remark, that slavery made white and black folks "into something else,"[45] McCauley calls into question who exactly is dehumanized by bid- ding in, and how the subject on the auction block is not the only "thing" to be examined.

I have suggested that McCauley's use of the auction block, as we en- counter it, continually establishes the limitations and the possibilities of black womanhood through and beyond bondage. More importantly, McCauley's auction block alters the terms of femininity and humanity by initiating a politics of what Sylvia Wynter calls "gender/beyond gender."[46] That is, the auction block can—in the past and the present—invoke a different, and underacknowledged, field of meaning. This field of meaning provides a frame of reference, which understands that bodily inscriptions be scrutinized not for their measurable oppressive corporeal identifiers, but rather for thinking about how practices of subjugation are socially produced and evidence of a larger, unfinished, geographic story. That is, the auction block is not only an underacknowledged human geography, situated right in the middle of our historical landscapes; it is also a site where structural forces can be, and are, called into question, where black humanness is wrapped up in the production of space. Gender/beyond gender, for sale on the auction block, insists on a different understanding of what it means to be human; the racialized body, stripped, displayed, emptied out, unfeeling, sexless and hypersexual, is explored in McCauley's work not only through historical re-visitation, but also for the ways in which a body for sale, on display, stripped, empty, is produced across time and space. This necessarily produces an alternative vantage point, which works to position how we, as audience and actors, function inside, and outside, and hopefully beyond, the dehumanizing act of Sally's rape.

# chapter 4

# Nothing's Shocking: Black Canada

Yet something more was going on; something more than a hot property of mayhem loaded with the thrill that a mixture of fame, sex, money, death and race produces . . .

—TONI MORRISON

There are only a handful of narratives about Marie-Joseph Angélique, the Portuguese-born slave who allegedly burned down most of Montreal, New France, in April 1734. Poems and a song, two plays and a film, a novel, historical footnotes, an art exhibit, brief historical inquiries, one extensive history. Accused of setting fire to her mistress's home and attempting to escape slavery while the fire spread throughout the city, Angélique was captured, arrested for arson, confessed under torture, was publicly executed by hanging, and cremated. Angélique's place in black Canadian history is, as far as counternarratives go, an important one. Not only does Angélique evidence slavery in Canada (a denied and deniable Canadian institution), the alleged act of arson led to a forced confession about the crime and her life in New France. This confession was recorded and archived, and has been re-narrated by scholars and writers who have an interest in exploring and re-imagining the history of Canada.

Within the context of Canadian historical geographies—a dominant narrative, Dionne Brand argues, which preserves a false legacy of whiteness by renouncing "race" and racial concerns—Marie-Joseph Angélique is a surprise.[1] By *surprise* I mean the outcome of wonder: an unexpected or astonishing event, circumstance, person, or thing; the emotion caused by this; astonishment, shock, or amazement; a gift or a present; a person or thing that achieves unexpected success; an attack or an approach made upon an unsuspecting victim; an act contrary to the expectations of a person; just as one might expect—no surprise at all.[2] Marie-Joseph Angélique invokes a number of surprises that are astonishing simply because they take place in Canada, a nation that has and is still defining its history as Euro-white, or nonblack. These surprises include, but are not limited to: black in/and Canada, black women in Canada, black resistances (to biological determinism, to racism, to sexism, to Canada and New France), eighteenth-century black "feminism," slavery in Canada, Canada as a site of permanent black residency. These people, place, events, and activities are not "Canada," are not supposed to be Canada, and contradict Canada; they are surprises, unexpected and concealed.[3]

In terms of geography, the element of surprise is contained in the material, political, and social landscape that presumes—and fundamentally requires—that subaltern populations have no relationship to the production of space. The surprise takes place when, as mentioned in chapter 1, these populations are recognized as viable geographic subjects who live and negotiate the world around them in complex ways. By defining and constructing the world they inhabit, black subjects challenge how we know and understand geography; by seriously addressing space and place in the everyday, through the site of memory and in theory and text, they also confront sociospatial objectification by offering a different sense of how geography is and might be lived. Within the context of historical and contemporary geographic expansion and the profitable displacement of difference, the surprise is an ongoing black refusal of a passive relationship with space and place; it is a dynamic interest in how geography is made and lived, through and beyond practices of domination. It could be argued, for example, that given the white colonial and geographic contexts of Canada, it is a surprise that black people are geographic at all due to spatial constraints that have an interest in sustaining black subordination and exclusion. More compelling, however, are the unexpected ways in which black geographic subjects differently produce space within this context of domination and objectification: specifically, the seeking out of alternative geographic options, and the coupling of geography with black matters, histories, knowledges, experiences, and resistances.

I am interested in exploring the element of surprise in black Canadian geographies, and through Marie-Joseph Angélique, because surprise presumes both blacklessness (prior to the surprise) and wonder (the emotion evoked by surprise, or in this case, blackness). Further, this suggests that after the surprise is uncovered, the unexpected event, person, or thing is warranted a particular kind of existence that is grounded in the idea that

something, or someone, was previously nonexistent: the wonder, following the surprise, gestures back to codes of representation and living that,
previously, did not expect a surprise. The element of surprise, then, holds
black Canada in tension with the nation's ceaseless outlawing of blackness:
blackness is surprising because it should not be here, was not here before,
was always here, is only momentarily here, was always over there (beyond
Canada, for example). This means, then, that black people in Canada are
also presumed surprises because they are "not here" and "here" simultaneously: they are, like blackness, unexpected, shocking, concealed in a
landscape of systemic blacklessness; and, they exist in a landscape of blacklessness and have "astonishingly" rich lives, which contradict the essential
black subject. In Canada, blackness and black people are altogether deniable *and* evidence of prior codes of representation that have identified
blackness/difference as irrelevant. But black existence is an actuality, which
takes on several different forms that do not (much to the surprise of some)
always conform to the idea of Canada.

As mentioned, the element of surprise permits an exploration of wonder. If blackness and black people in Canada can evoke wonder—emotions, such as admiration, perplexity, or curiosity—what does this mean
for Canada, black Canada, and black diaspora populations? Sylvia Wynter's discussion of wonder suggests that sites of representation, history, and
text cannot be examined as though they are freestanding events, people,
or things.[4] She argues that an exploration (rather than merely an expression) of wonder involves correlating embedded boundaries and hierarchies
and their experiential-contextual responses. Thus, we cannot just site/cite
wonder, we need to think about how wonder is made and always opens
up new inquiries. The surprise of blackness does not stand alone within
the confines of Canada; the surprise does not end after it has been encountered. Rather, it is followed by an experiential curiosity, wonder, which is
inevitably attached to new sensations, new ideas, that were previously unavailable. Let me give an example. In recently researching slavery in Upper
Canada/Ontario, I was told by a local archivist that slavery did not occur
in this particular province and that blacks did not reside in the city of York
(now Toronto) until the 1950s. While his assertion conflicted with some
of the general histories of urban Canada, this contradiction—I am familiar with a very different, specifically black, urban history—I was simultaneously surprised and unsurprised. To begin with the latter, these remarks

were unsurprising because they have repetitively constituted my experiences of/in black Canada. Institutionally, and socially, historical black existences are continually denied, for reasons I explore below. But my surprise at the remark is more interesting—I was, actually, also surprised at the archivist's impatient, comfortable, knowing denial, despite my handy history books, oral histories, and other archival explorations. This time, however, the surprise led me right into wonder, right into the historically present landscape of York/Toronto, to think about how projects of black "recovery" are not simply hindered by the denial of archivists, but actually structured by what might be called new histories or new genealogies. I began to wonder not about how black subjects are unavailable—in need of discovery—but rather how the *idea* of their previous lives shapes their absence and their presence. I began to consider, then, what happens when these historical lives are understood as new. Indeed, the connections between my surprise and the archivist's knowledge suggest that something is new, even though these past lives are long-standing black matters. So, what happens when we "wake up," to borrow Wynter's terminology, and find that Canada, and blackness, are no longer what we thought they were? What do we wonder? That is, my surprise and my "unsurprise"— the correlated embedded histories, the anticipated and unexpected denials, and my experiential responses to them—made me wonder how "conceptual otherness" is not simply missing or misread, but rather underwritten by new forms of knowledge that make Canada/York/Toronto what it is. Wonder invites new avenues for exploration that are both unexpected and underacknowledged and call into question the contexts that produce surprise and wonder in the first place: what makes blackness so surprising in Canada? And, what is curious about this surprise?

To examine black Canada and Marie-Joseph Angélique as surprises alone takes away from the possibilities implicit in the unfamiliar; black surprise, alone, undermines an examination of what was considered impossible under the paradigm of white Canada. The wonder of the unfamiliar and the impossible open up new avenues for research while also pointing to the ways in which blackness and black geographic subjects are not surprising at all—depending on one's vantage point. What do "surprise" and "wonder" offer black geographies in a nation that erases and demolishes black places and spaces and refuses to acknowledge the long-standing history of black peoples within its borders? Borrowing from theorist David

Scott, in the following section I suggest that the geographies of black Canada, and Marie-Joseph Angélique's Montreal, are not simply de-centering colonial and national geographies; rather, these black geographies cite a spatial terrain that makes available a place—and places—to produce and/or underscore varied responses to geographic domination.[5] The wonder implicit in black geographies thus refuses erasure by critically invoking the recognition that Canada is, in fact, racially produced—sometimes on different terms than expected.

## BLACK CANADA

The historical and contemporary geographies of Canada are colonial. Critical theories in Canadian native studies importantly highlight the ways in which exploration and conquest resulted in the violent displacement and genocide of First Nations communities. Indeed, this "making" of Canada situates a struggle that enmeshes race, whiteness, and the soil as they are attached to the nation's legal, political, and ideological claims of colonial superiority. Bonita Lawrence argues, for example, that claims to the land were deeply connected to human "exterminationist" practices, in effect "vanishing" native identities and communities through genocide and cultural imperialism.[6] Geographer Matthew Sparke argues, furthermore, that the struggles between native and nonnative populations rested on "cartographic" impulses, the desire of colonists to inhabit, map, and control what they considered an uninhabited (read: native-occupied) space.[7] These historical practices, of vanishing, classifying, objectifying, relocating, and exterminating subaltern communities, and desiring, rationally mapping, and exploiting the land and resources, are ongoing, firmly interlocked with a contemporary colonial agenda, which has material consequences.[8] Although the historically present struggles of Canada's First Nations are not my primary focus, nor identical to the history of black Canada, it is meaningful, in terms of geography and justice, to signal the ways in which the colonization of diverse native communities in Canada underscores how race is "placed" in Canada.

Two patterns of theorizing and "placing" blackness in Canada/nation emerge to challenge the seeming absence of the black diaspora. Here, I examine the ways in which specifying lost sites/citations of blackness and the analytical spaces of diaspora are cast as erasure and presence, concepts that are consequently used as oppositional strategies that fundamentally insist on a black presence. While some critics reverse narratives of elsewhere and absence in order to "find," "list," or "rediscover" black Canada, others analyze elsewhere and absence for their critical geographic possibilities, specifically how elsewhere and absence *are* in Canada, how black Canada is lived as unvisibility. Many black Canadian geographies offer a way into the nation without positing finished and transparent geographic projects; the struggle of asserting black in/and Canada necessitates an understanding of geography that is ongoing, connected to, yet displaced from, white geographic domination. This ongoing sense of place, and placing black in Canada through wonder, is also crucial to understanding the ways in which a figure such as Marie-Joseph Angélique, and a place such as Montreal, New France, figure into the broader geopolitics of Canada. I suggest that blackness has been geographically threaded through the colonial nation-space, despite the repression of ethnic geographies; it is through geographic threads that Marie-Joseph Angélique's ongoing sense of place can be imagined.

Giving access to otherwise lost histories, and spatializing processes of erasure, surprise and wonder disclose how a presumably Euro-white and colonial nation is concealing and/or obscuring unexpected social and geographic narratives. Concealment is accomplished at least in part by carefully landscaping blackness out of the nation: specifically, the demolition of Africville in Nova Scotia and Hogan's Alley in Vancouver; threatening and administering black diaspora deportation; the renaming of Negro Creek Road to Moggie Road in Holland Township, Ontario; the silence around and concealment of Canada's largest unvisible slave burial ground, Nigger Rock, in the eastern townships of Quebec; racist immigration policies; the ploughing over of the black Durham Road Cemetery in southwestern Ontario; the relocation, and recent renaming, of Caribana; and the commonly held belief that black Canada is only recent and urban.[9] When considered alongside other practices of discrimination, economic injustices, and racial-sexual oppressions, landscaping blackness out of the nation coincides with intentions to put blackness out of sight.

Unseen black communities and spaces thus privilege a transparent Canada/nation by rendering the landscape a "truthful" *visual* purveyor of past and present social patterns. Consequently, "truthful" visual knowledge regulates and normalizes how Canada is seen—as white, not blackless, not black, not nonwhite, not native Canadian, but white. "Other" geographic evidence is buried, ploughed over, forgotten, renamed, and relocated; this illustrates how practices of race and racism coalesce with racial and racist geographic demands. The surprise is produced, and wonder can be explored, the moment these hegemonic demands are called into question: displacement and blackness are implicated, unexpectedly, in the nation through black presence *and* blacklessness, burial, forgetfulness, renaming, relocation. The power-knowledge of what is "out of sight" is interrupted by the inadequate trickery of visual representation. We can begin to wonder, then, how the visual innocence of Canada and Canadian geographies are troubled, and sometimes re-ordered, by what Donna Haraway calls the topography of multidimensional positionings—those positionings, and subaltern subjects, that make unexpected openings (theoretical, geographic, philosophical, representational) possible and engaging.[10]

If black Canada is assumed to be nonexistent and/or recent, the work of scholars and writers investigating black Canada requires an engagement with wonder. More specifically, it is clear that several scholars and writers suspect and/or know of the long history of black Canada, but the evidence is thin, destroyed, or cast as non-Canadian. Slavery in Canada (British North America and New France), for example, is either forthrightly denied or deemed too brief and too small to warrant intellectual and political consideration. While the institution was certainly not comparable to large-scale slave institutions and economies in the United States or the Caribbean, it did last over 200 years.[11] The meaning of slavery in New France simultaneously represented brutal forms of captivity and small-scale enforced labor; this simultaneity, of "smallness" and violence against black subjects, renders the institution of slavery in New France difficult to detail: dehumanization and the smaller scale of Canadian slavery, together, make blackness erasable. Yet, as historians have shown, slavery in New France and British North America was maintained to uphold waves of European colonial settlements (new colonial subjects from France and Britain, Loyalists from the United States) and assist in the physical production of the nation.[12]

Because early black communities in Canada are erasable (which is not only shown in the national imaginary but also replicated vis-à-vis the paucity of investigations of black Canada during and after transatlantic slavery), Canada is often solely positioned as a safe haven (to U.S. fugitive slaves) and a land of opportunity (for black migrant workers, the Caribbean community, and migrants from the continent of Africa). Despite the extensive work by several theorists and activists in Canada, the black community and the struggles that coincide with being black in Canada, remain relatively unknown in the broader national discourse and non-Canadian black diaspora studies.[13] The intellectual and political terrain of historical black Canada is either absent or crosscut with narratives of Canadian paternalism and benevolence. One exception to absence, which also heightens paternalism and material marginalization, is Africville. The demolition of Africville in the 1960s scaled the nation vis-à-vis the media and provincial and national politics. The decision to relocate the Africville community illustrated both racism and the re-marginalization of the Nova Scotian black community. Although the initial decision to destroy Africville was couched in paternalistic health-conscious "cleaning up" of blackness, it was also an attempt to erase black lands through legal and social decentralization. The sociogeographic process itself soon became the site of obvious racist and economic assumptions and violations. Blackness was, arguably, exposed and became a multiscalar and ongoing debatable site.[14] Even so, I would suggest that the destruction of Africville, and the debates and reclamations surrounding this space, continue to be underwritten by an always already fleeting historic black community. Jennifer Jill Nelson importantly notes that recent reclamation attempts—the building of Seaview Memorial Park—does not adequately respatialize the legal violence imposed on the black community in Nova Scotia.[15] At the same time, Africville remains an imaginary past geography, a brief paternalistic governmental mistake, and often the only contested space of blackness in Canada. Africville, too, needs to be wondered.[16]

Despite Africville's historic legacy, to assert the possibility of black Canada—in the academy and the everyday—is often met with articulations of surprised disbelief. This surprise is followed by a panicked return to those events I have already mentioned: But they came here from the United States during slavery; but they only just arrived; but Canada was and is too progressive and too nice (or neutral) to engage in slavery and racism. And what about Africville? The panicked return to racial marginalization and denial is upheld by a nation that prides itself on two founding nations (French and British) and a multiculturalism that attempts to discursively and materially push nonwhite communities—including Native Canadians—outside its ideological and/or physical borders.

In terms of black Canada, the displacement of black subjects and histories is achieved by attaching categories such as race, ethnicity, nation, and home to the United States and the Caribbean. To belong as black in Canada is therefore to necessarily belong elsewhere.[17] This process of naming Canadian blackness as Caribbean or U.S. unhinges black people from Canada, while also reducing black specificities to an all-encompassing elsewhere (simply non-Canadian). The geographic terms of being black *in* Canada are, within the context of Canadian colonialism and nation-making, crucially nonphysical geographies unless they are outside the borders of the nation-state. This displaces black communities by refusing their social, economic, and political commitment to places and spaces both within and beyond Canada. It also reifies ideologies around nation-purities by insisting that black communities are non-Canadian, always other, always elsewhere, recent, unfamiliar, and impossible.

Because Canada is riddled with these different forms of disavowal, the geographies of black Canada also tend to be constructed according to narratives of absence or elsewhere. Susan Ruddick's discussion of race, scale, and place, in Toronto and Canada, outlines how blackness can be "comfortably" forgotten because Canadian racism effectively denies the black community any geographic relevancy.[18] If black geographies are, according to Canadian nationalism and its citizens of white and European descent, irrelevant and elsewhere, then the active production of black spaces in Canada is necessarily bound up with a contradiction: black Canada is simultaneously invisible and visibly non-Canadian. This contradiction demonstrates the subtle ways in which domination shapes what has been called "the absented presence"[19] of black Canada and black Canadian geographies: black people *in* Canada are geographically un-Canadian—their bodies (and therefore their histories) tell us so. This also suggests, to return to Ruddick's terminology, that historical and contemporary geographic dominations can be relatively comfortable processes because the domination is of something and someone that/who is not really Canadian, or is not really here/there at all.

The wonder of black Canada, however, discloses incomplete disavowal: places and spaces that leave ideological and material traces; locations that can and have been uncovered, sites that continually produce questions; historical and contemporary subjects who have an interest in missing persons, histories, and geographies; and positionings that revisualize and reorder the landscape. Historical and geographic disavowal produces something else, which does not entirely negate the presence of the subaltern, nor does it exactly replicate the past that it has attempted to erase. The tensions, between community and preservation, absence and erasure, scatter the Canadian landscape, illustrating that places, local and national, are inflected with unexpected, unacknowledged, historical maps. Geography and black Canadian geographies therefore demand an exploration of wonder in order to unravel what is beneath and beyond existing geopolitical landscapes.

Narratives of erasure and domination, as mentioned, make the possibility of black Canada surprising and unexpected. Several scholars who have examined black Canada have therefore spent considerable time making black Canada, and Canadian racism, unsurprising. George Elliot Clarke's "Africana Canadiana: A Select Bibliography of Literature by African-Canadian Authors, 1785–2001" is a perfect example of making black Canada unsurprising.[20] The document, which lists over 2,500 African-Canadian texts, suggests that the histories and writings of black Canada are not, as mentioned above, thin, destroyed, or non-Canadian. Clarke's meticulous and extensive list of black writings in and about Canada—each citation coupled with the (black) birthplace of the author—forces the reader to engage with thousands of black subjects who have, always or at some point, occupied Canadian spaces. The document, and Clarke's compulsion to list, suggest not only that black Canada is knowable, but that black Canadian presences are incontestable. Despite Clarke's attachment to processes of categorization and listing all that is black Canada (which necessarily also boxes in and excludes, and arguably truncates "wonder" through its definitive marking of what/who "black" is)—"Africana Canadiana" persuasively identifies that black Canada *is* and *was*, and is therefore unsurprising.

Texts such as Francis Henry's *The Caribbean Diaspora in Toronto: Learning to Live with Racism*, Sherene Razack's *Looking White People in the Eye*, Daniel G. Hill's *The Freedom-Seekers: Blacks in Early Canada,* and Cecil Foster's *A Place Called Heaven: The Meaning of Being Black in Canada* have theoretical underpinnings that illuminate the ways in which racial histories and contemporary experiences are repressed in Canada.[21] Historians of black Canada in particular, for example, tend to begin their analyses by outlining the frustrating ways in which black history is hidden, eradicated, and underexplored; they often begin their studies vis-à-vis the wonder of blackness—what might have been or who was and is historically present—in order to locate a lost and neglected black history.[22] In documenting the continued presence of black people and their racialized lives, the repression is overturned, exposing what Foster describes as both "predictable" and "culturally symbolic" black Canadian experiences: racial profiling, black celebratory events, institutionalized racism, violences, economic hardship, black music and music making, educational problems and possibilities.[23] The projects by Clarke, Henry, Razack, Hill, and Foster, among others, while very different, seek to explore social differences as they are produced in conjunction with a nation that continually refuses to acknowledge, or see, black communities. These projects reflect a pattern of antiracist and antiracist feminist theorizing in/on Canada, wherein blackness is repositioned as a relevant and imaginable part of the nation-state.[24] This work not only documents the material locations of blackness and black communities, it demonstrates that race, racism, and erasure shape black lives and black scholarship. Consequently, there is a push to *see* blackness, black people, and black histories, and oppose racist domination by acknowledging the varying spaces of black lives or black geographies.

What these different critics offer is a visual and discursive mapping of black Canada. They reorder the ways in which black peoples are situated in the nation due to white discourses and domination. Sociospatial reordering moves blackness away from nonexistence and into the nation, wherein the nation is asked to be held accountable for the ways in which domination reproduces different forms of black invisibility. White accountability for black discrimination, however, often mutates if and when it is addressed in the dominant Canadian discourse. An intelligible discursive conceptualization of black in/and Canada is often coupled with the suggestion that *if* blackness *is* in fact here—visual, Canadian, historic—it is also criminal and problematically black, or visually un-Canadian. Geographically, this tension between absence and hypervisual non-Canadian black subjects fulfills a nation-discourse that displaces black histories in similar ways that other nations, such as the United States, do: the spatialization of the underclass, stereotyping blackness, overpolicing black communities, racial profiling, criminalizing black communities, refusing black Canadian citizenship, and so on. The anxiety in Toronto, Ontario, over Jamaican criminals thus warrants an overpolicing of black Toronto communities in general; blackness is publicly collapsed, a criminal and suspect category, which belongs elsewhere, is ahistorical, is invading Canada, and is described as "spilling over" onto the streets of Toronto and the city-nation.[25] The public media discourse around black/Jamaican spillage, leaking into the city-nation, repeats Canada's history of marking nonwhite communities through discourses of disease, vice, cleanliness, and health.[26] It also discursively "places" blackness as ethnically outside the nation and criminally inside the nation—and always recent.

The geographic "problem" of blackness, after its existence is surprisingly unearthed, is often recast as something/someone who threatens to launch a criminal, or a non-Canadian, or a diseased surprise attack on the nation. The hypervisual black subject is dangerously un-Canadian and therefore geographically unacceptable. Black Canadian spaces and places of unacceptability go two ways at once—back in time, reestablishing that "black" has never been believably Canadian, or geographic, and forward again, reasserting that black subjects are perpetually and visibly non-Canadian. Antiracist approaches to black Canada work through these discourses of hypervisibility and lost histories, offering a critique of the ways in which geopolitical patterns push blackness out of the nation; their agenda refuses the racism that displaces black communities. Geographically, this refusal attends to a politics of location that sites/cites black Canada, warranting black existence and disclosing how Canadian racism shapes black lives.

Other scholars and writers have focused on making black Canada not only relevant, but also a part of broader critical debates around borders, exclusion, the black diaspora, and race and racism in the Americas. The linking up of black cultures within and beyond Canada demonstrates how the local is connected to transnational and supranational geographies and patterns of displacement.[27] These studies investigate black presences and erasures by suggesting that black Canada, and black Canadian geographies, are diasporic spatializations. These diasporic spatializations are situated in the local and are inflected with black historical and contemporary narratives that are not so local. Diaspora narratives reach back to the forced scattering of black subjects during and after transatlantic slavery, and are also premised on outernational connections and cultural borrowings, such as philosophies, musics, migrations, and memories. In this view, black Canada is not invisible, nor is it, as the above-mentioned scholars suggest, simply *in* Canada; rather, black Canada exhibits stories, places, and spaces that are materially detectable in the local landscape and through and beyond the nation-state.

This approach to black Canada takes those projects that are committed to making blackness a relevant and imaginable part of Canada in a slightly different direction. Black Canadian diaspora studies, seen in the work of Marlene Nourbese Philip, Dionne Brand, and Rinaldo Walcott, for example, suggest that absence and elsewhere, while putting blackness "out of sight" and attaching hypervisual meanings to black bodies, are also analytical categories. These studies and literatures have produced two connected geographic trajectories: first, are the ways in which black histories, geographies, and experiences in Canada are bound to non-Canadian sites and histories. Rather than insisting that black is elsewhere, these studies suggest that various local and outernational black geographies contribute to the production of spaces *within* the nation. Philip, for example, writes of Toronto's Caribana as a present-local celebration of blackness, which holds in it multiple past and present diaspora spaces: other carnivals in Canada, the United Kingdom, the United States, Africa, and the Caribbean; slavery; slave rebellions and escape; black labor and immigration patterns.[28] The kind of geography Philip employs in her discussion of Caribana is identifiably Canadian (Toronto, University Avenue, Lakeshore Boulevard) without being exclusively in Canada or in the present (Notting Hill Carnival in 1976, slaves ships, and so forth). Blackness is strategically used to recast how elsewhere, the "problem" of black un-Canadian-ness in fact produces local Canadian spaces.

Second, absence and elsewhere are, in fact, critical sites of nation, in that black subjects encountering and living the nation also expose its social, political, racial, and sexual limitations.[29] The limitations of space and place, then, are explored by illustrating how the local-present cannot do the work of black Canadian geographies alone. Thus, nation-borders are called into question, because they do not sufficiently speak to the ways in which black geographies in Canada are made and upheld. What I mean by this is that diaspora connections are necessary to many black geographies in that they configure how one lives absence and elsewhere within Canada. Diaspora geographies are demonstrated in two ways: if Canada refuses and displaces blackness, its seemingly democratic and benevolent geographies are overturned and aligned with other geopolitical refusals; outernational and Canadian black geographies are produced in tandem with these nation-limitations in order to validate and expand spatial options. Philip thus concludes her discussion of Caribana by outlining the ways in which this black Canadian space is policed, socially unacceptable, and underfunded; Caribana is, importantly, a festival of limitations, which informs geographic critiques of spatial domination.[30] If we recognize that the nation is both hostile and made up of places unbound, and recognize the complexities of black in/and Canada, nation-interrogation is produced on slightly different terms. Specifically, black Canadian diaspora spaces are not only *in* Canada, they are produced through the disappointments of Canada/nation (which assert unwelcoming and/or blackless discourses) and through alternative geographic possibilities that spatialize a different, less border-bound, sense of place. Implicit to these nation and border critiques is a reworking of traditional geographies; the politics of boundaries, nationhood, and race are replaced by experiential and material diaspora geographies, which insist that the Canadian nation-space is simultaneously occupied by and implicated in different forms of blackness.

Dionne Brand's *A Map to the Door of No Return* demonstrates a different sense of place by presenting conflicting geographic patterns, which trouble both Canada and blackness. Brand's uses throughout the text, on spaceless and placeless maps, and the pain traditional colonial maps inflict, suggests that diaspora geographies within and outside Canada are fostered by brutal conquests and subaltern disappearances: black diaspora subjects, enduring bodily/global geographic conquests, colonialism, and transatlantic slavery, are always landing "with no destination in mind."[31] She writes, "landing is what people in the Diaspora do. Landing at ports, dockings, bridgings, stocks, borders, outposts."[32] These landings are not predictable or premeditated; rather, they chart a different sense of place, which is simultaneously unexpected, rooted, and rootless: the diaspora subject exists, in place, without destination and, Brand argues, destination desire. The maps of diaspora subjects are placeless because a black claim to place is unavailable through traditional geographic means. Brand can land in place, but she will not claim it in ways with which we are familiar. By critically engaging with seductive landscapes that are "cut through with something terrible that happened," she is hesitant to own geography on familiar terms.[33]

While Brand is drawn to mapping, the limitations of traditional geographic patterns—such as regions, nations, boundaries, geometeries, maps, and paths—force her to scrutinize geography through the site of memory and different forms of black placelessness. *A Map to the Door of No Return* moves from mapping to the unmappable, back and forth, from page to page: detailed descriptions of physical locations, forced exiles, maps, travels, old geometry and history books, are set in and amongst her struggle with places unbound and undetectable sites of subaltern loss. Brand is caught up in the predicament of black geographies as they are understood beyond and through colonial and imperial projects. She invokes a different sense of place by presenting black diaspora geographies that are riddled with desire for place, the suspicion of the desire for place, and experiential physical place(s):

> I have not visited the Door of No Return . . . I am constructing a map of the region . . . The Door of No Return is of course no place at all but a metaphor for place . . . it is not one place but a collection of places. Landfalls in Africa, where a castle was built, a house for slaves, *une maison des esclaves* . . . a place where a certain set of transactions occurred, perhaps the most important of them being the transaction of selves . . . The door signifies the historical moment which colours all moments of the diaspora . . . A body pushing a grocery cart through the city housing at Lawrence and Bathurst in Toronto, her laundry, her shopping all contained there . . .[34]

These geographies exemplify local-global moments of pain and desire, locations that situate black diaspora populations both materially and imaginatively. The unknown (the door) is attached to, and "colours," local moments (Lawrence and Bathurst Streets) and black displacements (the transaction of selves, *une maison des esclaves,* class struggles in the diaspora).

Together, different local-global geographic moments are framed by a kind of compulsion to chart and map the environment beyond transparency. Unlike George Elliot Clarke's compulsion to list all that is, and was, and therefore can be black Canadian, in Brand's text, her yearning to map demonstrates her continued unwillingness to be geographic according to these rules: crucially, she cannot map all that is, was, and can be black, and she knows this. This knowledge forces her to come to terms with the ways in which her sense of place is inflected by unspeakable (unmapped) and speakable (mapped) displacements: racial-sexual discrimination, homophobia, uneven geographies. By working through the tensions between imaginary and real geographies—the door of no return, black geographies in the Americas, Africa, Europe—Brand illustrates the ways in which a specific time-space locality is unraveled by a sense of place that dislodges traditional geographic rules from black spatial experiences. These diaspora geographies invoke a politics of place which, through Brand's own exploration of geographic wonder, calls into question how racial-geographic liberation is not a matter of carving out a place, or a comfortable situatedness, or ownership; rather her discomfort with and her compulsion to map bring forth new cartographic processes: she can and cannot construct the map; the Door of No Return simultaneously offers no return and a return to different forms of spatial occupation and domination, including her own.

The context of absence and elsewhere pushes an exploration of what and where absence and elsewhere are, and how they are employed, lived, and expressed by black communities through and beyond disavowal. This process of mapping absence/elsewhere under the paradigm of Canadian disavowal and black existences illustrates how a geographic lack opens up critical commentaries about exclusion, racism, segregation, and spatial objectification; what is geographically missing, according to Brand—black histories, black geographies—is made into something politically possible: a space and place of critique and black diasporic occupancy in the nation. To posit that a geographer, a black feminist geographer, has no destination in mind, is a reconceptualization of how geography might be practiced.

Thus, it is not simply a matter of placing blackness within Canada, or the world; nor is it a matter of superimposing black maps atop the nation-space. Rather, black diaspora theories hold place and placelessness in tension, through imagination and materiality, and therefore re-spatialize Canada on what might be considered unfamiliar terms. Black discourses and sites of contestation, conflict, and displacement advance a different sense of place, which is tied to alternative geographic agendas: exposed are cartographic impossiblities, surprising black geographies, and black geographic subjects who are otherwise understood as beyond the comprehension of traditional Euro-white geographies and geographers; spatialized are different formations of black geographies and new analytical sites of social difference and social justice.

## EIGHTEENTH-CENTURY MONTREAL, NEW FRANCE

Marie-Joseph Angélique's Montreal is a site where Canada, as we are meant to know and encounter it, falls apart: it is where blackness and whiteness meet, historically, presently, imaginatively, and geographically. This meeting point is both a site of forgetting and wonder. The historical geography and legacy of colonial Montreal conceals blackness, privileges whiteness, and attaches black subjects to anywhere but Canada; because Angélique's story predates the arrival of U.S. black communities during the Underground Railroad, her geographies are often cast as impossible, or unacceptable, to the making of a benevolent Canadian space. Further, the eighteenth-century landscapes Angélique negotiated have not been mapped on her terms—her status as a slave, as property, and as a black woman forbade a deliberate black production of space. Yet she landed, against her will and enslaved, with no desired destination in mind and, we must imagine, a very complex sense of place. The town/city was not built to benefit Angélique specifically, but her material surroundings—the streets, the spatial order of Montreal, the côtes, the St. Lawrence River, the Hôtel-Dieu, Mont-Royal—matter, then and now. In what ways can these material geographies comprise part of black Canada? How does the presence of Angélique shape Canadian geographies? In what ways does Angélique's Montreal incite material and imaginative geographic patterns of social (in)justice? And, why is her presence, as George Elliot Clarke rightly argues, so irresistible?[35]

In *Montreal in Evolution,* architect and geographer Jean-Claude Marsen describes the town and island of Montreal as an "advantageous geography."[36] The colonial town, situated on the St. Lawrence and Ottawa Rivers, was indeed in an invaluable location (see Figure 4): the waterways provided a transit point between inland new world colonial points, the Great Lakes, the North Atlantic Ocean, and beyond. In addition to being an advantageous "connective" geography, colonial Montreal had what has been called "an orderly spatial disposition": agricultural land was divided into long and narrow lots, perpendicular to the St. Lawrence River, with several distinct strip developments, together, comprising côtes or "colonization districts."[37] Each of the colonization districts were inhabited by early colonial subjects and were sites of agricultural and habitation development.

The early "main" streets—Rue St. Paul and Rue Notre-Dame—ran close and parallel to the St. Lawrence River and were also early sites of colonial occupation. Rue St. Paul, where Marie-Joseph Angélique is said to have lived and worked, lies closest to the St. Lawrence River and encompassed the lower town.[38] Like other growing towns and cities, then, colonial Montreal was fashioned according to a fairly orderly geometric grid, with territorial divisions and "emblematic sites"—Place du Marché, St. Sulpice Seminary, Notre-Dame Church, L'Hôtel-Dieu, Mont-Royal—serving as sociospatial markers and sites of religious, social, and economic exchange. These emblematic sites (except, of course, Mont-Royal, which is part of the natural landscape), along with the colonial homes, were made with either, or a combination of, wood, stone, slate, tile, and tin; most colonial homes, up to and into the mid-1700s, were constructed with wood.[39]

The geographic layout of Montreal was intertwined with the social, economic, and religious activities of the town. At the end of the sixteenth century, the fur trade and religious evangelization dominated the colony as the primary economic and social practices. Until the British conquest of New France in 1763, Montreal did not have a diversified economic base and the organization of the colony, and the social regulation of Europeans and non-Europeans, was framed by religious proselytism and religious differences.[40] The local population included religious leaders (Jesuits, Dominicans, Franciscans), wealthy colonists, and tradespeople, French indentured laborers, black slaves, and Native slaves *(Panis)*. The social hierarchy was geographically mapped onto the city, with the aforementioned religious "emblematic sites" representing and distributing wealth, Catholicism, trade transactions, military decisions, infrastructure choices, and administrative order. Because agricultural and artisan skilled-work were undermined by the fur trade and religious expansion, colonial occupation of eighteenth-century New France remained small and bifurcated along class lines and population: wealthy, bourgeois, and religious French subjects maintained trade alliances and geo-economic control, and a relatively small number of peasant, poor, and enslaved peoples worked the land and in the homes of those in power.

In 1734, the year Marie-Joseph Angélique was accused of setting fire to her mistress's home and the surrounding buildings, New France had been practicing slavery for over a century. Black slaves from Africa, the United States and other European colonies, such as the Caribbean, as well as

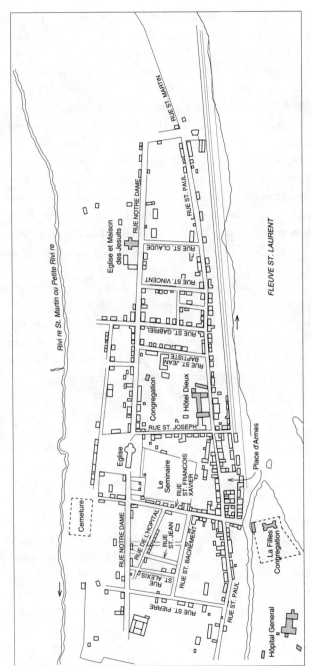

Figure 4. Map of the town of Montreal, circa 1730. Courtesy of Cartographic Office, York University; drawn by Carolyn King.

Native Canadians, were purchased for domestic, agricultural, and small-scale industrial labor. By 1734, slavery was entrenched, both legally and socially. The French colony had institutionalized slavery and sociopolitical control over the slave population through royal authorization of slave purchases in 1689 and 1709, and *The Code Noir* of 1685 and 1728.[41] Historians Robin Winks and Marcel Trudel have noted that while the exact population of black Canadian slaves is difficult to determine because they were considered a form of property, wealthy colonists, together, owned anywhere from 1,000 to 1,500 black slaves between the 1730s and the 1760s.[42] Compared with the French colonial population of New France at the time, which was approximately 38,000, it can be estimated that there was approximately one slave to every thirty colonial subjects during Angélique's enslavement.[43] Furthermore, historians also suggest that more than one-half of black slaves in New France were purchased by residents of the town of Montreal, a growing region of affluence.[44]

With more than one-half of the slave population concentrated in or near Montreal, Marie-Joseph Angélique's geographies are evidence of other undocumented stories; the landscape, industry, and infrastructure, as well as colonial properties (human and nonhuman), shed light on how Angélique and other black slaves may have encountered Montreal. Those who worked the land, as well as shopkeepers, domestics, and craftspeople, were inextricably tied to the French sanctioned socioreligious geography. For the black enslaved population of Montreal, these orderly and ideological spatial patterns determined their movement to and within the colony: socioeconomic needs imported blacks into Canada, while religious ideologies and geopolitical and legal patterns determined the meaning of "race" and racial movements within the colony. Purchasing black slaves in New France was, according to historians, primarily carried out by the elite class, although other groups (the gentry, merchants) also held *Panis* and black slaves. Maureen Elgersman, Robin Winks, and Charmaine Nelson all suggest that black slaves were symbols of wealth, purchased by elite colonial subjects (including religious leaders) to provide local and personal domestic and agricultural labor.[45] This suggests, then, that unlike the United States and the Caribbean, black slaves in New France were purchased primarily to work the immediate home-economy rather than the broader colonial-economy. This parallels the economic patterns in New France mentioned previously, which in the eighteenth century were centered on the fur trade and a mercantile system controlled by the French government: the labor implicit to the fur trade itself was carried out by French colonials and Native Canadians. The land in New France—the natural and agricultural resources beyond the fur trade—was yet to be exploited for regional, national, and international trade-profits. While the scale of the home-economy certainly stretches and sustains colonial and French European economies, the boundaries and definitions of domestic slave work surely limited the ways in which this labor was experienced; that is, while black slaves were purchased to sustain all sorts of economies, their geographic and economic contribution was localized and discursively prohibited by the terms of captivity.

If black slaves were purchased to function as working-sexual objects that symbolically elevated the status of the elite, Angélique's geographic opportunities and experiences were produced through and alongside geographic domination. I will address how her presence in New France and her workplace/home structured her surrounding and experiential geographies in three ways: through *The Code Noir*, emblematic "objecthood,"[46] and the spaces of the colonial domestic workplace.[47] I am addressing these three geographies for two reasons. First, in order to think about the ways in which black geographies might have been produced by and for black slaves in Montreal—and how the production of space by and for black people does not neatly parallel absence or captivity. And second, to delineate why geography matters so much to the story of Angélique, and why her relationships with space and place, including the alleged arson, create a terrain through which other black geographies and narratives are produced.

Marie-Joseph Angélique's status as a racialized-commodity-object contributed to the organization of the social and ethnic structures in New France—specifically through phenotype, gender, class, and sex. Introduced to protect Europeans in the French Caribbean and Louisiana from slave violence, such as theft, revolt, and escape, *The Code Noir* was only periodically enforced in New France. Because of the small white colonial population, the smaller slave population, and the high proportion of domestic slaves, the code was enacted "in spirit" when individual threats (or resistances) to the white population occurred.[48] This differs from other French colonies (such as Louisiana) in that large-scale plantations were said to be more at risk for large-scale black revolt and violence. It could be argued, then, that the uses of *The Code Noir* in New France echoed the ways in

which black slaves were spatially organized: there was less of a threat of
community revolt because black slaves were separated, often working alone
in homes rather than in groups; contact with other black slaves, *Panis,* and
indentured laborers was probably limited due to the particular geographic
regulations of slavery. *The Code Noir* thus perhaps gives one clue as to the
ways in which the geographies of slavery in New France were mapped out;
it was used to organize and adversely shape individual slave-spaces, such
as colonial homes.[49]

Regardless, *The Code Noir* ideologically entrenched the institution of
slavery within New France. The presence of the legal discourse naturalized
race hierarchies by legalizing, and ethnically coding, subordination. Lynn
Stewart has thus described *The Code Noir* as a "legal geography," which
regulated circuits of rational sociogeographic domination, through secur-
ing the slave body into the landscape.[50] This geographic domination required, furthermore, that slaves be cast as "immovable property," or, that
they would be severely punished, or killed, for moving ("moving" would
include, then, theft of slaves, revolt, and escape). The marking of blackness as immovable and subordinate within New France surely shaped the
geographies of black slaves by legally and socially enforcing "objecthood."
That is, within the context of eighteenth-century New France, *The Code
Noir* not only bound blackness to the landscape of Montreal by sanctioning punishment and determining the "immovable" terms of ownership, it
legally marked black bodies as objects in that landscape.

Black domestic slaves also represented, geographically, luxury items.
Thus, we can also imagine the ways in which the body of the domestic
slave in New France was understood and imagined as an "object in the
midst of other objects."[51] Blackness was, in part, considered a site of wealth
and therefore geographically emblematic. This emblematic positioning
of blackness and black people ties into questions of how ownership determines the production of space: the work black domestic slaves performed
unfolds as the production of white spaces rather than the production of
black spaces; white ownership of black human-property, and black labor,
discloses an explicit, top-down, production of space. The biological and
material reproduction of slave labor, the cleaning, cooking, and building,
the agricultural work, and so forth, were characterized by the ways in
which these tasks built up, and maintained, white dwellings, white infrastructures, white profit, white well-being, and racial hierarchies. Within the

domestic sphere, the practice of positioning blackness as a site of elite
"objecthood" marked black labor and lives (and therefore the production
of black spaces) as emblematic of whiteness and white profit. This suggests, moreover, that "seeing" blackness in New France—on the streets, in
the homes and yards of colonial elites, at the Place du Marché and the
Seminary—was also a process of engendering ethnic geographies: the kinds
of spaces black slaves did and did not occupy underscored, visually and
emblematically, different nonblack spaces, for example, *Panis* and white European spaces, as well as who constituted a human subject, and the extent to
which geographic mobility was possible for different people in New France.

Despite the restrictions and inscriptions that *The Code Noir* and emblematic objecthood imposed on black subjects in New France, the geographies of slavery were daily and experiential. I have suggested above that
black labor produced spaces that were identifiably white; in tandem with
this were spaces that, because they were occupied by black slaves, had to
be, at least in part, black geographies. More clearly, if identity and place
are understood as mutually constructed, then black slaves were implicated—experientially, imaginatively, and materially—in the production of
space. Of central importance are the spaces of the colonial domestic workplace: the homes and properties of the elite classes were, significantly, sites
of black occupation. Black slaves' quarters, as well as their workplaces and
duties, served to spatialize subordination and domination. Thus, there was
what Heidi Nast describes as a "denigrated placement" of black bodies,
which geographically determined who was, and who was not, black.[52]
Additionally, several black feminist historians and critics have outlined the
duties of black female domestics during slavery, suggesting that their labor
stabilized the home-economy: responsibilities included cooking, cleaning,
washing, sewing, needlework, tending to gardens, coordinating other slaves'
work, tending to children, and purchasing household items.[53] While this
labor was geographically differentiated and hierarchical across the black
diaspora, the work of black slaves in and around the home was, without a
doubt, an act of producing white and nonwhite spaces.

In addition to household duties, black women were often purchased for
sexual violence, sexual gratification, and sexual reproduction. Black slaves
were forced to make and maintain sexual spaces and deliver future working-
sexual bodies. The spatial expression of patriarchies—enacted through
sex, rape, and forced reproduction—inscribed colonial homes with violence,

sexuality, and racial hierarchies. The production of sexual spaces coincided
with control and access to blackness and, in Marie-Joseph Angélique's case,
black femininity. Thus, several homes within Montreal demonstrated a
different kind of "advantageous geography": geographies that correlate
blackness with spaces of profitable sex and violence. Work, sexuality, violence, gender, and race thus determined how the production of space was
enacted by and through black subjects in New France. The material locations of the white and black populations communicated and structured
race, gender, and class, illustrating how ideological codes contribute to the
place and placement of different racial identities.

The daily and experiential geographies of black slaves in New France
were evident through and beyond the home-place. Imagining the combination of daily domestic responsibilities, the threat of punishment and
sexual violence, the repetitive coding of blackness, the emblematic and
orderly spatial disposition of the streets, and the "small square domestic
fortresses" of elites, clarifies how black spaces may have been created in
eighteenth-century Montreal.[54] Slave labor, race, and sexuality structured
the lives of domestic slaves by implicating them in the production of space
without permitting explicit freedoms. Through stabilizing social, political,
and economic patterns, the presence of blackness in Montreal was implicit
to the production of racialized spaces. The black social and representative
presence in New France opens up new areas for inquiry: the landscape of
New France, the homes worked and occupied by black people, and the
culmination of being black and being geographic, challenges the immovability and absence of blackness. The uneven ethnic geographies in New France,
then, were in part produced by and because of the need for racialized
working-sexual colonial luxury "items" which, because they were also owned,
provided an unexpected, and radically different, terrain through which
black geographies, and Canadian geographies, can be understood. Importantly, then, the production of space in Montreal signals the ways in which
white European spaces were also spaces of black captivity. This black captivity, however, did not prohibit the production of black spaces; in fact,
black captivity defined exactly how Montreal was spatially created by way
of practices of domination. Thus, it is the landscape of Montreal that res-
onates with the lost geographies of black slavery in Canada; the erasure of
black Canada cannot be completely fulfilled if, for example, Rue St. Paul—
the center of the town of Montreal and where Angélique is said to have

resided—was walked, worked, and threatened by blackness/Marie-Joseph Angélique.

## THE FIRE: GEOGRAPHIES OF ARSON, PUNISHMENT, AND TRANSCENDENCE

The geographies of eighteenth-century Montreal provide a map through which Marie-Joseph Angélique can be imagined. Put simply, she participated in the production of space through captivity. The regulatory nature of slave geographies, the spatial organization of Montreal, and sexual-racial codes, together, demonstrate how she might have negotiated the colonial town; her dispossessed status, her experiential objecthood, suggest that the geographies of Montreal were produced in tandem with, rather than without, black captivity, black labor, and black subjectivity. I want to suggest that very important spatial occurrences come out of Marie-Joseph Angélique's Montreal; her captive and human geographies appear to transcend the spatial disposition of eighteenth-century Montreal and set the stage for the production of ongoing black Canadian debates. More clearly, the question of her alleged arson spatializes, in part, the terms through which blackness can become a convincing historical and contemporary Canadian geography. Those orderly places and spaces of captivity, gender, and race outlined above were radically challenged by Angélique, not only because she was a geographic subject, but also because she was and is so familiarly implicated in (and deemed responsible for) the fire of 1734. So, it is the alleged geographies of arson, and the consequential punishment/death of blackness, that signal a spatial politics through which other black Canadian geographies are created.

This is how Marie-Joseph Angélique's story of arson is generally told: Angélique's alleged arson of Montreal, and her escape, are said to be initiated by her imminent sale. Angélique's slave-master, Français Poulin de Francheville, had recently died; his wife, Thérèse Decouagne, was no longer able to afford a domestic slave and had made arrangements to sell Angélique. On April 10, 1734, a fire spread through Montreal, destroying forty-six buildings, including the famed hospital/convent Hôtel-Dieu. No one died, but in the aftermath it was discovered that the slave Marie-Joseph Angélique had escaped, allegedly in the company of her white lover, Claude Thibault, an indentured servant from France. Soon after the fire, authorities found and detained Angélique. She endured a two-month trial, which included her making "confessions" that documented the story of her life. On June 20, a day before her execution, Angélique underwent confession under torture. She confessed that she, alone, was the arsonist. On the morning of June 21, a cart carried her to the parish church, where she made honorable amends, as was traditionally required of convicted criminals in both France and New France. The cart took her to the public gallows, where the hangman, another slave named Mathieu, placed the noose around her neck and ended her life. Her body was later burnt and the ashes "cast to the four corners of the earth."[55]

Angélique's "new" spatial disposition of Montreal, specifically her alleged criminal geographies, offer what Toni Morrison calls "the production of belief."[56] Her implication in the fire makes her story believable; her alleged criminal resistance to captivity is, more often than not, cast as incontestably real. That she *may* not have set the fire is not an option; she did set the fire. Her race and gender reinscribe this believability: who else would do such a thing? Who else would threaten and respatialize the codes of colonial conduct but a black woman? The past accidental fires in the colonial town, the continued authorization of fire codes, before and after the 1734 fire, which indicate Montreal's "flammability," do not matter. Spatial resistance and the consequential "production of belief" not only create a verifiable black female criminal, they re-landscape the colonial town in two ways: first, by illustrating the lengths to which the local communities needed to go to name and defy Angélique's production of (now believable) criminal black geographies; and second, by positing Angélique's geographies as evidence of blackness, and therefore the site through which other stories can be narrated. Either way, the fire and the threat to space create a believable black story and the kind of black geography that can only partially be erased.

This story, of the sale of humans, escape, miscegenation, arson, torture, confession, and death, is a story of spatial politics and spatial processes. If we believe that Angélique in fact set the fire, her story could be considered an ideal example of black (or black feminist) political, racial, and spatial opposition. Historian Maureen Elgersman argues, for example, that Angélique's arson is indicative of a "spectrum of resistance."[57] Elgersman writes that the arson was "one of the most serious and dramatic material forms of resistance undertaken by a black slave woman" and that it was almost certainly an act that deliberately "destroyed the material comfort of her owner."[58] Like other geographies of resistance—such as maroonage, abortion, violence—the arson/fire had geographic beginnings and geographic consequences: captivity, imminent sale and violent exile, illegal interracial couplings, and escape are fundamentally about the ways in which blackness was spatially regulated and transcended by the alleged arsonist.

The arson and consequential punishment of Angélique illustrates how blackness could and could not be tolerated in New France. The fire, the confessions, the public torture all reconfigured the local streets of Montreal by demonstrating the ways in which an unacceptable black geographic subject is mapped onto the landscape. Not only was slavery and escape chronicled on public record, Angélique apparently, and singlehandedly, destroyed the city: the forty-six buildings that were destroyed in 1734 made up most of Montreal. To threaten the spatial disposition, the racial codes, and the emblematic order of the colonial town was surely a radical form of geopolitical resistance and transcendence—which Angélique paid for with her life. Immovability and subordination were called into question by her movement; a new kind of spatial disposition, one that interrupted the existing landscape and disregarded local slave boundaries, was momentarily available.

Regardless of the identity of the actual arsonist (or the possibility of an accidental fire), the accused confessed, and in a Foucauldian manner, her confession under torture reinscribed race and gender hierarchies and affirmed existing assumptions: the unruly black slave was, as the local population knew, subhuman, primitive, and negligent. The appropriate formations of power and knowledge stayed in place. Although the city was destroyed, Angélique's punishment also demonstrates how the locals needed to publicly reaffirm these dynamics by parading, and then killing and burning, blackness. While this type of punishment reflects the time and place—specifically the imposition of *The Code Noir*—the fact that this is one of the most-cited records of slavery and blackness in New France, and Canada, makes it all the more meaningful: parading a black woman through local Montreal in the eighteenth century, executing her, and burning her remains, achieved two important spatial projects: spectacular punishment of someone and something that is said not to exist, and the destroying of bodily evidence: or, blackness is located, assessed as deviant, punished, erased, and cast beyond the nation (to the four corners of the earth).

Notwithstanding the historical attempts to punish and erase her, Marie-Joseph Angélique matters to Canada because her story overturns the geographies of nation-purity in ways that permit spatializing the nation on different terms. Angélique is a geographic subject that can unmake and remake the nation: it does not matter if she set the fire; what matters is that she represents a long-standing racial meeting-point that discloses geographies of wonder. That is, Angélique left behind primarily spatial clues, and an important sense of place, and it is these geographies that make her story so compelling and open to re-narration. Marie-Joseph Angélique's Montreal does not, then, de-center colonial New France (or France, or white Canada); rather it is a spatial terrain that makes available a place—and places—to produce and/or underscore varied responses to geographic domination.[59] Thus, it is not simply a matter of "exhuming" Angélique, and revealing a past "true life," which will help us know our history and ourselves, as George Elliot Clarke contends.[60] Rather, Angélique makes plausible a new terrain—a different material and imaginative geography—of Canada and the black diaspora. Her story is an excellent example of how the poetics of landscape and black expressions remake geography in a meaningful way: she does not simply recuperate the past and evidence black Canada, she also symbolically respatializes, and therefore politicizes, the ways in which practices of domination both disrupt and enable black Canadian geographies through re-narration.

The process of re-narration has not only legitimated Angélique's presence, it has repositioned Canadian history through her presence. Scholars and writers as diverse as Afua Cooper, George Elliot Clarke, Daniel G. Hill, and Maureen Elgersman have thus written Angélique into their discussions of Canada and black Canada, suggesting that her story implicates the nation in slavery, sexism, and racism: Angélique was enslaved; she resisted slavery by (allegedly) setting fire to her mistress's home; she escaped; she is feminist, resistant, heroic—a black martyr who refused Canada and refused racial-sexual objectification.[61] This re-narration—whether it is re-imagined through Angélique's eyes (as with Cooper), documenting the validity of slavery in Canada (as with Hill), or utilized to explore Angélique in tandem with other black histories (as with Elgersman and Clarke)—continually posits an enslaved black women who is at odds with the nation. For these scholars, her presence troubles Canada's historical and contemporary terrain because it does not neatly parallel how we are supposed to know, or encounter, the nation. Angélique was, and is, a radical historical subject because she secures blackness and black subjectivities in a nation that has an ostensibly blackless past.

Nowhere is this geographic respatialization made clearer than in Lorena Gale's play *Angélique*. Gale recalls Angélique's life through nonlinear time, setting the play in "The present and the 1730s. Then is now. Now is then."[62] This allows her to shape the text according to different kinds and moments of blackness. When the character of the reporter conveys the news of the fire of 1734, Gale has him explain: "In dramatic new developments in the O. J.—I mean M. J. Angélique case . . ."[63] Gale's conflation of time-space-gender and use of the U.S.-Simpson trial—the "hot property of mayhem loaded with the thrill that a mixture of fame, sex, money, death and race produces"—indirectly connects Marie-Joseph Angélique to Simpson. It also, however, discloses the ways in which constructions of race and criminality make Canada work. That is, once she is believable, the fire and the arsonist, the story of unsurprising black criminality becomes the narrative of Angélique.[64]

Marie-Joseph Angélique overturns the myths of Canadian neutrality and paternalism by racializing the nation and reconfiguring the ways in which the nation is inhabited by black and other subaltern communities. Her story documents Canadian slavery as well as the lengths to which local communities will go to secure racial, economic, and gender hierarchies. Angélique also calls into question the workings of the Canadian nation by shattering the safe-haven myth—one of the key ways in which the nation secures both its disconnection from blackness and its seeming exoneration from difficult histories. By exposing how transatlantic slavery played a key role in the making of the nation (through enforced labor and the entrenchment of racial hierarchies), Canada is exposed as both materially complicit to, and discursively innocent of, racial domination. More clearly, Angélique's narrative suggests that slavery is possible, but that this possibility holds in it a series of comfortable erasures, in which the nation is always positioned as opposed to both blackness and racial domination. This produces the aforementioned unexpected or alternative geographies, where the "true-north-strong-and-free" is pitted against a singular black woman, who is not only an unrecognizable historical subject, but also an unruly historical subject whose unitary presence asks for a re-assessment of the "who" and "where" and "how" of race in Canada.

# chapter 5

# Demonic Grounds: Sylvia Wynter

There is no end
To what a living world
Will demand of you.
—OCTAVIA BUTLER

The discussion of black geographies in the previous chapters has demonstrated that racial-sexual domination is an ongoing spatial project. I have been suggesting that the ideological naturalization of black women is correlated to the production of space, highlighting three processes. First, ideas about black femininity, racial superiority, and difference are spatialized, consequently curtailing subaltern geographic desires and opportunities. In this case, the historical and historically present body is at stake, frequently returning us to questions of geographic captivity, ownership, and dispossession as they are connected to corporeal schemas. Second, black women's unique geographic concerns are concealed by racial, sexual, and economic processes. That is, the dispossessed black female body is often equated with the ungeographic, and black women's spatial knowledges are rendered either inadequate or impossible. While dispossession and the ungeographic are certainly not guaranteed, traditional social paradigms, such as implementation of transparent space and the geographic manifestation of racial-sexual classificatory systems, shape how we see, or do not see, black women's geographies. Finally, these real and discursive sociospatial processes evidence struggles—over the soil, the body, theory, history, and saying and expressing a sense of place. Importantly, the real and imaginary geographic processes important to black women are not just about limitations, captivities, and erasures; they are also about everyday contestations, philosophical demands, and the possibilities the production of space can engender for subaltern subjects. Black women's geographies—produced in the margins, on auction blocks, in garrets, through literatures, and in "the last place they thought of"—indicate that traditional spatial hierarchies are simultaneously powerful and alterable. This simultaneity suggests that human geographies are unresolved and are being conceptualized beyond their present classificatory order.

What can these unresolved sociospatial ideas do for us philosophically? If black women's geographies illustrate that our ideological models and the three-dimensional physical world can, indeed, be alterable and reimagined, *where* do their sense of place, and their conceptual interventions, take us? Can black women's geographies also open up the possibility to rethink, and therefore respatialize, our present sociogeographic organization? In order to think about these questions, I turn to philosopher Sylvia Wynter and integrate some of her "creative and world constitutive activities" into my discussion.[1] Wynter's work and ideas demonstrate that the material and conceptual geographies of the black diaspora are not simply "marginal" or "different" or "unacknowledged." Rather, her interest in "new forms of life" opens up philosophical configurations that posit a flesh-and-blood worldview implicit to the production of space. Wynter allows us, then, to imagine black women's geographies not simply as descriptive areas of complex "differences." She also allows us to consider the ways in which space, place, and poetics are expressing and mapping an ongoing human geography story.

It is not within the scope of this chapter to delineate Sylvia Wynter's philosophies in their entirety. As David Scott rightly notes, "the scale and ambition of [her] project is as vast as it is complex."[2] My interest in Wynter's work here is threefold. First, she is a skilled and rigorous interdisciplinary scholar. The range of her textual sources—she engages and interweaves, for example, physics, film, musics, economics, history, neurobiology, critical theory, literature, Christianity—and the depth with which she reads these texts, demonstrate exceptional interdisciplinarity. Although Wynter is not cited as an interdisciplinary scholar per se—she is most notably a critical theorist and the author of *The Hills of Hebron*—the breadth of her analytical interests unsettle knowledge categories and boundaries.[3] Indeed, she writes and thinks deeply across texts to articulate her arguments "outside the terms of the disciplinary discourses of our present epistemological order" and she encourages her readers to struggle with what they know, and where they know from.[4] Second, Wynter's philosophies, while vast, are secured to her ongoing struggle to re-present the fullness of human ontologies, which have been curtailed by what she describes as an over-representation of Man (Western bourgeois Man) as if it/he were the only available mode of complete humanness.[5] Spanning roughly 1492 to the present, Wynter's analyses of the inventions of Man/human and his human Others are genealogies, which trace how racial-sexual-economic categories get made, remade, and disrupted through the production of knowledge and conceptions of time-space. Finally, and related to both of the above points, Wynter's work addresses geographic matters. In addressing the ways in which space and place impact upon knowledge, subaltern political aims, and the overrepresentation of Man, her work is anchored to multiple and multiscalar "grounds"—demonic grounds, the space of Otherness, the grounds of being human, poverty archipelagos, archipelagos of human Otherness, les damnés de la terre/the wretched of the earth, the color-line, terra nullius/lands of no one. In addition to this, the geographies Wynter is interested in are unfinished, in the sense that she insists that there is "always something else besides the dominant cultural logic going on, and that something else constituted another—but also transgressive—ground of understanding . . . not simply a sociodemographic location but the site both of a form of life and of possible critical intervention."[6]

It is on this last point, Wynter's geographic interests, that I will focus in this discussion. I am interested in following alongside her argument re-garding the invention of Man, and discussing this in relation to what might be called Man's geographies. So, how do Man's geographies get for-mulated, cast as natural truths, and become overrepresented? How does this politics of mapping, of making space, shed light on the repetitive dis-placement of the planet's nonwhite subjects? Can the naturalized but alterable geographies of black women, and subaltern subjects in general, be understood in ways that do not replicate our historically present spatial patterns? What kinds of new and possible spaces are made available through our past geographic epochs? And finally, what can Wynter's discussions of "our fully realized autonomy of feeling, thoughts behaviour," her re-presentation of the human subject, bring to bear on geography and geo-graphic knowledge? I hope to answer these questions by working through three points—the inventions of Man, Man's geographies, and interhuman geographies—as they relate to some of the concerns I have developed in earlier chapters.

## THE INVENTION OF MAN1 AND MAN2, OR,
## THE INVENTIONS OF MAN

Sylvia Wynter is interested in sociospatial and intellectual epochs wherein the category of human, and representations of humanness, come to be represented as Man. She suggests the European arrival in the New World, economic expansions, and new religious and secular politics ruptured existing planetary organization and forced a reconsideration of how the self, other, and space are imagined. These sociointellectual ruptures were poignant—the inhabitants of Europe had to grapple with the psychic-unimaginable—and created an opening through which the conceptions of humanness began to be organized differently. Wynter's theoretical strategy is to trace how Man comes to represent the only viable expression of humanness, in effect, overrepresenting itself discursively and empirically. In order to elaborate on the formations of Man, she considers two overlapping knowledge shifts prompted by fifteenth- and sixteenth-century voyages to the New World. These moments correspond with the conceptualization of the encountered and encountering human (Man1), who has traveled (materially and imaginatively) to the New World for socioreligious exploratory purposes; and the imperialist political human (Man2), who has traveled outside Europe for territorial expansion, conquest, wealth.[7] Both of these inventions are struggling to develop a cohesive human subject that can consistently correspond with changing intellectual fields. Man1 was invented alongside the rise of the physical sciences, the decline of supernatural planetary sociospatial organization, and evangelistic contact. Man2 was invented alongside the rise of the biological sciences, transatlantic slavery, and land exploitation. In both cases, humanness was re-evaluated, produced in a classificatory, contextual, ideological manner—theologically/scientifically and then secularly/biologically. And both inventions of Man required a differential production of humanness. That is, Man and his human Others came to represent and produce themselves in relation to each other.

The inventions of Man are, Wynter argues, syncretized. The arrival in the New World surely ruptured European understandings of physiology, religion, politics, and geography. Humanness was thrown into crisis by the seeable, ungodly, indigenous peoples and their lands. Two entwining processes took place that initiated the reorganization of humanness. First, early explorers and religious evangelists had to make sense of a world, and cultures, they had previously considered nonexistent; and they could only make sense of the world through their subjective knowledges and positionalities. In the Middle Ages the New World, like southern Africa, was convincingly *physically uninhabitable* to Europeans. Upon encounters, and alongside Decartes's newly mathematizable world and Copernican theory, the question of humanness became wrapped up in the differences between Man's embodiment of the image of God and the New World inhabitants. The physical sciences and new struggles over religious frameworks (new heavens, new earths, a moving planet) produced a reasonable Man (Man1), located between "the lower natures of brutes" and divine natures. Here, human Others—inside and outside Europe—were identifiable "enemies of Christ," irrational and abnormal; the creed-specific, seemingly universal, conception of the human was a natural and rational "Godded" Man.[8]

Second, indigenous communities, the brutes/enemies of Christ, instigated a philosophical conundrum. They could not, in fact, be identified as enemies of Christ because of their geographic location—Christ's apostles did not reach the New World; Christ was an absolutely unavailable and unrepresentable image/idea for indigenous cultures (just as New World indigenous cultures and their geographies were truly unimaginable to Europeans prior to contact). Thus, the question of humanness had to be pondered in a new way: in what ways can subjugation be justified, and territorialization advanced, if indigenous communities are understood by Christian evangelist travelers—specifically the priest Bartolomé de Las Casas—to be embodying culturally specific and local "truths" that are radically outside a Christian worldview?[9] To put it another way, if these communities were not "enemies of Christ," and had not encountered—or even imagined—the Word, the Church, the orthodox theology of Christianity, how can their relationship to the divine be measured? And what of the local cultural *worldview* of indigenous populations? On what religious terms can their demonization be warranted? And more importantly, for Las Casas, what will become of *his* Christian soul if he spiritually and politically invests in the violent demonization of human Others?[10]

The conundrum noticed by Las Casas had to be resolved. And it was already in the process of being resolved as slave ships were increasingly transporting indigenous African subjects to the New World and indigenous populations in the Americas were, in fact, rendered "ungodly" by Las Casas's contemporaries. Man had to be worked out differently, humanness altered, on terms that spiritually legitimated a nonindigenous New World presence and the profitable dehumanization of indigenous and enslaved black cultures. This set in motion a second, interrelated, invention of Man (Man2), strikingly brought into focus in the seventeenth and eighteenth centuries. Man2 was a more secularized, political state actor whose planetary interests were/are underwritten by bodily schemas and their attendant geopolitical constructs: "'the rise of Europe' and its construction of the 'world civilization' on the one hand, and, on the other, African enslavement, Latin American conquest, and Asian subjugation."[11] Man2 reconfigured humanness by ideologically re-presenting itself as "world" humanness. The indigenous and black categories, conceptualized as an abnormal "enemy of Christ," were understood according to a new biocentric logic that systematized "differential/hierarchical degrees of rationality" and distinguished "different populations, their religions, cultures, forms of life; in other words their *modes* of being human."[12] The inventions of Man paralleled vast and violent colonial and slavery projects, increasingly heightening the meaning of phenotype and physiology and centralized economic power. Man2 and his ideologies set the stage for Darwinian theories to tell "accurate" bodily stories; for W. E. B. Du Bois to identify the color-line; for civil rights activists and academics (feminist, gay and lesbian, nonwhite, aboriginal) to struggle against the overrepresentation of Man; for contemporary capitalist global processes to naturalize and stigmatize the homeless, the underdeveloped, the jobless, the incarcerated.

The inventions of Man are neither guaranteed nor absolute. Implicit to Wynter's argument are two disruptions to Man. First is the ongoing social production of humanness, which compels us to recognize the ways in which we normatively conceptualize difference, cast our present hierarchical order as a truth, and site Man as a location of desire. That is, it is *conceptions* of Man/humanness that denaturalize Man and yet ground our present social systems through discourses of normalcy. Let me give an example from Wynter's interview with David Scott:

> The conception is *the* imperative. This is why, however much abundance we produce, we cannot solve the problem of poverty and hunger. Since the goal of our mode of production is *not* to produce for human beings in general, it's to provide for the material conditions of existence for the production

and reproduction of our present conception of being human: to secure the well-being, therefore, of those of us, the global middle classes, who have managed to attain its ethno-class criterion.[13]

Second, and related, are the underlying histories and philosophies of other truths, the *local contextual* criteria of humanness that prompted Las Casas's dilemma, which are in contradistinction with, yet substantiate, the making of Man: new and alternative forms of life that are implicit to Man yet totally interlinked with a different *conception* of humanness. In the process of making religious, intellectual, and physiological distinctions between Man and his human Others, varying *genres* or *modes* of the human are being constituted and *lived*. Race, gender, sexuality—biocentric differences—are the terms through "which we can alone experience ourselves as human."[14] Human genres simultaneously make and disrupt Man and open up the possibility for citing and imagining alternative forms of being, knowledge, and geography—from an interhuman/species perspective.

To sum up, our present order of existence centers on the inventions of Man that are anchored and constituted by discourses of normalcy. Normalcy is made and remade in relation to historically specific shifts that critically change the planetary order of things. The making of Man is a process, connected to broad and violent classificatory systems and local contextual experiences. The hierarchy of human normalcy is a dilemma, furthermore, because it is difficult to think outside of what appears to be a natural human story: we are bound to it, anchored to a familiar plot that "should not be taken as any index of [ . . . ] justness."[15] Humanness is, then, both Man made and human made, pivoting on the displacement of difference and alternative forms of life, which can be articulated, Wynter argues, through a new poetics.[16]

## MAN'S GEOGRAPHIES: THE UNINHABITABLE, ARCHIPELAGOS, AND THE MAKING OF DEMONIC GROUNDS

As mentioned previously, the inventions of Man coexisted with important geographic processes and sociospatial ruptures. Following Sylvia Wynter's model, it can be suggested that in order to come into being, Man has to encounter the unimaginable and unrepresentable. I consider here the ways in which Man comes into being through encountering geographic unknowns and making them biocentrically knowable. Here I focus on two concepts signaled by Wynter in her essay, "1492: A New World View"—the uninhabitable and archipelagos—to think about how the production of space is worked out through mapping and attempting to constitute the space of human Others as disembodied and then transparently abnormal. The interrelated quest to map the unknown—the geographic unknown, the corporeal indigenous/black unknown—sets forth what Neil Smith calls "uneven development," albeit from a very different analytical perspective: the systematic production of differential social hierarchies, which are inscribed in space and give a coherence to disproportionate geographies.[17] I suggest that the negotiation of social, corporeal, and spatial human configurations, initiated by encounters with the unknown, created new spaces, specifically Man's geographies, which are overdetermined, normalized, and naturalized. The inventions of Man come to be reflected in spatial queries and arrangements. If Man is an overrepresentation of humanness, Man's human geographies are an extension of this conception. The development and mapping of the uninhabitable and uneven archipelagos are two important ways Man's geographies are overrepresented.

In "1492: A New World View," Wynter describes how the seemingly complete world geography of explorer Christopher Columbus shaped his spatial expectations. The land of the Western hemisphere (the "New World"/various Caribbean islands) should not have been there upon Columbus's arrival. These landmasses should have been, according to "the earth" and accepted geographies of his Latin Christian Europe, submerged: these areas were comprehensively non-navigable, uninhabitable, unlivable, and oceanic.[18] Columbus's geographic "discovery"—and his *personal* belief that God did put land in the Western Hemisphere—radically challenged the embedded geo-religious rules of his time; geographic imaginations were stretched and forced to confront the unimaginable: landmasses above the water! This "discovery," like the discovery of populations inhabiting what were considered "torrid zones" (present-day Senegal) signaled a geographic disruption of Eurocentric space: a newly expanded ecological, geological, environmental planet, new spaces of Man, alterity, and difference:

> The series of fifteenth-century voyages on whose basis the West began its global expansion voyages (one of which proved that the earth was homogeneously habitable by humans, seeing that the Torrid Zone was indeed inhabited as

was that of the land of the Western hemisphere that turned out to be above water), together with Copernicus's new astronomy (which proposed that the earth also moved about the Sun, projected as the center, and was therefore of the same substance as, homogenous with, the heavenly bodies), were to initiate . . . a new order of cognition in which "the objective set of facts" of the physical level of reality was to now be gradually freed from having to be known in the adaptive terms of . . . the nonhomogeneity of the geography of the earth and . . . the nonhomogeneity of the earth and the heavens.[19]

The uninhabitable landmasses were initially disembodied by European cartographers and explorers. In naming them "terra nullius/lands of no one" and mapping them as "peopleless" voids, the uninhabitable was abstracted by cartographic translations of where and who can constitute the terms of normal habitability.[20] This cartographic abstraction corresponded with claims to sovereignty, and the lands were perceived as legitimately appropriable in the name of the (Spanish, European) state. The spatial concerns of Mani became wrapped up in an ideological perspective that dehumanized and disembodied subaltern populations by conflating their beingness with *terra nullius,* places and bodies outside God's grace: idolaters in the uninhabitable; uninhabitable idolaters. Remember, however, that *terra nullius,* the lands of no one, incited the philosophical conundrum with which Bartolomé de Las Casas was faced. It was precisely *the geographic location* of the New World, radically outside the conceptual/imaginary categorical models of Christian Europe, that disclosed the *worldviews* of indigenous/black populations in *local-cultural* terms. This Other local-cultural worldview, notably, identifies Mani's geographic perspective (his Godly claim to indigenous lands) as mad, irrational, drunk.[21]

The uninhabitable—the nonexistent lands and underwater places— were existent, occupied, and above water. But what becomes of the native-occupied "uninhabitable" zones is a geo-racial reorganization. The "new symbolic construct of race," which coincided with post-1492 colonial arrangements, was spatially organized according to a new biocentric logic.[22] This spatial organization did not completely replace existing indigenous worldviews, arrangements, and geographies, but it did thrive on geo-racial management. Wynter traces the biocentric codes that arose out of these new encounters and examines how ideologies of "difference" were extensions

of what Columbus's contemporaries considered geographically uninhabitable and unimaginable. She does this by looking specifically at what
Columbus's contemporaries and his colonial descendants assumed to be
"naturally geographic" (Europe prior to his first voyage) and "naturally
ungeographic" (the uninhabitable/underwater). This geographic dichotomy,
*after* 1492, unraveled into New World cultural exchanges that settled into
a rigorous nonhomogeneous human model. Humanness became a classificatory text, distinguishing white, native (nonwhite), African (native/
Other/nigger) from one another and identifying subtypes of human Otherness, such as class, gender, sexuality. This model, traceable into the present, comes to pivot on the middle-class model of Man2 and guarantees a
foundation for what constitutes a "normal being" and therefore a normal
way of life.[23]

Keeping in mind Wynter's focus on modes of humanness, I want to
address the ways in which the uninhabitable still holds currency in the
present, and how conceptions of what I call "the inhabitability of the normal" organizes contemporary geographic arrangements. Wynter only briefly
suggests that the uninhabitable, like biocentric human hierarchies, is a
presently traceable category. Building on this, I argue that the uninhabitable is especially traceable vis-à-vis uneven geographies: while encounters
with the unknown made the uninhabitable a newly available geography
for exploration and economic gain, it also translated places that were previously deemed nonexistent (underwater, unlivable) into conquerable and
profitable spatial categories. Post-1492, what the uninhabitable tells us,
then, is that populations who occupy the "nonexistent" are *living* in what
has been previously conceptualized as the unlivable and unimaginable. If
identity and place are mutually constructed, the uninhabitable spatializes
a human Other category of the unimaginable/native/black.

It follows, then, that the question of geographic interrelatedness—colonial geographies—came to be coded in much the same way as described
above: spaces for white/nonwhite/African(black). The now profitable and
workable lands of the uninhabitable are not so much unlivable and unimaginable as they are grids of racial-sexual management and geographic
growth (which "grew" due to free slave labor). That is, the uninhabitable
creates an opening for a geographic transformation that is underscored by
racial and sexual differences. To transform the uninhabitable into the inhabitable, and make this transformation profitable, the land must become

a site of racial-sexual regulation, a geography that maps "a normal way of life" through measuring different degrees of inhabitability. This geographic transformation, then, does not fully erase the category of "uninhabitable," but rather re-presents it through spatial processes as a sign of social difference. This is expressed through uneven geographies: spatial arrangements that map and measure populations according to "normal," "a normal way of life," or the normally inhabitable. Presently, this spatial re-presentation brings to mind the discussions advanced by Angela Davis and Ruth Wilson Gilmore on U.S. (California) prison expansion, which Davis describes as the "perfect site for the simultaneous production and concealment of racism."[24] What their work shows is not only the (concealed) spatial management of race/gender/class, but also the ways in which new geographic formulations are produced according to "normative views of how people fit into and make places in the world."[25] The extension of what Columbus's contemporaries assumed was "nonexistent" is a geographic system that comes to organize difference in place: the color-line, the wretched of the earth. Clyde Woods has described these places of difference as: burned, toxic, unhealthy, incarcerated, killing fields, extinct, starved, torn, endangered, impoverished, while Wynter describes them as "poverty archipelagos."[26] These places, global in existence are, from the view of what is "normal" or inhabitable, new versions of the unlivable-uninhabitable. I am going to quote Wynter at length in order to illustrate *where* archipelagos take place and how the overrepresentation and normalization of Man's geographies underwrite dispossessions and desires:

> . . . all our present struggles with respect to race, class, gender, sexual orientation, ethnicity, struggles over the environment, global warming, severe climate change, the sharply unequal distribution of the earth's resources (20 per cent of the world's peoples own 80 per cent of its resources, consume two-thirds of its food, and are responsible for 75 per cent of its ongoing pollution, with the leading two billion of earth's peoples living relatively affluent lives while four billion still live on the edge of hunger and immeseration, to the dynamic overconsumption on the part of the rich techno-industrial North paralleled by that of overpopulation on the part of the dispossessed poor, still partly agrarian worlds of the South)—these are all differing facets of . . . Man vs. Human struggle . . . [poverty archipelagos,

spaces of the Other are categories] defined at the global level by refugee/eco-
nomic migrants stranded outside the gates of the rich countries, as the postcolonial variant of Fanon's category of les damnés . . . with this category in
the United States coming to comprise the criminalized majority of Black
and dark-skinned Latino inner-city males now made to man the rapidly
expanding prison-industrial complex, together with their female peers—the
kicked-about welfare moms—with both being part of the ever expanding
global, transracial category of the homeless/jobless, the semi-jobless, the criminalized drug-offending prison population. So that if we see this category
of les damnés that is internal to (and interned within) the prison system of
the United States as the analog form of a global archipelago, constituted by
the Third- and Fourth-World peoples of the so-called "underdeveloped"
areas of the world—most totally of all by the peoples of the continent of
Africa (now stricken with AIDS, drought, and ongoing civil wars, and
whose bottommost place as the most impoverished of all the earth's conti-
nents is directly paralleled by the situation of its Black Diaspora, with Haiti
being produced and reproduced as the most impoverished nation of the
Americas). . .[27]

The inhabitability of the normal, consequently, also produces two forms
of geographic nonexistence, which differ from what was assumed was "not
there." First, what Audre Lorde describes as the "institutionalized rejection of difference": invisible workforces, sites of homelessness, unproper-
tied communities, undocumented and/or "justified" violences; marginalized,
silent women, men, and children; what has been described as "the rest"
beyond the West (the South, the Caribbean, the non–United States, and so
forth). And second, what Édouard Glissant describes as the "real but long
unnoticed" places of interhuman exchanges: cultural sharings, new poetics, new ways of being, "a new world view," human struggles.[28]

The uninhabitable and archipelagos of difference signal the conceptual
openings 1492 made possible and the incompleteness of geographic processes and note where poetics might disrupt the habitability of normal.
These conceptions of space and place, Man's geographies, are important because they reveal the limitations of existing geographic arrangements and,
consequently, put demands on the ways in which we presently organize the
world. The overrepresented spaces of Man disclose that space is socially
constituted—and that historical epochs are underwritten by differential

encounters with geography. These encounters always include the under-represented conceptions of being *in place*—the spaces of Otherness, subjective worldviews—that may not be immediately available in our geographic imaginations because Man's sense of place is naturalized as normal. However, archipelagos of poverty, hemmed in and categorized by global color-lines and biocentric logics—are, like Man's geographies, inhabited. And, if we return to Glissant and connect his poetics of landscape to this present discussion, encountering, saying, and living geography brings the subject into being—regardless of place. Those who occupy the spaces of Otherness are always already encountering space and therefore articulate how genres or modes of humanness are intimately connected to where we/they are ontologically as well as geographically. To return to an earlier discussion, spaces of Otherness are "palpitating with life."[29] What do we do with the biocentric spaces of unevenness that are life-filled and poetic? And what are the poetics saying about space and place, and a new world-view? Can this lead to another geographic disruption—one which, in noting the alterability of our present geographic organization, takes seriously the possibility of more humanly workable geographies? I now turn to demonic grounds in order to think about how the habitable/uninhabitable can perhaps be reframed as interhuman geographies.

As mentioned in my introductory remarks, the *place* of black women is deemed unrecognizable because their ontological existence is both denied and deniable as a result of the regimes of colonialism, racism-sexism, transatlantic slavery, European intellectual systems, patriarchy, white femininity, and white feminism. Correlated, their grounds are silent and their place is uninhabitable within the given frameworks of Man's geographies.[30] Placeless and silent black women, if legitimately posited in the world (placed, unsilenced), call into question our present geographic organization. The geographies of black womanhood, as demonic grounds, put forth a geographic grammar that locates the complex position and potentiality of black women's sense of place.

Demonic grounds can be detected through the biocentric categories of race and sexuality (black femininity), political locations (black/Caribbean feminism), and alongside social theories and ideologies, such as white European and Euro-American feminism, patriarchy, and black/Caribbean studies. By adding the variable of race-sexuality to existing grounds of human being, black femininity establishes a slightly different path through social theories and ideologies as well as material and conceptual geographies. This path does not have to be understood as entwined with erasures and absences but rather indicates the human, expressive, and geographic terms of disavowal *and* black women's geographies. Where demonic grounds differ from, say, other black feminist and feminist geographies is in their function. Specifically, it is the making and meaning of black womanhood and black feminism that discloses the *purpose* of race/racism within feminism and sex/sexism within black social movements. To put it another way, and to expand on one theme discussed earlier, it is not simply a marginal special-partial vantage point that divulges the workings of black womanhood or black feminism or feminism. And this is exactly where feminism(s) and other identity-theories sometimes get stuck, by recycling and politicizing biocentric modes of humanity *in* the margins, in the classroom, in theory; this emphasizes that hierarchical *genres* of human/gender difference will somehow complete the story. Instead, it is useful to imagine the ways in which the margin is a serious conceptual intervention into what it means to be/not be a black woman: the margin (or "race-class-gender-sexuality," or the garret, or "difference," and so forth) is part of the story, not the end of the story. As I began to ask in chapter 2, through Marlene Nourbese Philip, and what thinking about black women's geographies as "demonic" opens up is: what happens when black womanhood, black femininity, black women's spaces, places, and poetics are "*Not* on the margins"?[31]

If the grounds of black femininity and black feminism, what Wynter describes as the terrain of "Caliban's woman," *is* inhabited, it is therefore part of a larger human geography story. This story indicates that the grounds of what is considered "the inhabitability of normal" are socially produced and alterable. Black femininity and black feminism are therefore also establishing new oppositional demands that recast human normalcy through the politics/poetics of black femininity. Importantly, black feminism and the discourses of marginality-identity have made a difference to feminism and to other social theories by: disrupting the category of "woman" and the centered subject (race, class, gender, location); calling into question the patriarchal and feminist meanings of private/public, home, work, motherhood, selfhood, nation; critiquing black political movements, black popular culture, feminist theory, and activism; reshaping women's studies, black studies, cultural studies; re-historicizing transatlantic slavery and post-slavery landscapes. If these conceptual and political differences are not simply cast as marginal, they do not have to replicate marginality. Demonic grounds are not, then, only reifying and politicizing marginality in itself (black women's identities = margin/position = difference in/ and feminism; or, our present form of life). Rather they are also a projection of what the biocentric human (*genres* of black womanhood) means in relation to "the normally inhabitable." This troubles a formerly familiar landscape and reveals that the places of black womanhood—the garrets and auction blocks, the streets of Montreal, the political interventions—can be conceptualized as particular, contested moments, which necessarily connect Man's geographies to ongoing locations of subaltern struggle.

What is compelling about Wynter's discussions—and where she differs, sometimes radically, from antiracist and/or feminist theories of "inclusivity" and "special vantage points"—is how seriously she takes the flesh-and-blood human species and the grounds of the subaltern to fashion a workable and new politics. This politics recognizes our present history as simultaneously "interhuman and environmental."[32] Specifically, Wynter asks that we recognize that the making of the Americas was/is an (often dangerously genocidal and ecocidal) interhuman and environmental project through which "new forms of life" can be conceptualized. Recognizing that new forms of life, occupying interhuman grounds (beneath *all* of our feet), can perhaps put forward a new worldview from the perspective of the species—that is, from outside the logic of biocentric models: not as a *genre* or *mode* of human but as human. Consequently, if the flesh-and-blood human can know from outside the logic of biocentric models, special/partial vantage points only make sense as indicative of patterns that are *inside* the logic of biocentric models and familiar plots—because special-ness and inclusions, in these theories and through our existing sociospatial arrangements, are necessarily produced in conjunction with (repeating and/or undermining) Man's geographies, old hierarchical tensions, old grounds, partial histories, and partial interests.

Sylvia Wynter's work entails not only "deconstructing" or denaturalizing categories such as "race"; it also means envisioning what is beyond the hierarchical codes and partial human stories that have, for so long, organized our populations and the planet. This means accepting that global, human, and environmental *connections*—of cultural histories, exchanges, "discoveries," experiences—are evidence of a conceptual shift. This shift, while overrepresented as hinging on the voyages of Christopher Columbus

and subsequent intellectual and global expansions, also brought into being
our present world order and a single world history, and therefore new culturally connective subject positions.[33] It is the geographic and human con-
nectiveness that makes possible envisioning and accepting flesh-and-blood
humans as an interrelated, co-identified species.

## REVISITING THE POETICS OF LANDSCAPE

I want to turn to two examples—one historical and one contemporary—
to clarify how the uninhabitable and demonic grounds relate to Wynter's
framework and geography. These examples return me to black Canada
and the body, and I suggest that the poetics of landscape is perhaps one
way to think through and trouble biocentric geographic organization. In
seventeenth-century Montreal, in response to increased colonial demands
for free labor, Louis XIV gave limited approval to institute slavery in New
France. In his statement sanctioning the institution, the monarch also
commented that the project of slavery may fail in Canada—black slaves,
he suggested, coming from such a different climate might perish due to
the cold Canadian weather.[34] That New France might be an uninhabitable
site for blackness collapses biocentric categories and geographic categories.
While the weather certainly did not prevent slavery in New France, and
black communities did not perish, the monarch's comments did affirm a
discourse through which black in/and Canada could be imagined—as unacceptably impossible or geographically inappropriate. This discourse continued, long after the execution of Marie-Joseph Angélique, attaching itself
to other black diaspora populations from Africa and the Caribbean. Among
other reasons for immigration prohibition between the 1900s and the 1950s
were the potential immigrants' "geographical area of origin" and his/her
"unsuitability" to the Canadian climate.[35] The question of the uninhabitable Canadian nation was established in relation to the normally inhabitable (livable cold, white, Canadian-European geographies), allowing the
*idea* of the cold land to determine the natural place or placelessness of
black diaspora communities. Thinking about this in relation to Wynter's
discussion of 1492 reveals three important moments: the ideological turn
away from "what is not there, submerged, unlivable"; the ideological shift
that demonstrates that "what is here, above water, livable, conquerable"
requires a biocentric logic through which Canadian geography could be

managed; and a reassertion of the uninhabitable—the erasure of black histories, impossible black geographies, nonexistence. By institutionalizing and
recycling natural connections between geography and the biocentric body,
the uninhabitable becomes a meaningful racial category utilized to reassert
how livable Canada is, and for whom it is appropriately livable.

The meaning of Canada/place thus came to underpin the "institutionalized rejection of difference" and the "real but long unnoticed" sites of interhuman exchanges. But as unacceptably impossible, and keeping in mind
what demonic grounds disclose, the uninhabitable, cold landscape in fact
houses a new form of blackness. I am thinking in particular of Dionne
Brand's discussion of Bathurst Street in Toronto, Ontario. This piece not
only places blackness right in the middle of the black-uninhabitable (Canada), it identifies how genres or modes of humans put new demands on the
nation on interhuman terms:

> Bathurst Subway. I say it like home. It's an uneasy saying . . . They first took
> you to Bathurst and Bloor to locate you, your place, the point from which
> you would meet this country. And your relationship to it was clear since this
> was the only oasis of Blacks in the miles and miles to be learned of in the
> white desert that was a city. They took you here for you to get a sense of
> your new identity, the re-definitions you knew were coming but could never
> have anticipated though you had some sense when you gave yourself up to
> the journey you'd emptied a place for them. Bathurst was the site of new
> definitions . . . in 1978 we were working the four corners of the intersection
> [protesting/flyering] just after the killing of Albert Johnson by the cops. Only
> months before they had killed Buddy Evans down on Spadina Avenue. And
> those who could have saved his life said that he was just a nigger and left
> him to die. Now Albert Johnson was shot on the staircase of his house on
> Manchester.[36]

What is interesting about Brand's recollection is not only her description
of Toronto, Ontario, as a "white desert" (biocentrically black-habitable,
what Wynter might call a "torrid zone," seemingly geographically suitable
for the black diaspora), but the ways in which she mixes geographic possibilities with the uninhabitable. She writes an incomplete human geographic story, and she situates this incomplete story under the familiar
geographic sign of "Canada," signaling how these unfinished projects are

particular to the nation (projects of, then, Canadian benevolence, safe havens, Underground Railroads to freedom). As a site of new definitions and death, Bathurst Street proves demonic for Brand, a site where she can map a location of new inhabitability ("home," "your place") with an uneasiness that accentuates the discomfort and pain of the uninhabitable. Interhuman exchanges are premised on the politics of the four corners of Bathurst, where sites of protest, community, "newness" (or alterable geographies) intersect with the logic of the uninhabitable and unacceptable (he was left to die, an incomplete human geography story). Incomplete human geography stories are, in part, disclosed through the poetics of landscape. Brand's imaginative and real geographies insert "past" spaces of blacklessness and death into contemporary geographic matters.

Dionne Brand's poetics, her mapping of Bathurst Street, Toronto, Canada, cold torrid zones, urban archipelagos for "just a nigger," bring the city, and her selfhood, into existence on new terms. I want to turn to the ways in which contemporary black expressive cultures have also contributed to what might be considered new and contestatory geographic acts. These geographic acts communicate the livability of the world through mapping it as a terrain that can publicly and creatively express blackness and black femininity. Here I am thinking specifically about music and music-making as geographic acts—soundscapes that are implicit technologies of the poetics of landscape. The terrain of music and music-making is, as many have argued, one of the more vibrant, creative, and complexly private/public spaces in which blackness is articulated.[37] It stages and presents creativity, politics, sex, violence, struggle, and diaspora connections; it is a site of invention, reinvention, parody, performativity, community, and critique. Music expresses a wide range of emotions and ideas; it establishes and severs human relationships; it is buyable, transferable, and sometimes free. Musical expressions are also geographic. Musical expressions are fundamentally about place because they alter the soundscape. The art of noise is not just about listening, it is also about dancing, seeing, not listening, and (in)voluntarily listening to other people's music; it also enhances our privacy, wards off loneliness, and simulates aloneness (through use of Walkmans, for example).

In his discussion of black musics and economics in the Mississippi Delta, geographer Clyde Woods has argued that the act of making music paralleled an intellectual transformation that has been overlooked. Woods is not arguing that black musics were not heard or listened to—indeed, musicians and musics were worshipped, celebrated, envied, and feared. But an intellectual "mutation," to borrow from Sylvia Wynter, expressing "the origins, consequences, and varieties of life lived in a brutal and love-less society," has been ignored. Black musics, evidencing a *mutation* and arranging a viable participatory soundscape through which blackness can say itself and its history, is often rendered trivial.[38]

There are geographic and social demands implicit in the soundscape. For example, contemporary music and music-making has, geographically, contributed to the spatialization of blackness. It has publicly presented a kind of blackness that cuts across the hierarchical genres of human nor-malcy and re-presents the ways in which black artists (sometimes but not always) embrace and/or perform the normal and change the stakes of nor-malcy. The consumption of contemporary black musics and black video has established an arena through which the artist, musician, dancer, can publicly disclose the contradictions, possibilities, and histories of black-ness: at an awards show, the hip-hop act Outkast restaged a plantation, populating it with minstrel images: "the whole world," they sang, "loves you when you: don't get down, when you sing the blues, when you're in the news." In her hit video "Get Ur Freak On," artist Missy Elliott uses lynch symbolism as a backdrop: live pained bodies, hanging upside down (and dead/dying lynched bodies)—a demonic landscape that creates a provocative space for Elliott to sing about and expose the connections between black sex, violence, and pleasure in the historical present.[39] New and old archipelagos mapped across Man's and black geographies, unset-tling how the "whole world" is imagined by Man and his human others. Music, as a geographic act, is an available space through which blackness can be read as an integral and meaningful part of the landscape.[40] This identifies the soundscape as a contestation, which publicly and privately communicates geographic possibilities. It is a space and place used by sev-eral black artists to "say" the historical present. It is this "sayability" that I am interested in here, and how singer-songwriter Macy Gray uses the sphere of the soundscape to integrate a seeable and critical intervention into the normal.

At the 2001 MTV music awards, Macy Gray arrived in a dress with a message sewn on the front which read: "My new album drops Sept. 18 2001." The back of her dress read: "Buy my album."[41] Whether or not the legacy Gray invoked with her dress was intended, her public body-self, her expressive dress, worked its way into the space of the music awards in a provocative way. When discussing this occasion with a class of under-graduate students—alongside a discussion of black feminist thought—several students asserted that Gray's fashion choice was an inappropriate and an unstylish catastrophe: she exhibited desperation which was wrapped up in a "bad" dress.[42] The student responses to Gray's popular presenta-tion indicated their comfort zones—in terms of femininity, popular cul-ture, music marketing, and blackness. Their responses demanded a kind of black femininity Macy Gray refused to deliver. Gray's expressive fash-ion act at the MTV music awards inappropriately exceeded the bounds of public self-presentation and respectable womanhood. Or did it?

Macy Gray's use of her body and fashion at the MTV awards tells us something interesting about blackness: in a way, she wrote the historical weight of black womanhood on her body. She was not articulating wom-anhood; she was expressing black womanhood, in the flesh. That Gray could enter hyperpublic space and "say" her body in this way was an im-portant expressive act: it was, to borrow from Stuart Hall, "a profoundly mythic use of public space."[43] In choosing to write "buy my album" across her back she created a space of parody, one that distorts who she is sup-posed to be (as a woman) by invoking the ways in which her historical body is shaped by another, less familiar, legacy (as a black woman).

Like other human geographies, black expressive cultures do not com-municate whole geographies. Instead, the mixture of presentation, music, noise, bodies, performance, and musical arrangements are used to exploit existing geographic arrangements and push narratives of normalcy out of the comfort zone. The geographic act of expressing blackness and black femininity illustrates what happens when gender and race are overtly attached to public space. It points to how uncomfortable the normal can be and how the "sayability" of place is caught up in the expressive econ-omy of the racial-sexual. But singing and writing the unspeakable can, to return to Macy Gray, allow her to also utter her "unedited" newness, her freaky-ness, and her loving-human/freak-connection with others "deep in the struggle": "you are relating to a psychopath/your role model is in ther-apy/you must be real far gone/you're relating to a psychopath"; or, "I wanna be with you for all of my life/I'm so glad you're a freak like me."[44]

Gray's biocentric body and her sense of place, she suggests, are not quite normal: she produces and lives, then, a mutation, which is evidence of the ways in which black femininity is implicated in an unjust, but speakable, human geography story: "Ask if I'm free and I'll say 'oh yes'/ but down here in reality everybody knows there ain't/no such thing/. . . What I'm looking for is not here on earth."[45] Gray's expressive acts are musical geographies that call into question "down here in reality," through poetically expressing that "down here" is an uneasy social reality. She provides a communicative act that is a respatialization because "down here in reality" is not, in fact, a humanly workable place. Gray, momentarily, leaves her historically present geographic story behind, imagines another place for her blackness beyond the "no such thing," or the impossible, and invites her audience into a different spatiality, "beyond the moon," or outside the anticipated realms of the normal.[46]

Is it feasible, then, to link respatialization to practices of subaltern expression? Or, to put it differently, what is different about geography—in the material and the imaginary—if we "say" geography on new poetic terms? Is saying geography a respatialization and therefore a repoliticization? Can creative expressions of new geographic forms—interhuman, in the beyond, outside the normal, "not here on earth"—widen our understanding of human geography and loosen the ties between biocentric categories and what are now familiar, and for some, comfortable, locations? In chapter 1, I mentioned that geography is deeply dependent on imaginary work. This is where I think Sylvia Wynter's contribution to black geographies is most important. She not only advances a way to reconceptualize black women's geographies, she also insists that creatively communicating this reconceptualization formulates geographic options in a way that is more humanly workable; she makes us think hard about what we imagine, what we want to imagine, and what we can imagine for human geographies. It is, then, new forms of life, imagining, expressing, and living geography that put demands on spatial arrangements, that contest, respatialize, and inhabit the uninhabitable. If "there is no end/to what a living world/will demand of you,"[47] how are we living this present world? If our expressive demands can demonstrate a new worldview, in what ways can ethical human geographies, or interhuman geographies, be mapped?

*Conclusion*

# Stay Human

What Sylvia Wynter's analytical grounds make available, for geography, is a space to rethink the complex linkages between history, blackness, race, and place. Rather than situating the grounds of blackness within antici-pated realms of existing geographic arrangements (inside/outside, or, as I have mentioned in earlier chapters, descriptively paradoxical and across), I have tried to use Wynter's ideas to notice where black human geogra-phies might take us. What I mean by this is that Wynter opens up a new function for human geographies, one that takes "new forms of life" as seri-ously as it takes biocentric spatial organizations (or present forms of life). The geographic meaning of racialized human geographies is not so much rooted in a paradoxical description as it is a projection of life, livability, and possibility. Poetics, real and imagined geographies, put demands on traditional geographic arrangements because they expose the racial-sexual functions of the production of space and establish new ways to read (and perhaps live) geography.

Geographic alternatives are best displayed through communicative acts—geographic expressions that, as mentioned in previous chapters, cite/site underacknowledged black geographies. I want to conclude by dis-cussing black women's geographies as communicative expressions of what Wynter calls "a third perspective," those new forms of life that assert new geographic formulations. I am in part returning, then, to deep space and a poetics of landscape (as they are expressive) and the conundrum of geography as it is produced in relation to imaginative-real black human geographies.

Throughout several of Sylvia Wynter's essays, she notes that communicative acts—such as poetry, fiction, film, theory—can uncover the particularities of black cultures. She argues that such acts name the world, conceptualize the world, and therefore give the writer/reader access to new forms of life.[1] Through the work of Édouard Glissant, I have also suggested that geographic expressions and poetics are important to uneven geographies, in that "saying," imagining, and living geography locates the kinds of creative and material openings traditional geographic arrangements disclose and conceal. I want to suggest here that the poetics of landscape are particularly important to black women's geographies not only because they function to name and conceptualize the world, but also because they advance complex respatializations that can perhaps move beyond descriptive paradoxical geographies. That is, the poetics of landscape, as a projection of black femininity, can provide a moment to imagine new forms of geography, seeing the world from an interhuman (rather than partial) perspective.[2]

So, in what ways can the garret, the auction block, and Marie-Joseph Angélique's New France function as new forms of geography and a respatialization of present geographic forms? What do these communicative acts of place invoke? In terms of Jacobs/Brent, I argued that the attic serves as a workable paradoxical space, one that positions her across the regime of slavery and begins her emancipation. I also suggested that the garret is a painful geographic expression of black emancipation. When Hortense Spillers creatively recasts the garret to insinuate a black project of "garreting" in and beyond slavery, a different expression of space, place, race, and gender is made possible. Specifically, Brent's story functions to spatialize Spillers's theoretical concerns and invoke the ideological and geographic "captivities" black women continue to endure. More than this, the geographic perspective of slavery is widened and understood as an *alterable* geographic device—a new geographic form—which counters the naturalization of race, gender, and place: it precedes and corresponds with other feminist geographies, allowing Spillers to integrate black femininity into the historical present "in the flesh," not on the margins, no longer in the last place they thought of.[3] The geographic possibility of the garret can make and remake black femininity not simply as a garreted/marginal "way of being" but as a geographic project that is respatializing and shifting the grounds of black womanhood.

Similarly, Robbie McCauley's use of the auction block in her play *Sally's*

*Rape* replays the unresolved story of (white-black) feminism and woman-hood and the violent legacy of transatlantic slavery. But McCauley's dramatic choices, as writer, director, character, and self, establish new poetic functions for the auction block: as a site of white womanhood, black womanhood, and interhuman dialogue. The geography and meaning of the auction block, in our present, is renewed not to descriptively re-marginalize black femininity, nor to put Sally/Robbie/Jeannie up for sale, but rather to work out how a radically racial-sexual biocentric geography can be transformed into a critical site of correlation. New France and Canada, as well, were transformed by a black woman: Marie-Joseph Angélique's execution, death, and absented presence suggest that blackness can be expunged from the nation; but this story of black femininity also contributes to making Canada possible, through Angélique's permanent and long-standing geographic subjectivity. Marie-Joseph Angélique thus becomes a historical and geographic device through which new respatializations can be imagined and lived: the launching of Lorena Gale's play *Angélique* in Calgary, New York City, Detroit, and Toronto, is then a dramatic and transferable spatialization of Canada's uneasy relationship with transatlantic slavery and contemporary black residencies. Angélique is not, then, just a presence or an absented presence; she also evidences how the livability of black worlds are necessarily expressive tactics that can alter the seeming transparency of (blackless/ungeographic) space.

More humanly workable geographies are not always readily available. Dominant geographic patterns can often undermine complex interhuman geographies by normalizing spatial hierarchies and enacting strict spatial rules and regulations. More than this, "normal" places and spaces—of comfort, wealth, peace, safety—are hopefully seductive: they allude to the idea that finding and living the "normal" within existing spatial hierar-chies is a geographic achievement, a fulfilling geographic story. "Normal" and seductive geographies contribute to the ways in which geography appears to be fixed and draw us to this fixity as though it is natural—there-fore "naturally" excluding "difference" from the normal. Our environment, our cities and towns, our borders, our maps, continually render the world around us as simply given; we move through and around its familiar and unchanging arrangements: space just is. To challenge something that "just is," as many subaltern subjects have, can be a very threatening geographic act; it is punishable, erasable, and oppositional.

Yet black women's geographic experiences and expressions reveal new and innovative spatial practices: if one moves through, rebuilds, contests, or even "says" space, "natural" geographic arrangements are called into question. There are other available geographic patterns at work and they perhaps gesture to more just and humanly workable geographic possibilities. While geography, space, and place are useful to thinking about ways in which we are differently "in place" and implicated in the production of space, they are also useful in signaling the alterability of "the ground beneath our feet." The poetics of landscape and local-contextual experiences, of garrets, auction blocks, and Canada, might therefore be read beyond the margins, as part of an interhuman story that unhinges the body-self from its anticipated realms. Black women's geographies disclose that black femininity or body-histories are connected to a long and inter-human geographic story; they illustrate the ways in which the act of ex-pression reveals *why* these geographies are important and how they express new forms of life that contest our historically present, and uneven, genres of human geography.

The title of this conclusion, "Stay Human," is borrowed from musicians Michael Franti and Spearhead.[4] The title of their album *Stay Human* suggests that we can drift in and out of humanness—and that humanness, like geography, is alterable. Setting their music and music-making within the context of industrial prison expansion and the story of a black woman activist on death row—archipelagos of death and activism—*Stay Human* asks that we look and listen closely to the ways in which human normalcy is spatialized and resisted. Black women's geographies and poetics chal-lenge us to stay human by invoking how black spaces and places are inte-gral to our planetary and local geographic stories and how the question of seeable human differences puts spatial and philosophical demands on geography. These demands site the struggle between black women's geog-raphies and geographic domination, suggesting that more humanly work-able geographies are continually being lived, expressed, and imagined. And staying human, these struggles suggest, offers a different entry point into human geography: one that recognizes the alterability of humanness, space, and place, and one that imparts the understanding that this alter-ability is a pathway into new geographic practices.

# Acknowledgments

Thank you to Linda Peake, Leslie Sanders, and Rinaldo Walcott for reading and thinking with me, for rereading and discussing the ideas, problems, and spaces of *Demonic Grounds*. Each of you, in very different ways, has been so encouraging and thoughtful: I am grateful for your patience, intelligence, friendship, openness, and calm coolness, and I am very appreciative for dinners, drinks, and for your support of demonic grounds—the place and the work.

I thank Jenny Burman and Clyde Woods for their thorough reading and critiques of *Demonic Grounds* and to Neil Smith for his meaningful comments on an earlier draft of this manuscript. Thanks also to Kamala Kempadoo and Warren Crichlow for comments and discussion.

I am appreciative of a Social Science and Humanities Postdoctoral Fellowship, which assisted in getting *Demonic Grounds* "off the ground," and grateful to Carolyn King for mapping eighteenth-century Montreal. I am indebted to Robbie McCauley and Ed Montgomery for providing me with a live taped version of *Sally's Rape*. Thanks also to Renie Howard, Carrie Mullen, and Jason Weidemann at the University of Minnesota Press for your assistance and for paying attention to big and small details.

Thank you, Dionne Brand and Gayle Jones and Marlene Nourbese Philip, for writing.

The thoughts of Sylvia Wynter, conveyed through the post, are still inspirational and insightful.

My thanks also to Valerie Brodrick, Bob McKittrick, Ned Morgan,

Anne Brierley, Bryan Grundmann, Sharon Morgan Beckford, and Dina Georgis. I am also grateful to those families and friends, brothers and sisters, colleagues, writers, and musicians who have inspired, listened to, or lived with *Demonic Grounds*.

To Liz Millward, an extra-special thank you for long conversations about everything, for your intelligence and thoughtfulness.

Jennifer McKittrick, I am so grateful to you for making me laugh (hard), for being so bright and encouraging and always knowing my sense of place, for being so loving.

Ray Zilli, thank you for your creativity and confidence and for bringing me so much peace.

# Notes

## INTRODUCTION

1. Sylvia Wynter, "Beyond the Word of Man: Glissant and the New Discourse of the Antilles," 640.

2. Olaudah Equiano, *The Interesting Life of Olaudah Equiano, or Gustavus Vassa, The African*, 35–36.

3. Dionne Brand, *Land to Light On*, 48.

4. Kathleen Kirby, *Indifferent Boundaries: Spatial Concepts of Human Subjectivity*, 9.

5. Neil Smith and Cindi Katz, "Grounding Metaphor: Towards a Spatialized Politics," in Michael Keith and Steve Pile, eds., *Place and the Politics of Identity*, 80. My emphasis.

6. See: Gillian Rose, "Progress in Geography and Gender. Or Something Else?" 531–37; Derek Gregory, *Geographical Imaginations*, 5–9. It is important to note, then, that "traditional geography" and "traditional geographies," throughout the study, refer to both the discipline of human geography and dominant geographic patterns.

7. Saidiya Hartman, *Scenes of Subjection: Terror, Slavery, and Self-Making in Nineteenth Century America*, 5.

8. The production of space refers to: any landscape that arises out of social practices; the historical production of spatiality through racialized, gendered, and classed forms of geographic organization. Derek Gregory, *Geographical Imaginations*, 356; Neil Smith, *Uneven Development: Nature, Capital and the Production of Space*, 78. And a note on "blackness": throughout the study, I borrow from Rinaldo Walcott, *Black Like Who?* xiv–xv. Walcott writes that blackness is most usefully understood as "a sign, one which carries with it particular histories of resistance and domination . . . questions of blackness far exceed the categories of the biological and ethnic . . . [it is] a discourse, but that discourse is embedded in a history or a set of histories which are messy and contested."

9. Audrey Kobayashi and Linda Peake, "Unnatural Discourse: 'Race' and Gender in Geography," 227. Emphasis in the original.

10. Ruth Wilson Gilmore, "Fatal Couplings of Power and Difference: Notes on Racism and Geography," 16.

11. Ibid., 16.

12. For example, compare the slave narratives in Henry Louis Gates Jr., *The Classic Slave Narratives,* Olaudah Equiano, Mary Prince, Frederick Douglass, Harriet Jacobs/Linda Brent, whose narratives span 1789–1861, are gendered, and are authored by one African, two African Americans, and one Caribbean. For recollections, see also B. A. Botkin, ed., *Lay My Burden Down: A Folk History of Slavery;* Ira Berlin, Marc Favreau, and Steven F. Miller, eds., *Remembering Slavery.* Finally, see David Barry Gasper and Darlene Clarke Hine, eds., *More Than Chattel: Black Women and Slavery in the Americas,* for essays examining gender and slavery in different historical and geographic contexts.

13. Jenny Sharpe, *Ghosts of Slavery: A Literary Archaeology of Black Women's Lives,* xxi.

14. For example see: Hortense J. Spillers, "Mama's Baby, Papa's Maybe: An American Grammar Book," 454–81; Marlene Nourbese Philip, "Dis Place—The Space Between," *A Genealogy of Resistance and Other Essays,* 74–112; Patricia Hill Collins, *Black Feminist Thought.*

15. Carole Boyce Davies and Monica Jardine, "Imperial Geographies and Caribbean Nationalism: At the Border between 'A Dying Colonialism' and U.S. Hegemony," 162.

16. Avery Gordon, *Ghostly Matters: Haunting and the Sociological Imagination,* 195. My emphasis.

17. Paul Gilroy, *The Black Atlantic: Modernity and Double Consciousness,* 16.

18. Exceptions include some of the essays collected in the special "Black Atlantic" issue of *Research in African Literatures.*

19. Joan Dayan, "Paul Gilroy's Slaves, Ships, and Routes: The Middle Passage as Metaphor," 7–14.

20. Neil Smith and Cindi Katz, "Grounding Metaphor: Towards a Spatialized Politics," in Michael Keith and Steve Pile, eds., *Place and the Politics of Identity,* 80.

21. Paul Gilroy, *The Black Atlantic,* 48.

22. Édouard Glissant *Caribbean Discourse: Selected Essays,* 4–11.

23. Sylvia Wynter, "Beyond the Word of Man," 638–39. See also: Sylvia Wynter, "Ethno or Socio Poetics," 87.

24. Édouard Glissant, *Caribbean Discourse,* 75, 105.

25. Ibid., 130–31.

26. Ibid., 160.

27. Sylvia Wynter, "Beyond Miranda's Meanings: Un/Silencing the 'Demonic Ground' of Caliban's 'Woman'," 365.

28. Ibid., 364.

29. In terms of her focus on feminism, see also Sylvia Wynter, *Beyond Liberal and Marxist Leninist Feminisms: Towards an Autonomous Frame of Reference,* and Sylvia Wynter and David Scott, "The Re-Enchantment of Humanism: An Interview with Sylvia Wynter," 183–85.

30. Audre Lorde, *Sister Outsider,* 117.

31. I expand on demonic grounds and Wynter's work in chapter 5.

32. Sylvia Wynter and David Scott, "The Re-Enchantment of Humanism: An Interview with Sylvia Wynter," 121. Emphasis in the original.

33. Sylvia Wynter, "Beyond Miranda's Meanings," 366.

34. Carole Boyce Davies, "Negotiating Theories or 'Going a Piece of the Way with Them'," *Black Women, Writing and Identity: Migrations of the Subject,* 38–58; Zora Neale Hurston, "How It Feels to Be Colored Me," 152. Drawing on Zora Neale Hurston, Carole Boyce Davies suggests that we only "go a piece of the way"—rather than all the way home—with our academic and scholarly theories in order to unsettle knowledge hierarchies and eschew practices of discursive ownership and therefore cite/site the multiple positions and "syncretic articulations" of subaltern knowledges.

35. Marlene Nourbese Philip, *A Genealogy of Resistance and Other Essays,* 25. My emphasis.

## I. I LOST AN ARM ON MY LAST TRIP HOME

1. Octavia E. Butler, *Kindred,* 264.

2. Avery Gordon, *Ghostly Matters: Haunting and the Sociological Imagination,* 8.

3. Kathleen Kirby, *Indifferent Boundaries,* 11–36.

4. Glissant writes: "We know that we must exhaust the rhythms of the land and expose the landscape to those various kinds of madness that they have put us in." Édouard Glissant, *Caribbean Discourse: Selected Essays,* 160.

5. Morrison explains: "Slavery broke the world in half, it broke it in every way. It broke Europe. It made them into something else, it made them slave masters, it made them crazy. You can't do that for hundreds of years and it not take a toll. They had to dehumanize, not just the slaves but themselves . . . The idea of scientific racism suggests some serious pathology." Paul Gilroy, "Living Memory: A Meeting with Toni Morrison," 178.

6. For a thorough analysis of scale see: Neil Smith, "Homeless/Global: Scaling Places," 87–119.

7. This reclamation is spatialized, for example, in musician Prince's contractual disputes with the Warner Brothers record label over owning his own material, name, and controlling his music distribution. During the disputes (1992–96) the artist changed his name to an unutterable symbol and made all public appearances with "slave" written across his face. Equally interesting, at least in terms of geography, is the way Prince describes what he calls his emancipation from Warner Brothers: " . . . [with Warner Brothers] I wasn't free. Now I can make an album with Lenny [Kravtiz] if I want to. But he can't 'cause he's still under a contract . . . He's still on the plantation . . . he's down south. I'm up north." Dimitri Ehrlich, "Portrait of the Artist as a Free Man," 94. I want to reiterate, then, that practices of black spatial reclamation are not important only to geography, they continue to be haunted by racial dispossession and segregation, and in this case U.S. geographic regionalism and history. That is, black geographic ownership is coupled with *re*possession and displacement rather than easy, fulfilled acquisitions. Emphasized is the longing or struggle for equality, freedom,

safety in place. Clyde Woods carefully analyzes this relationship between geographic dispossession and reclamation with specific reference to black musics in his *Development Arrested: The Blues and Plantation Power in the Mississippi Delta*.

8. Nell Irvin Painter, "Hill, Thomas, and the Use of Racial Stereotype," 201.

9. Toni Morrison, "Introduction: Friday on the Potomac," in Toni Morrison, ed., *Race-ing Justice, En-Gendering Power: Essays on Anita Hill, Clarence Thomas, and the Construction of Social Reality,* vii–xxx.

10. I briefly discuss this question of African American class differences, property ownership, and geography in "Black and 'Cause I'm Black I'm Blue: Transverse Racial Geographies in Toni Morrison's *The Bluest Eye*," 125–42.

11. Henri Lefebvre, *The Production of Space*, 27–29. My understanding of transparent space throughout this study also draws on: Alison Blunt and Gillian Rose, *Writing Women and Space: Colonial and Postcolonial Geographies*, 1–25.

12. Henri Lefebvre, *The Production of Space*, 28. See also Donna J. Haraway, *Simians, Cyborgs, and Women: The Reinvention of Nature*, 188–96.

13. Susan Ruddick, "Constructing Difference in Public Spaces: Race, Class and Gender as Interlocking Systems," 132–51; Linda Peake, "Toward an Understanding of the Interconnectedness of Women's Lives: The 'Racial' Reproduction of Labour in Low-Income Urban Areas," 414–39.

14. Neil Smith, *Uneven Development: Nature, Capital and the Production of Space*, 155.

15. David Scott, *Refashioning Futures: Criticism After Postcoloniality*, 31. Emphasis in the original. On the imperative of a perspective of struggle, see Sylvia Wynter, "Beyond the Word of Man: Glissant and the New Discourse of the Antilles," 640.

16. Neil Smith and Cindi Katz, "Grounding Metaphor: Towards a Spatialized Politics," Michael Keith and Steve Pile, eds., *Place and the Politics of Identity*, 68.

17. Paul Gilroy, *The Black Atlantic*, 28; Carole Boyce Davies, *Black Women, Writing and Identity: Migrations of the Subject*, 38–58; Robin Cohen, *Global Diasporas: An Introduction*, 31–42, 127–53; Clyde Woods, *Development Arrested: The Blues Plantation and Power in the Mississippi Delta*, 39; W. E. B. Du Bois, *The Souls of Black Folk*, 3; Frantz Fanon, *The Wretched of the Earth*, 41.

18. Neil Smith, *Uneven Development: Nature, Capital and the Production of Space*, 169.

19. "In place" as in "staying put" and as in staying in one's place (gratefully subservient and respectful to authority).

20. Laura Pulido, "Reflections on a White Discipline," 46.

21. Linda Peake and Audrey Kobayashi, "Policies and Practices for an Antiracist Geography at the Millennium," 50.

22. In addition to the writings in *Professional Geographer*, see: Audrey Kobayashi and Linda Peake, "Unnatural Discourse: 'Race' and Gender in Geography," 225–43; Linda Peake and Richard Schein, "Racing Geography into the New Millennium: Studies of 'Race' and North American Geographies," 133–41; Minelle Mahtani, "Women Graduate Students of Colour in Geography: Increased Ethnic and Racial Diversity, or Maintenance of the Status Quo?" 11–18; Felix Driver, "Geography's Empire: Histories of Geographical Knowledge," 23–40; Owen J. Dwyer, "Geographical Research about

African Americans: A Survey of Journals, 1911-1995," 441–51; Katherine McKittrick and Linda Peake, "What Difference Does Difference Make to Geography?" in Noel Castree, Ali Rogers, and Douglas Sherman, eds., *Questioning Geography,* 39–54.

23. Linda Peake and Audrey Kobayashi, "Policies and Practices for an Antiracist Geography at the Millennium," 50–51.

24. It is important to underscore, then, that the gap in the academy is not simply discursive—a conceptual omission of "race" or blackness: there is a *physical* distance between black subjects, black geographers, black philosophers and the discipline of geography itself. See Linda Peake and Audrey Kobayashi, "Policies and Practices for an Antiracist Geography," 51; Laura Puildo, "Reflections on a White Discipline," 44–45.

25. Ruth Wilson Gilmore, "Fatal Couplings of Power and Difference," 16.

26. Ibid., 22n3. Emphasis in original.

27. For example: John W. Frazier, Eugen Tetty-Flo, Florence Margai, eds., *Race and Place: Equity Issues in Urban America;* Joe T. Darden, "Black Residential Segregation: Impact of State Licensing Laws," 415–26; Joe T. Darden, "Residential Segregation and the Quality of Life: The Black Ghetto of Pittsburgh Revisited," 11–20; Joe T. Darden and Sameh M. Kamel, "Black Residential Segregation in the City and Suburbs of Detroit: Does Socioeconomic Status Matter?," 1–13; Thomas J. Cooke, "Geographic Context and Concentrated Poverty within the United States," 552–66; Kwadwo Konadu-Agyemang, "Characteristics and Migration Experiences of Africans in Canada with Specific Reference to Ghanaians in Greater Toronto," 400–14.

28. In addition to analyses that "place" race, some recent empirical studies on health and geography have demonstrated how spaces of racial and economic difference, those geographies where black, hispanic, and other lower-class communities reside, experience higher and more dangerous health issues in the United States: Laura Pulido, "Rethinking Environmental Racism: White Privilege and Urban Development in Southern California," 12–40; Gerald F. Pyle, "The Diffusion of HIV/AIDS and HIV Infection in an Archetypal Textile County," 63–81; Sarah McLafferty and Barbara Templaski, "Restructuring Women's Reproductive Health: Implications of Low Birthweight in New York City," 309–23.

29. Don Mitchell, *Cultural Geography: A Critical Introduction,* 17–20. See also Oscar Lewis's *La Vita: A Puerto Rican Family in the Culture of Poverty: San Juan and New York,* which argues that the pathological behaviors related to poverty prevent the social advancement of the poor. Lewis's "culture of poverty" thesis, which mirrors environmental determinism, has been taken up to justify class hierarchies. For critiques that demonstrate the limitations of the culture of poverty thesis, see: Eleanor Leacock, ed., *The Culture of Poverty: A Critique;* Judith G. Good and Edwin Eames, "An Anthropological Critique of the Culture of Poverty"; George Gmelch and Walter P. Zenner, eds., *Urban Life: Readings in Urban Anthropology,* 405–17.

30. Richard Dyer, "White," 44–64; bell hooks, "Representations of Whiteness in the Black Imagination," *Black Looks: Race and Representation,* 165–78. Examples of the geographic pull into different kinds/places of blackness include: Evelyn Brooks Higginbotham, *Righteous Discontent;* Tracey Skelton, "Ghetto Girls/Urban Music: Jamaican Ragga Music and Female Music," 142–54; Laura Pulido, "Community, Place and Identity," 11–28; Naz Rassool, "Fractured or Flexible Identities: Life Histories of 'Black'

Diasporic Women in Britain," 187–204; bell hooks, "Homeplace: A Site of Resistance," *Yearning: Race, Gender and Cultural Politics,* 41–49.

31. Sylvia Wynter, "Rethinking Aesthetics," 243; Sylvia Wynter and David Scott, "The Re-Enchantment of Humanism: An Interview with Sylvia Wynter," 195.

32. "Mapping man's inhumanity to man" is taken from David Harvey, *Social Justice and the City,* 144–45.

33. Neil Smith, *Uneven Development,* 161.

34. Ibid.

35. Ibid., 167.

36. Ibid., 169.

37. Sylvia Wynter, "1492: A New World View," 5–57; "Rethinking Aesthetics," 238–79.

38. Édouard Glissant, *Caribbean Discourse,* 64; see also 150.

39. Ibid. *cf.* Trevor Barnes and Derek Gregory, *Reading Human Geography: The Politics and Poetics of Inquiry,* for a different discussion of poetics and geography.

40. bell hooks, *Yearning: Race, Gender, and Cultural Politics,* 41–50 and 145–54; bell hooks, *Feminist Theory: From Margin to Center;* Houston A. Baker Jr., *Blues, Ideology, and Afro-American Literature: A Vernacular Theory,* 139–72; Marlene Nourbese Philip, "'Dis Place—The Space Between," *A Genealogy of Resistance and Other Essays,* 74–112; Dionne Brand, *A Map to the Door of No Return: Notes to Belonging;* Ralph Ellison, *Invisible Man;* Paul Gilroy, *The Black Atlantic: Modernity and Double Consciousness;* Carole Boyce Davies, *Black Women, Writing and Identity,* 152–55. Davies is perhaps recasting Adrienne Rich's "politics of location," from her "Notes Toward a Politics of Location," in *Blood Bread and Poetry: Selected Prose, 1979–1985,* 239–56.

41. Frederick Douglass, *Narrative of the Life of Frederick Douglass, an American Slave,* 138.

42. Ibid.

43. *cf.* Rinaldo Walcott, "Pedagogy and Trauma: The Middle Passage, Slavery and the Problem of Creolization," 135–51.

44. *cf.* Ralph Ellison, "Introduction," *Invisible Man,* xii; Avery Gordon, *Ghostly Matters,* 17.

45. I am referring to the photograph "I AM A MAN" by Ernest C. Withers, which was part of the 2001 *Committed to the Image: Contemporary Black Photographers* exhibit at the Brooklyn Museum of Art. See also Homi Bhabha, "Are You a Man or a Mouse?," 61.

46. See: Michael Keith and Steve Pile, "Introduction: The Politics of Place," in Steve Pile and Michael Keith, eds., *Place and the Politics of Identity,* 1–21; Gillian Rose, *Feminism and Geography: The Limits of Geographical Knowledge;* Peter Jackson, "Constructions of 'Whiteness' in the Geographical Imagination," 99–106; Edward Soja and Barbara Hooper, "The Space That Difference Makes: Some Notes on the Geographical Margins of the New Cultural Politics," 183–205. Katherine McKittrick, "bell hooks," 189–94. For a discussion of reducing black women and black women's experiences to an absolute conceptual arena, see: Valerie Smith, "Black Feminist Theory and the Representation of the 'Other'," 38–58.

47. Linda McDowell, *Gender, Identity and Place: Understanding Feminist Geographies,* 94.

48. Audre Lorde, *Sister Outsider,* 117.

49. Michael Keith and Steve Pile, "Introduction: The Politics of Place," in Steve Pile and Michael Keith, eds., *Place and the Politics of Identity,* 16–20.

50. Paul Gilroy, *There Ain't No Black in the Union Jack: The Cultural Politics of Race and Nation.*

51. Toni Morrison, Bob Marley, Jimi Hendrix, Ralph Ellison, C. L. R. James, Edward Kamu Braithwaite/Édouard Glissant, Carole Boyce Davies, Dionne Brand, Janet Jackson, Public Enemy, Frantz Fanon, Jamaica Kincaid, Julie Dash, Zora Neale Hurston, W. E. B. Du Bois.

52. Dorothy Allison, "Public Silence, Private Terror," 103–14.

53. Dionne Brand, *Land to Light On;* Dionne Brand, *A Map to the Door of No Return;* Toni Morrison, *The Bluest Eye;* Toni Morrison, *Paradise;* C. L. R. James, *Beyond a Boundary;* Melvin Dixon, *Ride Out the Wilderness: Geography and Gender in Afro-American Literature;* Audre Lorde, "The Master's Tools Will Never Dismantle the Master's House," *Sister Outsider,* 110–13.

54. W. E. B. Du Bois, *The Souls of Black Folk.*

55. Ibid., 134–35.

56. Ibid., 3–4.

57. Ibid., 92.

58. Ibid., 3, 35.

59. Neil Smith, *Uneven Development,* 161.

60. Ato Sekyi-Otu, *Fanon's Dialectic of Experience,* 100. I am very grateful to Jenny Burman for encouraging me to return to Sekyi-Otu's text—his valuable discussion of Fanonian space has been both valuable and instructive to my understanding of human geographies and ontology.

61. Ibid., 25.

62. Frantz Fanon, *Black Skin, White Masks,* 111.

63. Ibid., 113. For a different discussion of Fanon's schemas see Steve Pile, "The Troubled Spaces of Frantz Fanon," 260–77. My reading of Frantz Fanon's "schemas" differs slightly from Pile's. He conflates corporeal, epidermal, historio-racial, bodily, and racist schemas, suggesting that they are all evidence of Fanon's struggle with objectification (Pile, "The Troubled Spaces," 263–66). However, Fanon (*Black Skin, White Masks,* 112) makes a distinction between corporeal and historio-racial epidermal schemas, suggesting that the former is undermined by the latter vis-à-vis racism and the gaze, and that although race-difference, history-difference, and body-difference are intertwined, the corporeal schema is in fact "assailed" by historio-racial schemas. This suggests to me that the corporeal/bodily schema is not, for Fanon, simply skin, but skin-self, and therefore a much deeper site of human existence than Pile suggests.

64. Sylvia Wynter, "Towards the Sociogenic Principle: Fanon, Identity, The Puzzle of Conscious Experience," 49. Emphasis in the original.

65. Frantz Fanon, *Black Skin, White Masks,* 112.

66. Ibid., 115.

67. Ibid., 112.

68. Ibid., 113.

69. Frantz Fanon, *The Wretched of the Earth,* 52.

70. Ibid., 51–52.

71. Ato Sekyi-Otu, *Fanon's Dialectic of Experience,* 82.

72. *cf.* Frantz Fanon, *Black Skin, White Masks,* 113.

73. Ato Sekyi-Otu, *Fanon's Dialectic of Experience,* 83.

74. Frantz Fanon, *Black Skin, White Masks,* 109–40.

75. Katherine McKittrick, "The Uncharted Geographies of Frantz Fanon in *The Wretched of the Earth.*"

76. Neil Smith, "Homeless/Global: Scaling Places," 101.

77. Frantz Fanon, *Black Skin, White Masks,* 109–40. See also Steve Pile, *The Body and the City,* 250–56.

78. Frantz Fanon, *Black Skin, White Masks,* 229.

79. Ibid., 128.

80. Ibid., 135.

81. Ibid., 140.

82. As an aside, we might therefore also consider the new theoretical spaces and debates Frantz Fanon's discussions have raised within black studies, Caribbean studies, diaspora studies, African studies—and whether or not these spaces and debates carry with them a change in the material geography of the university, the classroom, the library, disciplines, and so forth. For a summary of "Fanon Studies," see David Scott, *Refashioning Futures,* 195.

83. Stuart Hall, "New Ethnicities," 445.

84. Ibid., 447.

85. Ibid.

86. Dionne Brand, "Job," *Bread Out of Stone,* 41–42.

87. Toni Morrison, "The Site of Memory," 305.

88. Ibid., 304.

89. Ibid., 299–305.

90. Dionne Brand, "Notes for Writing Thru Race," *Bread Out of Stone,* 187–92; Rinaldo Walcott, *Black Like Who?,* 37.

91. Stuart Hall, "New Ethnicities," 449.

92. Octavia E. Butler, *Kindred,* 9.

93. Sojourner Truth, "Ain't I a Woman?," 93–95; Toni Morrison, *Beloved,* 82.

94. Octavia E. Butler, *Kindred,* 264.

## 2. THE LAST PLACE THEY THOUGHT OF

1. Harriet A. Jacobs [Linda Brent], *Incidents in the Life of a Slave Girl: Written by Herself.* Linda Brent is the pseudonym Jacobs used to conceal her identity in *Incidents in the Life of a Slave Girl.* Born in slavery, Jacobs could read and write; the text was produced with the assistance of Lydia Marie Child.

2. Ibid., 114.

3. Ibid., 127, 147, 148, 156. Brent makes several more comments about the ways in which the attic disabled her body and threatened her emotional well-being.

4. Angelyn Mitchell, *The Freedom to Remember: Narrative, Slavery and Gender in Contemporary Black Women's Fiction*, 22.

5. Hazel V. Carby, *Reconstructing Womanhood: The Emergence of the Afro-American Woman Novelist*, 45–61; Valerie Smith, "'Loopholes of Retreat': Architecture and Ideology in Harriet Jacobs's *Incidents in the Life of a Slave Girl*," 212–26; Hortense J. Spillers, "Mama's Baby, Papa's Maybe: An American Grammar Book," 454–81; Saidiya V. Hartman, *Scenes of Subjection: Terror, Slavery, and Self-Making in Nineteenth-Century America*, 105–12. See also the collected essays in *Harriet Jacobs and Incidents in the Life of a Slave Girl*.

6. Jenny Sharpe, *Ghosts of Slavery: Literary Archaeology of Black Women's Lives*, xx.

7. Jenny Sharpe outlines some of the key debates concerning Brent's agency/victimization in her introduction to *Ghosts of Slavery*, xviii–xxii. See Saidiya V. Hartman, *Scenes of Subjection*, 105–12; as her discussion asks: can any sexual relationship under slavery *not* be rape? And, is Brent's sexual "choice" of her white lover, Mr. Sands, nullified by her enslaved status and the normative patterns of sexual violence under slavery? See also Angelyn Mitchell, *The Freedom to Remember*, 22–41.

8. Harriet A. Jacobs [Linda Brent], *Incidents in the Life of a Slave Girl*, 123.

9. Paul Gilroy, *The Black Atlantic: Modernity and Double Consciousness*, 68.

10. Harriet A. Jacobs [Linda Brent], *Incidents in the Life of a Slave Girl*, 123–24.

11. See Henri Lefebvre, *The Production of Space*, 41, on the logic of visualization.

12. Harriet A. Jacobs [Linda Brent], *Incidents in the Life of a Slave Girl*, 114.

13. Ibid., 28.

14. Gillian Rose, *Feminism and Geography: The Limits of Geographical Knowledge*, 140.

15. Harriet Jacobs [Linda Brent], *Incidents in the Life of a Slave Girl*, 116–17.

16. Angelyn Mitchell makes this important point concerning Brent's retreat to the garret and the letters she arranges to have posted from New York and Boston: "The tables are turned dramatically when she finds a way to manipulate her oppressor economically. Eluding Dr. Flint, Brent forces him to spend a great deal of money in pursuit of her. Her strategy, in turn, causes Dr. Flint, in need of money, to sell her two children indirectly to their father [Mr. Sands]" (Angelyn Mitchell, *The Freedom to Remember*, 38). Houston A. Baker Jr. also discusses the economic consequences of Brent's retreat in *Blues, Ideology, and Afro-American Literature: A Vernacular Theory*, 53–55.

17. Harriet Jacobs [Linda Brent], *Incidents in the Life of a Slave Girl*, 147.

18. On "disembodied eye" see: Heidi J. Nast and Audrey Kobayashi, "Re-Corporealizing Vision," 75–93. See also Donna Haraway's discussion of "seeing from below" and privileging the partial perspective in her *Simians, Cyborgs, and Women: The Reinvention of Nature*, 190–91.

19. Harriet A. Jacobs [Linda Brent], *Incidents in the Life of a Slave Girl*, 117.

20. Dionne Brand, "This Body for Itself," *Bread Out of Stone*, 101.

21. Harriet Jacobs [Linda Brent], *Incidents in the Life of a Slave Girl*, 145.

22. I have also discussed the geographies of Marlene Nourbese Philip and "Dis Place" in "Who Do You Talk to, When a Body's In Trouble? Marlene Nourbese Philip's (Un)Silencing of Black Bodies in the Diaspora," 223–36.

23. Marlene Nourbese Philip, "Dis Place—The Space Between," *A Genealogy of Resistance and Other Essays*, 74.

24. E. Francis White and Joy James differently discuss the ways in which codes of respectability are integrated into post-slave black identities. E. Frances White, *Dark Continent of Our Bodies: Black Feminism and the Politics of Respectability;* Joy James, *Transcending the Talented Tenth: Black Leaders and American Intellectuals.*

25. I am thinking specifically about Linda McDowell, *Gender, Identity and Place: Understanding Feminist Geographies,* 34–70. McDowell summarizes feminist geographers' work on the body in addition to social theories on the body. In her essay, she does not discuss nonwhite racial bodies and theories and fails to acknowledge that whiteness is also a racialized construction. This hinders her discussion of how identity, gender, space, and place are mutually produced. Overall, she repeats white feminist critiques of white sex-gender binaries and consequently implies that theories of the body are primarily concerned with what she calls "Western bodies." She does not consider that black bodies are Western bodies, nor that black women impact upon the meaning of "Western bodies" (as working bodies, leisure bodies, inscribed bodies, adorned bodies, private bodies, public bodies, natural bodies, sick bodies, pregnant bodies, sexual bodies—these are just some of the "Western bodies" McDowell discusses). While I understand McDowell's intention in this essay (it is, for the most part, a literature overview), and I do not want to linger on her absences, her essay evidences how easy it is to simply dismiss the work of nonwhite women and men and ultimately *miss* how complicated bodily geographies can be. Importantly, McDowell acknowledges that a discussion of "skin colour" is absent from her text (what color is white Western skin?) and she supports this absence by adding that "to date there is little explicit work by geographers [on skin colour]" (70). However, it is interesting that McDowell finds it useful to draw heavily on key *non-geographers* to frame her ideas on Western (white) bodies—Michel Foucault, Elizabeth Grosz, Judith Butler, Pierre Bourdieu. She does not attempt to consider that nonwhite non-geographers might also be useful to her corporeal geographic theories. Her justification for excluding "skin colour" falls apart right in front of this reader's eyes.

26. Marlene Nourbese Philip, "Dis Place," 94.

27. Ibid., 91.

28. Ibid., 95. Emphasis in the original.

29. Ibid., 104–105.

30. Ibid., 77. Emphasis in the original.

31. Ibid., 99.

32. Compare, for example, the battle cries between the two competing gangs of Jamettes, or, the black middle-class critiques of Jamettes and the opposing interpretations of space/place/the streets. Philip, *The Streets,* 79–81, 108, and especially 83 (Act II, Scene iii).

33. Marlene Nairbese Philip, "Dis Place," 78–83, 107–110.

34. There are few feminist or human geographers who extensively engage with black studies and particularly with black feminist studies (rather than antiracist, critical race, or "race" studies). In terms of interdisciplinary and conceptual connections across black feminism, black studies, and feminist geographies, exceptions include:

Linda Peake and Alissa Trotz, *Gender, Ethnicity and Place: Women and Identities in Guyana;* Susan Ruddick, "Constructing Difference in Public Spaces: Race, Class and Gender as Interlocking Systems," 132–51; Peter Jackson, "Constructions of 'Whiteness' in the Geographical Imagination," 99–106. I also find the interdisciplinary work of geographer Ruth Wilson Gilmore useful: "Fatal Couplings of Power and Difference: Notes on Racism and Geography," 15–24; "Globalisation and U.S. Prison Growth," 171–88; "Public Enemies and Private Intellectuals," 69–78; "Terror Austerity Race Gender Excess Theatre," 23–37; "'You Have Dislodged a Boulder': Mothers and Prisoners in the Post-Keynesian California Landscape," 12–38.

35. Joy James and T. Denean Sharpley-Whiting, "Editor's Introduction," *The Black Feminist Reader,* 1–7.

36. The editors write that the "best-known documentation of [black feminist] endeavors is found in the historical and contemporary works of black women in the United States." Joy James and T. Denean Sharpley-Whiting, "Editor's Introduction," 1. The essays in the reader written by U.S.–Caribbean scholars Barbara Christian and Sylvia Wynter are cited by the editors as African American *and* Caribbean. However, James and Sharpley-Whiting make clear, through their review of black feminism and the locations of feminist struggles, that the focus is primarily on U.S. black feminism. This does not mean, however, that the geographic *intent* of all of the essays is the United States only; nor does it suggest that black feminism(s) produced in the United States is always already bound to a U.S. (national) feminist mandate. It does, however, reveal the weight of U.S. black feminism and U.S. black studies in general.

37. bell hooks, *Feminist Theory: From Margin to Center,* 15.

38. For example, note the ongoing and intertextual discussions of the *Moynihan Report* as a spatial expression of racism-sexism, which entered into and pathologized black, poor, urban women as well as their homes and communities: Hortense Spillers, "Mama's Baby, Papa's Maybe"; Angela Davis, *Women, Race and Class;* Wahneema Lubiano, "Black Ladies, Welfare Queens, and State Minstrels: Ideological War by Narrative Means," 323–61; Dorothy Roberts, *Killing the Black Body: Race, Reproduction and the Meaning of Liberty,* 15–17.

39. The Combahee River Collective, "A Black Feminist Statement," 14.

40. See also Patricia Hill Collins, *Black Feminist Thought,* 13, 27–28, 222–23. Hill Collins sharpens the ethnic-geographic possibilities of identity-location by asserting that black women's unique positions provide Afrocentric worldviews and Afrocentric feminist politics. Geographically, Collins's theoretical framework hinges on "the long-standing belief systems among African peoples" and how these belief systems have been denied and asserted in the United States. In gendering this geo-ideological connection with Africa, Collins suggests that black U.S. women's "standpoint" is a combination of Afrocentrism and feminism.

41. Iris Marion Young, *Justice and the Politics of Difference,* 9.

42. bell hooks, *Feminist Theory: From Margin to Center,* 12.

43. bell hooks, *Yearning: Race, Gender and Cultural Politics,* 149–50.

44. Patricia Hill Collins, *Fighting Words: Black Women and the Search for Justice,* 129.

45. Ibid.

46. Barbara Christian, "The Race for Theory," 15–16.

47. Ibid., 19.

48. I thank April Sharkey for introducing me to Ellen Driscoll's work.

49. Carole Boyce Davies, "Hearing Black Women's Voices: Transgressing Imposed Boundaries," 3–14. See also: Carole Boyce Davies and Elaine Savory Fido, eds., *Out of the Kumbla: Caribbean Women and Literature;* Carole Boyce Davies, *Black Women, Writing and Identity: Migrations of the Subject;* Carole Boyce Davies, ed., *Black Women's Diaspora: Critical Responses and Conversations.*

50. Hortense J. Spillers, "Mama's Baby, Papa's Maybe," 475. Spillers is drawing on Valerie Smith's conference paper on Harriet Jacobs, revised and published as "Loopholes of Retreat." I am drawing on Spillers's discussion here, rather than Smith's, because Smith does not use the word "garreting" in her published article (although it is implied).

51. Hortense Spillers, "Mama's Baby, Papa's Maybe," 478–80.

52. This includes, importantly, practices too terrible, and too beyond gendered respectability, for Jacobs to write out and/or recollect at the time of the publication of *Incidents in the Life of a Slave Girl*—experiences and incidents Jacobs/Brent describes as "the degradation, the wrongs, the vices . . . [which] are more than I can describe." Harriet Jacobs [Linda Brent], *Incidents in the Life of a Slave Girl,* 28. Spillers and Valerie Smith explain that these degradations, wrongs, and vices are only legible "between the lines" of the narrative, while Saidiya Hartman explains that the "unspoken and the censored haunt the narrative . . . the constraints on what can be said, the impossibility of representing the magnitude of slavery's violence, and the pain of recollection account for the selective character of the narrative." Hortense J. Spillers, "Mama's Baby, Papa's Maybe," 475; Valerie Smith, "Loopholes of Retreat," 214; Saidiya Hartman, *Scenes of Subjection,* 108.

## 3. THE AUTHENTICITY OF THIS STORY HAS NOT BEEN DOCUMENTED

1. Orville W. Carroll, "Green Hill Slave Auction Block," *Historic American Buildings Survey.* Carroll wrote that the slave block, in 1960, was still in "good condition." While the plantation itself has been restored and modified since it was built in 1797, the slave block and the accompanying auctioneer's stand have not been removed because of the support of the Virginia Department of Historic Resources. See Cheryl Simpson-Freeman, "Green Hill Plantation Offers Look Into Past." Although the Green Hill Plantation is not, to my knowledge, a formal tourist site, there has been interesting work done in geography on tours and pilgrimages to plantations in the United States. See Steven Hoelscher, "Making Place, Making Race: Performances of Whiteness in the Jim Crow South," 657–86.

2. Orville W. Carroll, "Green Hill Slave Auction Block."

3. William Wells Brown, *Clotel, or, The President's Daughter: A Narrative of Slave Life in the United States,* 88. For a more extensive discussion of the selling of "fair-skinned" and "white" slaves on the auction block, see Walter Johnson, "The Slave Trader, the White Slave, and the Politics of Racial Determination in the 1850s," 13–38.

4. While I am not including the additional sketches I examined at the Library of Congress here, several images are available in George Bourne's antislavery text, *Picture of Slavery in the United States*. Or, see Edward D. C. Campbell Jr. and Kym Rice, eds., *Before Freedom Came: African American Life in the Antebellum South*. This latter text has reprinted most of the images of auction blocks available at the Library of Congress. With regards to material sites: while my research was limited to representations at the Library of Congress, it is important to note that auction-house ruins, locations for public auctions that have since been transformed into markets or public buildings, and other geographic evidence of slave auctions are available.

5. The political agenda of the Green Hill survey is, indeed, very different from antislavery campaigns. Orville W. Carroll was working on behalf of the U.S. Historic American Buildings Survey and the National Park Service. The surveys began in 1933 and were designed to have unemployed architects document unique buildings and structures that were identified with historic events. It was a systemic project, originally underwritten by a Depression economy, designed to preserve representations of the U.S. landscape in the face of fires, natural diminishment, natural disasters, and real estate renovations. Charles E. Peterson, "The Historic American Buildings Survey Continued," 29–31.

6. Marcus Wood has recently published an important and extensive study on representations of slavery (paintings, songs, pamphlets, advertisements, and so forth): *Blind Memory: Visual Representations of Slavery in England and America, 1780–1865*.

7. Saidiya Hartman, *Scenes of Subjection: Terror, Slavery and Self-Making in Nineteenth Century America*, 17–18.

8. Walter Johnson, *Soul by Soul: Life Inside the Antebellum Slave Market*, 17–18.

9. Neil Smith, *Uneven Development: Nature, Capital and the Production of Space*, 41–54.

10. Frederick Douglass, *Narrative of the Life of Frederick Douglass, an American Slave*, 49; Saidiya Hartman, *Scenes of Subjection*, 21.

11. Walter Johnson, *Soul by Soul;* Thomas J. Durant Jr. and J. David Knotterus, eds., *Plantation Society and Race Relations: The Origins of Inequality;* David Barry Gasper and Darlene Clarke Hine, *More than Chattel: Black Women and Slavery in the Americas*.

12. Some descriptions of the auction block were gathered at the Library of Congress and are not included here. As mentioned above, see Edward D. C. Campbell Jr. and Kym Rice, eds., *Before Freedom Came*, as it contains several of the images available at the Library of Congress. Other descriptions of auction blocks have come from: B. A. Botkin, ed., *Lay My Burden Down: A Folk History of Slavery;* Ira Berlin, Marc Favreau, and Steven F. Miller, eds., *Remembering Slavery;* Frederic Bancroft, *Slave Trading in the Old South*.

13. James Martin, "Interview with James Martin," *Born in Slavery: Slave Narratives from the Federal Writers Project, 1936–1938*, 3.

14. Saidiya Hartman, *Scenes of Subjection*, 36–38.

15. Sallie A. Marston, "The Social Construction of Scale," 220.

16. Ollie Gary Christian, "The Social Demography of Plantation Slavery," *Plantation Society and Race Relations: The Origins of Inequality*, 149–61. See also: Theresa A. Singleton, ed., *The Archaeology of Slavery and Plantation Life*.

17. Clyde Woods, *Development Arrested: The Blues and Plantation Power in the Mississippi Delta*, 46–50.

18. Saidiya Hartman, *Scenes of Subjection*, 31.

19. Walter Johnson, *Soul by Soul: Life Inside the Antebellum Slave Market;* Walter Johnson, "The Slave Trader, The White Slave," 16–20; James O'Breeden, ed., *Advice Among Masters: The Ideal Slave Management in the Old South.*

20. Mary Prince, *The History of Mary Prince, A West Indian Slave. Related by Herself,* 191; B. A. Botkin, ed., *Lay My Burden Down: A Folk History of Slavery,* 106, 155; Deborah Gray White, *Ar'n't I a Woman? Female Slaves in the Plantation South,* 32.

21. Nicholas Blomley, "Law, Property, and the Geography of Violence: The Frontier, the Survey, and the Grid," 121–41.

22. Hortense Spillers, "Mama's Baby, Papa's Maybe: An American Grammar Book," 458–59; Angela Davis, *Women, Race and Class,* 25.

23. Angela Davis, *Women, Race and Class,* 3–29; Deborah Gray White, *Ar'n't I a Woman;* bell hooks, *Ain't I a Woman: Black Women and Feminism,* 15–49; Hortense Spillers, "Mama's Baby, Papa's Maybe," 454–81; Kamala Kempadoo, "Continuities and Change: Five Centuries of Prostitution in the Caribbean," 5–10.

24. Audre Lorde, *Sister Outsider,* 117.

25. Angela Davis, *Women, Race and Class,* 25.

26. Marlene Nourbese Philip, "Dis Place—The Space Between," *A Genealogy of Resistance and other Essays,* 74–77.

27. Hortense Spillers, "Mama's Baby, Papa's Maybe," 427.

28. Heidi J. Nast, "Mapping the Unconscious: Racism and the Oedipal Family," 215–55.

29. Neil Smith, *Uneven Development: Nature, Capital and the Production of Space,* 173.

30. Donna J. Haraway, *Simians, Cyborgs, and Women: The Reinvention of Nature,* 183–201.

31. Delicia Patterson, "The Faces of Power: Slaves and Owners," *Remembering Slavery,* Ira Berlin, Marc Favreau, and Steven F. Miller, eds., 44.

32. Sherley Anne Williams, *Dessa Rose,* 192–233.

33. My reading of the play draws on the 1994 text and the 1998 performance. I am extremely grateful to Robbie McCauley and Ed Montgomery for providing me with the 1998 VHS version of *Sally's Rape,* performed live at the Penumbra Theatre, St. Paul Minnesota. Viewing the play has greatly enhanced my reading and understanding of *Sally's Rape.* Robbie McCauley, "Sally's Rape," 212–38.

34. Ann E. Nymann, "*Sally's Rape:* Robbie McCauley's Survival Art," 577–87; Deborah Tompson, "Blackface, Rape, and Beyond: Rehearsing Interracial Dialogue in *Sally's Rape,*" 123–39; Arlene Croce, "Discussing the Undiscussable," 54–60; Cynthia Carr, "Talk Show," *On Edge: Performance at the End of the Twentieth Century,* 201.

35. Robbie McCauley, *Sally's Rape,* 218.

36. Ibid.

37. Ibid.

38. Deborah Britzman, *Lost Subjects, Contested Objects: Toward a Psychoanalytic Inquiry of Learning,* 117–18.

39. Ibid., 117.

40. Robbie McCauley, *Sally's Rape*, 230–231.

41. Angela Davis, *Women, Race and Class*, 25.

42. The second scene with the auction block is Jeannie's occupation of it. Robbie asks the audience to "bid in" on Jeannie. Jeannie, reluctant to fully participate in the sale, refuses when Robbie asks her to take off her dress. This is an equally complex scene, wherein white womanhood is put up for sale and Jeannie stands in for white feminine "respectability," a woman who can refuse to participate in the geographic violence of the block. Yet what McCauley makes clear is that white womanhood is, in fact, a rape-able bodily site; Jeannie has a *different* body history and "bodymemory," which endures and perpetuates uneven sexual violences because of the ways in which white femininity is valued. Can these different body histories, McCauley asks, invoke a moment of communion?

43. Robert Crossley, "Introduction," *Kindred*, xiv.

44. Robbie McCauley, *Sally's Rape*, 231.

45. Toni Morrison, "Living Memory: A Meeting with Toni Morrison," 178.

46. Sylvia Wynter, "Afterword: Beyond Miranda's Meanings: Un/Silencing the 'Demonic Ground' of Caliban's 'Woman'," 364. See my discussion of Wynter in chapter 5.

## 4. NOTHING'S SHOCKING

1. Dionne Brand, *Bread Out of Stone*, 187–92.

2. *The Canadian Oxford Dictionary*, s.v. "surprise."

3. Additionally, knowledge of Angélique is useful, in that she can startle unsuspecting subjects: she can be drawn on in crises to surprise and bewilder those who refuse the legacies of black Canada; she is needed to invoke a lost history, to potentially disarm unbelievers.

4. Sylvia Wynter, "But What Does Wonder Do? Meanings, Canons, Too? On Literary Texts, Cultural Contexts, and What It's Like to Be One/Not One of Us," 129.

5. David Scott, *Refashioning Futures: Criticism After Postcoloniality*, 24–26.

6. Bonita Lawrence, *"Real" Indians and Others: Mixed Blood Urban Native Peoples and Indigenous Nationhood*, 25–63.

7. Matthew Sparke, "Mapped Bodies and Disembodied Maps: (Dis)placing Cartographic Struggle in Colonial Canada," 305–36.

8. Bonita Lawrence, *"Real" Indians and Others*; Kim Anderson, *A Recognition of Being: Reconstructing Native Womanhood*; Sherene Razack, "Gendered Racial Violence and Spatialized Justice: The Murder of Pamela George," 121–56; Patricia Monture-Okanee, "The Violence We Women Do: A First Nations View," 193–203.

9. Caribana was renamed Toronto International Carnival in 2002. For examples of landscaping blackness out of Canada and/or relocating black diaspora populations, see: Rinaldo Walcott, *Black Like Who?*; George Elliott Clarke, "Honouring African-Canadian Geography: Mapping Black Presence in Canada," 35–38; Katherine McKittrick, "'Their Blood Is There and You Can't Throw It Out': Honouring Black Canadian Geographies," 27–37; Linda Peake and Brian Ray, "Racializing the Canadian Landscape: Whiteness, Uneven Geographies and Social Justice," 180–86; Peter Jackson, "The Politics of the Streets: A Geography of Caribana," 130–57.

10. Donna Haraway, *Simans, Cyborgs, and Women: The Reinvention of Nature,* 188–96.

11. Maureen G. Elgersman, *Unyielding Spirits: Black Women and Slavery in Early Canada and Jamaica;* Robin W. Winks, *The Blacks in Canada: A History.*

12. Robin W. Winks, *The Blacks in Canada;* Daniel G. Hill, *The Freedom-Seekers: Blacks in Early Canada;* Sylvia Hamilton, "Naming Names, Naming Ourselves: A Survey of Early Black Women in Canada," Peggy Bristow, et al., *"We're Rooted Here and They Can't Pull Us Up": Essays in African Canadian Women's History,* 13–40.

13. See, for example, Rinaldo Walcott, *Black Like Who?;* Robin W. Winks, *The Blacks in Canada;* Peggy Bristow, et al., *"We're Rooted Here and They Can't Pull Us Up": Essays in African Canadian Women's History;* Daniel G. Hill, *The Freedom-Seekers;* Rinaldo Walcott, ed., *Rude: Contemporary Black Canadian Cultural Criticism;* Cecil Foster, *A Place Called Heaven: The Meaning of Being Black in Canada;* George Elliot Clarke, *Odysseys Home: Mapping African-Canadian Literature;* Marlene Nourbese Philip, *A Genealogy of Resistance and Other Essays;* David Chariandy, "'Canada in Us Now': Locating the Criticism of Black Canadian Writing," 196–216.

14. Donald H. Clairmont and Dennis William Magill, *Africville: The Life and Death of a Canadian Black Community;* Robin W. Winks, *The Blacks in Canada,* 452–56; Jennifer Jill Nelson, "The Space of Africville: Creating, Regulating, and Remembering the Urban 'Slum'," 211–32.

15. Jennifer Jill Nelson, "The Space of Africville," 211–32.

16. And it has begun to be wondered. See: Dana Inkster, dir., *Welcome to Africville,* and Rinaldo Walcott's discussion of Inkster's film in "Isaac Julien's Children: Black Queer Cinema after *Looking for Langston,*" 10–17.

17. Rinaldo Walcott, "Caribbean Popular Culture in Canada; Or, the Impossibility of Belonging to the Nation," 123–39. For a different perspective, see Andre Alexis, "Borrowed Blackness," 14–20.

18. Susan Ruddick, "Constructing Difference in Public Spaces: Race, Class, and Gender as Interlocking Systems," 132–51.

19. Rinaldo Walcott, "Caribbean Popular Culture in Canada," 129; see also Dionne Brand, *Bread Out of Stone,* 139.

20. George Elliot Clarke, "Africana Canadiana: A Select Bibliography of Literature by African-Canadian Authors, 1785–2001, in English, French and Translation," 339–448. This is an update of Clarke's earlier document, "Africana Canadiana: A Primary Bibliography of Literature by African-Canadian Authors, 1785–1996, in English, French and Translation," 107–209.

21. Francis Henry, *The Caribbean Diaspora in Toronto: Learning to Live with Racism;* Sherene Razack, *Looking White People in the Eye;* Cecil Foster, *A Place Called Heaven;* Daniel G. Hill, *The Freedom-Seekers.*

22. For example, see the introductions to: Robin W. Winks, *The Blacks in Canada,* ix–xviii; Peggy Bristow, et al., *"We're Rooted Here and They Can't Pull Us Up,"* 3–12; Dionne Brand, *No Burden to Carry,* 11–36; Adrienne Shadd, "300 Years of Black Women in Canadian History: circa 1700-1980," 4–13; Maureen G. Elgersman, *Unyielding Spirits: Black Women and Slavery in Early Canada and Jamaica.*

23. Cecil Foster, *A Place Called Heaven,* 9, 248.

24. In addition to Henry, Razack, and Foster, see: Rella Braithwaite and Tessa Benn-Ireland, *Some Black Women: Profiles of Black Women in Canada;* Joseph Mensah, *Black Canadians: History, Experiences, Social Conditions;* Carol Tater, Frances Henry, and Winston Mattis, *Challenging Racism in the Arts;* George Elliot Clarke, "Honouring African-Canadian Geography," 35–38; Himani Bannerji, ed., *Returning the Gaze: Essays on Racism, Feminism, and Politics;* Enakshi Dua and Angela Robertson, eds., *Scratching the Surface: Canadian, Anti-Racist, Feminist Thought.*

25. "Fantino Talks with Police in Jamaica," A3; Dale Brazao, "Fantino Tours Jamaican Slums," A1; "Robbery Suspects Had Been Deported Twice," A1.

26. Kay Anderson, "Engendering Race Research: Unsettling the Self-Other Dichotomy," 197–211; Sarah Carter, "Categories and Terrains of Exclusion: Constructing the 'Indian Woman' in the Early Settlement Era in Western Canada," 177–95; Susan J. Smith, "Immigration and Nation-Building in Canada and the United Kingdom," 50–77.

27. Linda Peake and Brian Ray, "Racialising the Canadian Landscape," 180–86; Rinaldo Walcott, "'Who Is She and What Is She to You?': Mary Ann Shadd Cary and the (Im)Possibility of Black/Canadian Studies," 27–47; Dionne Brand, *Bread Out of Stone.*

28. Marlene Nourbese Philip, "African Roots and Continuities: Race, Space and the Poetics of Moving," 201–33.

29. Rinaldo Walcott, *Black Like Who?* 40–41.

30. Marlene Nourbese Philip, "African Roots and Continuities," 227–33.

31. Dionne Brand, *A Map to the Door of No Return: Notes to Belonging,* 150.

32. Ibid.

33. Ibid.

34. Ibid., 18–27. Emphasis in original.

35. George Elliot Clarke, "Raising Raced and Erased Executions in African-Canadian Literature: Or, Unearthing Angélique," 42.

36. Jean-Claude Marsen, *Montreal in Evolution,* 6.

37. Annick Germain and Damaris Rose, *Montréal: The Quest for a Metropolis,* 37–38.

38. Marcel Trudel, *L'Esclavage au Canada Français: Histoire et Conditions De L'Esclavage,* 227; Lorena Gale, *Angélique,* 8.

39. Annick Germain and Damaris Rose, *Montréal,* 38; Jean-Claude Marsen, *Montreal in Evolution,* 44, 74, 82.

40. Annick Germain and Damaris Rose, *Montréal,* 16–18.

41. *The Code Noir* was instituted in French colonies and had fifty-five provisions relating to slaves and slave ownership. For example, religious instruction, food and clothing regulations, and antimiscegenation laws were included in the laws. *The Code Noir* also legalized slave punishments and violences and thus was also designed to sanction subordination, objectification, and slaves' immobility. Lynn Stewart, "Louisiana Subjects: Power, Space and The Slave Body," 228; Charmaine Nelson, "Slavery, Portraiture and the Colonial Limits of Canadian Art History," 24–26.

42. Robin Winks, *The Blacks in Canada,* 9; Marcel Trudel, *L'Esclavage,* 86–87. See also Ken Alexander and Avis Glaze, *Towards Freedom: The African Canadian Experience,*

37. It is important to note that black slaves constituted about one-third of all slaves in New France when Marie-Joseph Angélique was alive, and that the number of black slaves significantly increased after British conquest.

43. *Census of Canada, 1665–1871.* This census indicates there were 37, 716 people in New France.

44. Robin Winks, *The Blacks in Canada,* 9; Maureen G. Elgersman, *Unyielding Spirits,* 15–16. The majority of other black slaves were concentrated in other New France towns: the towns of Québec and Trois-Riviéres.

45. Charmaine Nelson, "Slavery, Portraiture and the Colonial Limits of Canadian Art History," 24, 26; Maureen Elgersman, *Unyielding Spirits,* 4–5; Robin Winks, *The Blacks in Canada,* 10–15. Elgersman thus suggests that most agricultural labor was performed by *Panis.*

46. "Objecthood" is taken from Frantz Fanon, *Black Skin, White Masks,* 109.

47. Although I am not detailing the socioreligious spaces, it is important to note that French Catholicism underpinned these geographies. As mentioned, French religious leaders owned slaves; furthermore, many slaves were encouraged and rewarded for conversion. See Robin Winks, *The Blacks in Canada,* 12–15.

48. Ibid., 7.

49. This does not mean, however, that individual (rather than groups of) slaves did not pose a threat in other French colonies.

50. Lynn Stewart, "Louisiana Subjects," 227.

51. Frantz Fanon, *Black Skin, White Masks,* 109.

52. Heidi Nast, "Mapping the 'Unconscious': Racism and the Oedipal Family," 226.

53. Angela Davis, *Women, Race and Class,* 3–29; Linda Carty, "African Canadian Women and the State: 'Labour Only Please'," 202–3; Hilary Beckles, "Black Female Slaves and White Households in Barbados"; David Barry Gasper and Darlene Clarke Hine, eds., *More Than Chattel: Black Women and Slavery in the Americas,* 111–25; L. Virginia Gould, "Urban Slavery-Urban Freedom: The Manumission of Jacqueline Lemelle," 302–4; Julia Burkart, "Gender Roles in Slave Plantations," 125–35.

54. Jean-Claude Marsen, *Montreal in Evolution,* 110.

55. This summary is taken from Marcel Trudel, *L'Esclavage,* 226–29; Afua Cooper, *The Hanging of Angélique.*

56. Toni Morrison, "The Official Story: Dead Man Golfing," xvi.

57. Maureen Elgersman, *Unyielding Spirits,* 101.

58. Ibid., 115, 116.

59. David Scott, *Refashioning Futures,* 24–26.

60. George Elliot Clarke, "Raising Raced and Erased Executions in African-Canadian Literature," 51. Clarke's word choice—exhuming the dead—forces me to ask: how exactly do we exhume Angélique? She was burned, her ashes cast "to the four corners of the earth." If her bodily remains are gone, her ashes global, does it not follow that we must exhume her on different terms than he proposes or not exhume her at all?

61. Maureen G. Elgersman, *Unyielding Spirits;* George Elliot Clarke, "Raising Raced and Erased Executions in African-Canadian Literature: Or, Unearthing Angélique," 30–61; Daniel G. Hill, *The Freedom-Seekers,* 91; Afua Cooper, "Confessions of a Woman Who Burnt Down a Town," 81–85.

62. Lorena Gale, *Angélique,* 3.

63. Ibid., 69,

64. Toni Morrison, "The Official Story," xv.

## 5. DEMONIC GROUNDS

1. Paget Henry, "Sylvia Wynter: Poststructuralism and Postcolonial Thought," *Caliban's Reason: Introducing Afro-Caribbean Philosophy,* 118.

2. Sylvia Wynter and David Scott, "The Re-Enchantment of Humanism: An Interview with Sylvia Wynter," 121. While I am not taking on all of Sylvia Wynter's literatures and ideas in this chapter, a fairly comprehensive list of her collected works is included in my bibliography. For additional engagements with Wynter's work, see the special issue of *The Journal of West Indian Literatures,* 10:1/2 (2001) and the "Coloniality's Persistence" issue of *CR: The New Centennial Review,* 3:3, (Fall 2003).

3. Sylvia Wynter, *The Hills of Hebron: A Jamaican Novel.* Wynter is also known as an actor, dancer, playwright, short story writer, and translator.

4. Sylvia Wynter, "Unsettling the Coloniality of Being/Power/Truth/Freedom: Towards the Human, After Man, Its Overrepresentation—An Argument," 331, n1.

5. Ibid., 257–337.

6. Sylvia Wynter and David Scott, "The Re-Enchantment of Humanism," 164.

7. Sylvia Wynter, "Unsettling the Coloniality of Being/Power/Truth/Freedom," 264, 286. Man1 and Man2 are Wynter's framings.

8. Ibid., 284, 299.

9. Ibid., 293–95.

10. Ibid., 298.

11. Ibid., 263.

12. Ibid., 300. My emphasis.

13. Sylvia Wynter and David Scott, "The Re-Enchantment of Humanism," 160. Emphasis in the original.

14. Ibid., 183. This argument is elaborated on through Wynter's analysis of Frantz Fanon in her "Towards the Sociogenic Principle: Fanon, Identity, the Puzzle of Conscious Experience," 30–66.

15. Sylvia Wynter, "Rethinking 'Aesthetics'," 271.

16. Sylvia Wynter, "1492: A New World View," 46–49.

17. Neil Smith, *Uneven Development: Nature, Capital and the Production of Space,* xi–xvii.

18. Sylvia Wynter, "1492," 18.

19. Sylvia Wynter, "Unsettling the Coloniality of Being/Power/Truth/Freedom," 280.

20. Ibid., 293; Matthew Sparke, "Mapped Bodies and Disembodied Maps: (Dis)-Placing Cartographic Struggle in Canada," 305–36.

21. Sylvia Wynter, "The Pope Must Be Drunk, The King of Castile a Madman: Culture as Actuality and the Caribbean Rethinking of Modernity," 17–41.

22. Sylvia Wynter, "1492," 34. See also Édouard Glissant, *Caribbean Discourse: Selected Essays,* 13–52; Anne McClintock, *Imperial Leather: Race, Gender and Sexuality in the Colonial Conquest,* 21–74.

23. Sylvia Wynter, "1492," 42–43.

24. Avery Gordon, "Globalism and the Prison Industrial Complex: An Interview with Angela Davis," 147; Ruth Wilson Gilmore, "Globalisation and U.S. Prison Growth: From Military Keynesianism to Post-Keynesian Militarism," 171–88.

25. Ruth Wilson Gilmore, "Fatal Couplings of Power and Difference: Notes on Racism and Geography," 16.

26. Clyde Woods, "Life After Death," 62–66; Sylvia Wynter, "Rethinking 'Aesthetics'," 243. See also Sylvia Wynter and David Scott, "The Re-Enchantment of Humanism," 195.

27. Sylvia Wynter, "Unsettling the Coloniality of Being/Power/Truth/Freedom," 260–61.

28. Audre Lorde, *Sister Outsider,* 115. Édouard Glissant, "Creolization and the Making of the Americas," 268. See also Rinaldo Walcott's discussion of creolization and new human forms in "Pedagogy and Trauma: The Middle Passage, Slavery and the Problem of Creolization," 135–51.

29. Ato Sekyi-Otu, *Fanon's Dialectic of Experience,* 100.

30. Sylvia Wynter, "Beyond Miranda's Meanings," 355, 364.

31. Marlene Nourbese Philip, "Dis Place—The Space Between," *Genealogy of Resistance and Other Essays,* 94. Emphasis in the original.

32. Sylvia Wynter, "1492," 8. In terms of the "special vantage point," I am referring to bell hooks's *From Margin to Center,* 15, and Donna Haraway's "privileging of the partial perspective" found in her *Simians, Cyborgs, and Women: The Reinvention of Nature,* 190–91. See also the discussion of marginality and feminism in chapter 2. With regard to "inclusivity," I am thinking in particular about Angela Miles's *Integrative Feminism: Global Perspectives on North American Feminism.* This is not meant to suggest that partial perspectives and inclusion are not useful ways to think about social differences, but rather to signal Wynter's call for a "new world view from the perspective of the species, with reference to the interests of *its* well-being." (Emphasis in the original.) So, for example, what happens to the margin if it is analyzed as evidence of biocentricity and an assertion of black women's humanity *as connected to* the species?

33. Sylvia Wynter, "1492: A New World View," 47, 13.

34. Maureen G. Elgersman, *Unyielding Spirits: Black Women and Slavery in Early Canada and Jamaica,* 11; Robin Winks, *The Blacks in Canada: A History,* 5, 8. Importantly, some black slaves were purchased from other "cold" locations in the northern United States.

35. Robin Winks, *The Blacks in Canada,* 436–38. Remember, as well, Frantz Fanon's discussion of winter wherein the cold weather assists in producing Fanon's inhumanity *and* transforms him into a black man who is not shivering, but "quivering with rage." Frantz Fanon, *Black Skin, White Masks,* 114.

36. Dionne Brand, "Bathurst," *Bread Out of Stone,* 28–33. Albert Johnson, thirty-five, was shot and killed in his home on August 26, 1979. Toronto Police Constables Inglis and Walter Cargnelli were charged with manslaughter but were later acquitted. Buddy Evans, twenty-four, was shot and killed on August 9, 1978, by Toronto Police Constable Clark. No charges were laid against this officer.

37. For example: Paul Gilroy, *The Black Atlantic: Modernity and Double Consciousness;*

Angela Davis, *Blues Legacies and Black Feminism;* Clyde Woods, *Development Arrested: The Blues and Plantation Power in the Mississippi Delta.*

38. Clyde Woods, *Development Arrested,* 288.

39. Outkast, "The Whole World"; Missy Elliot, "Get Ur Freak On."

40. See Stuart Hall on the complexities and contradictions in black popular culture: "What Is This 'Black' in Popular Culture?" 465–75.

41. Soon after, Black Entertainment Television Internet voters chose Gray as "Tackiest Diva of the Year," who fashioned the "The Worst Awards Show Ensemble" of 2001. Laini Madhubuti, "2001 BET Fashion Disaster Awards."

42. Indeed, several students also commented on Gray's surprisingly "huge" tall body and strange (speaking) voice.

43. Stuart Hall, "What Is This 'Black' in Popular Culture?" 474.

44. Macy Gray, "A Moment to Myself"; Macy Gray, "Relating to a Psychopath" and "Freak Like Me."

45. Macy Gray, "The Letter."

46. Ibid. Here, of course, Gray may be signaling death and also returning us to slave resistances, such as suicide.

47. Octavia E. Butler, *Parable of the Sower,* 137.

## CONCLUSION

1. Sylvia Wynter, "Ethno or Socio Poetics," 78–94; Sylvia Wynter, "Rethinking Aesthetics," 238–79.

2. Sylvia Wynter, "1492: A New World View," 8.

3. Hortense J. Spillers, "Mama's Baby, Papa's Maybe: An American Grammar Book," 454–81.

4. Michael Franti and Spearhead, *Stay Human.*

# Bibliography

Alexander, Ken, and Avis Glaze. *Towards Freedom: The African Canadian Experience.* Toronto: Umbrella Press, 1996.

Alexis, Andre. "Borrowed Blackness." *This Magazine* (May 1995): 14–20.

Allen, John, and Doreen Massey, eds. *Geographical Worlds.* Oxford: Oxford University Press, 1995.

Allison, Dorothy. "Public Silence, Private Terror." In Carole S. Vance, ed., *Pleasure and Danger,* 103–14. London: Pandora Press, 1989.

Anderson, Kay. "Engendering Race Research: Unsettling the Self-Other Dichotomy." In Nancy Duncan, ed., *BodySpace: Destabilizing Geographies of Gender and Sexuality,* 197–211. New York and London: Routledge, 1996.

———. "The Racialization of Difference: Enlarging the Story Field." *The Professional Geographer* 54 no. 1 (2002): 25–30.

Anderson, Kim. *A Recognition of Being: Reconstructing Native Womanhood.* Toronto: Second Story Press, 2000.

Armstrong, Douglas V. "Archeology and Ethnohistory of the Caribbean Plantation." In Theresa A. Singleton, ed., *"I, Too, Am American": Archaeological Studies of African-American Life,* 173–92. Charlottesville and London: University Press of Virginia, 1999.

Baker, Houston A., Jr. *Blues Ideology and Afro-American Literature: A Vernacular Theory.* Chicago: University of Chicago Press, 1984.

Bancroft, Frederick. *Slave Trading in the Old South.* New York: Frederick Ungar Publishing, 1959.

Bannerji, Himani. *Returning the Gaze: Essays on Racism, Feminism, and Politics.* Toronto: Sister Vision Press, 1994.

Barnes, Trevor, and Derek Gregory. *Reading Human Geography: The Politics and Poetics of Inquiry.* London: Arnold, 1997.

Beckles, Hilary. "Black Female Slaves and White Households in Barbados." David Barry Gasper and Darlene Clark Hine, eds. *More Than Chattel: Black Women and*

*Slavery in the Americas*, 111–25. Bloomington and Indianapolis: Indiana University Press, 1996.

Berlin, Ira, Marc Favreau, and Steven F. Miller, eds. *Remembering Slavery*. New York: The New Press, 1999.

Bhabha, Homi K. "Are You a Man or a Mouse?" In Maurice Berger, Brian Wallis, and Susan Watson, eds., *Constructing Masculinity*, 57–65. New York and London: Routledge, 1995.

———. *The Location of Culture*. New York and London: Routledge, 1994.

Blomley, Nicholas. "Law, Property and the Geography of Violence: The Frontier Survey and the Grid." *Annals of the Association of American Geographers* 93 no. 1 (2003): 121–41.

Blunt, Alison, and Gillian Rose. *Writing Women and Space: Colonial and Postcolonial Geographies*. New York: The Guilford Press, 1994.

Botkin, B. A., ed. *Lay My Burden Down: A Folk History of Slavery*. Athens and London: University of Georgia Press, [1945] 1989.

Bourne, George. *Picture of Slavery in the United States*. Michigan: The Negro Press, [1834] 1972.

Braithwaite, Rella, and Tessa Benn-Ireland. *Some Black Women: Profiles of Black Women in Canada*. Toronto: Sister Vision Press, 1993.

Brand, Dionne. *A Map to the Door of No Return: Notes to Belonging*. Toronto: Doubleday, 2001.

———. *At the Full and Change of Moon*. Toronto: Vintage, 1999.

———. *Bread Out of Stone: Recollections on Sex, Recognition, Race, Dreaming and Politics*. Toronto: Coach House Press, 1994.

———. *In Another Place, Not Here*. Toronto, Vintage, 1996.

———. *Land to Light On*. Toronto: McClelland and Stewart, 1997.

———. *No Burden to Carry: Narratives of Black Working Women in Ontario, 1920s to 1950s*. Toronto: Women's Press, 1991.

Brazao, Dale. "Fantino Tours Jamaican Slums." *The Toronto Star*. February 13, 2003: A1.

Bristow, Peggy, Dionne Brand, Linda Carty, Afua P. Cooper, Sylvia Hamilton, and Adrienne Shadd, eds. *"We're Rooted Here and They Can't Pull Us Up": Essays in African Canadian Women's History*. Toronto: University of Toronto Press, 1994.

Britzman, Deborah P. *Lost Subjects, Contested Objects: Toward a Psychoanalytic Inquiry of Learning*. New York: State University of New York Press, 1998.

Brown, William Wells. *Clotel; Or, The President's Daughter*. Robert S. Levine, ed. Boston: Bedford, [1853] 2000.

Burkart, Julia. "Gender Roles in Slave Plantations." In Thomas J. Durant Jr. and J. David Knottnerus, eds., *Plantation Society and Race Relations: The Origins of Inequality*, 125–35. Westport: Praeger, 1999.

Butler, Octavia E. *Kindred*. Boston: Beacon/Bluestreak, 1979.

———. *Parable of the Sower*. New York: Time Warner, 1993.

———. *Parable of the Talents*. New York: Time Warner, 1998.

Campbell, Edward, D. C. Jr., and Kym Rice, eds. *Before Freedom Came: African American Life in the Antebellum South*. Charlottesville: University Press of Virginia, 1991.

Carby, Hazel V. *Reconstructing Womanhood: The Emergence of the Afro-American Woman Novelist*. New York and Oxford: Oxford University Press, 1987.

Carr, Cynthia. *On Edge: Performance at the End of the Twentieth Century.* Hanover and London: Wesleyan University Press, 1993.

Carroll, Orville W. *Historic American Buildings Survey.* Washington: Library of Congress, 1960: VA-605.

Carter, Sarah. "Categories and Terrains of Exclusion: Constructing the 'Indian Woman' in the Early Settlement Era in Western Canada." In Ken S. Coates and Robin Fisher, eds., *Out of the Background: Readings on Canadian Native History,* 177–95. Toronto: Copp Clarke, 1996.

Carty, Linda. "African Canadian Women and the State: 'Labour Only Please.'" In Peggy Bristow, ed., *"We're Rooted Here and They Can't Pull Us Up": Essays in African Canadian Women's History,* 192–229. Toronto: University of Toronto Press, 1994.

Case, Frederick Ivor. *Racism and National Consciousness.* Toronto: Plowshare Press, 1977.

Castree, Noel, Ali Rogers, and Douglas Sherman, eds. *Questioning Geography: Essays in a Contested Discipline.* Oxford: Blackwell, 2005.

Chariandy, David. "'Canada in Us Now': Locating the Criticism of Black Canadian Writing." *Essays on Canadian Writing* 75 (Winter 2002): 196–216.

Christian, Barbara. "The Race for Theory." In Joy James and T. Denean Sharpley-Whiting, eds., *The Black Feminist Reader,* 11–23. Oxford: Blackwell, 2000.

Christian, Ollie Gary. "The Social Demography of Plantation Slavery." In Thomas J. Durant Jr. and J. David Knottnerus, eds., *Plantation Society and Race Relations: The Origins of Inequality,* 149–61. Westport: Praeger, 1999.

Clairmont, Donald H., and Dennis William Magill. *Africville: The Life and Death of a Canadian Black Community.* Toronto: McClelland and Stewart, 1974.

Clarke, George Elliot. "Africana-Canadiana: A Primary Bibliography of Literature by African-Canadian Authors, 1785–1996, in English, French and Translation." *Canadian Ethnic Studies* 28 no. 1 (1996): 107–209.

———. "Honouring African Canadian Geography: Mapping Black Presence in Atlantic Canada." *Border/Lines* 45 (December 1997): 35–38.

———. *Odysseys Home: Mapping African-Canadian Literature.* Toronto: University of Toronto Press, 2002.

———. "Raising Raced and Erased Executions in African-Canadian Literature: Or, Unearthing Angélique." *Essays in Canadian Writing* 75 (Winter 2002): 30–61.

Coates, Ken S., and Robin Fisher, eds. *Out of the Background: Readings on Canadian Native History.* Toronto: Copp Clarke, 1996.

Cohen, Robin. *Global Diasporas: An Introduction.* Seattle: University of Washington Press, 1997.

Cooke, Thomas J. "Geographic Context and Concentrated Poverty within the United States." *Urban Geography* 20 no. 1 (1999): 552–66.

Cooper, Afua. "Confessions of a Woman Who Burnt Down a Town." In Afua Cooper, ed., *Utterances and Incantations,* 81–85. Toronto: Sister Vision Press, 1999.

———. *The Hanging of Angélique.* Toronto: Harper Collins, 2006.

Cooper, Carolyn. *Noises in the Blood: Orality, Gender and the "Vulgar" Body of Jamaican Popular Culture.* Durham: Duke University Press, 1995.

Croce, Arlene. "Discussing the Undiscussable." *New Yorker* (December 1994–January 1995): 54–60.

Crossley, Robert. "Introduction." In Octavia Butler, *Kindred,* ix–xxvii. Boston: Beacon/Bluestreak, 1979.

Darden, Joe T., and Sameh M. Kamel. "Black Residential Segregation: Impact of State Licensing Laws." *Journal of Black Studies* 12 (1984): 415–26.

———. "Black Residential Segregation in the City and Suburbs of Detroit: Does Socioeconomic Status Matter?" *Journal of Urban Affairs* 22 no. 1 (2000): 1–13.

———. "Residential Segregation and the Quality of Life: The Black Ghetto of Pittsburgh Revisited." *Pennsylvania Geographer* 24 no. 3/4 (1985): 11–20.

Davies, Carole Boyce. *Black Women, Writing and Identity: Migrations of the Subject.* New York and London: Routledge, 1994.

———, ed. *Black Women's Diaspora: Critical Responses and Conversations.* New York: New York University Press, 1995.

———. "Hearing Black Women's Voices: Transgressing Imposed Boundaries." In Carole Boyce Davies and 'Molara Ogundipe-Leslie, eds., *Moving Beyond Boundaries: International Dimensions of Black Women's Writing,* 3–14. New York: New York University Press, 1995.

Davies, Carole Boyce, and Monica Jardine. "Imperial Geographies and Caribbean Nationalism: At the Border between 'a Dying Colonialism' and U.S. Hegemony." *CR: The New Centennial Review* 3 no. 3 (Fall 2003): 151–74.

Davies, Carole Boyce, and 'Molara Ogundipe-Leslie. *Moving Beyond Boundaries: International Dimensions of Black Women's Writing.* New York: New York University Press, 1995.

Davies, Carole Boyce, and Elaine Savory Fido, eds. *Out of the Kumbla: Caribbean Women and Literature.* Trenton, New Jersey: Africa World Press, 1990.

Davis, Angela. *Blues Legacies and Black Feminism.* New York: Random House, 1998.

———. *Women, Race and Class.* New York: Vintage, 1981.

Dayan, Joan. "Paul Gilroy's Slaves, Ships, and Routes: The Middle Passage as Metaphor." *Research in African Literatures* 27 no. 4 (1996): 7–14.

Delaney, David. "The Space That Race Makes." *The Professional Geographer* 54 no. 1 (2002): 6–14.

Dixon, Melvin. *Ride Out the Wilderness: Geography and Identity in Afro-American Literature.* Urbana and Chicago: University of Illinois Press, 1987.

Douglass, Frederick. *Narrative of the Life of Frederick Douglass, An American Slave.* Houston A. Baker Jr., ed. New York: Penguin [1845] 1982.

Driver, Felix. "Geography's Empire: Histories of Geographical Knowledge." *Environment and Planning D: Society and Space* 10 (1992): 23–40.

Dua, Enakshi, and Angela Robertson, eds. *Scratching the Surface: Canadian, Anti-Racist, Feminist Thought.* Toronto: Women's Press, 1999.

Du Bois, W. E. B. *The Souls of Black Folk.* New York: Vintage, [1903] 1986.

Duncan, Nancy, ed. *BodySpace: Destabilizing Geographies of Gender and Sexuality.* New York and London: Routledge, 1996.

Durant, Thomas J. Jr., and J. David Knotterus, eds. *Plantation Society and Race Relations: The Origins of Inequality.* Connecticut and London: Praeger, 1999.

Dwyer, Owen J. "Geographical Research about African Americans: A Survey of Journals, 1911–1995." *Professional Geographer* 49 no. 4 (1997): 441–51.

Dyer, Richard. "White." *Screen* 29 (1998): 44–64.

Ehrlich, Dimitri. "Portrait of the Artist as a Free Man." *Notorious* 4 (2000): 86–94.

Elgersman, Maureen G. *Unyielding Spirits: Black Women and Slavery in Early Canada and Jamaica.* New York and London: Garland, 1999.

Elliott, Missy. *So Addictive.* Elektra, 2001.

Ellison, Ralph. *Going to the Territory.* New York: Vintage, 1986.

———. *Invisible Man.* New York: Vintage, 1952.

Epperson, Terrance W. "Constructing Difference: The Social and Spatial Order of the Chesapeake Plantation." In Theresa A. Singleton, ed., *"I, Too, Am American": Archaeological Studies of African-American Life,* 159–72. Charlottesville and London: University Press of Virginia, 1999.

"Fantino Talks with Police in Jamaica." *The Toronto Star.* February 10, 2003: A3.

Fanon, Frantz. *Black Skin, White Masks.* Trans. Charles Lam Markmann. New York: Grove Press, [1952] 1967.

———. *The Wretched of the Earth.* Trans. Constance Farrington. New York: Grove Press, [1961] 1963.

Foster, Cecil. *A Place Called Heaven: The Meaning of Being Black in Canada.* Toronto: Harper Collins, 1996.

Franti, Micheal, and Spearhead. *Stay Human.* Six Degrees, 2001.

Frazier, John W., Eugen Tetty-Flo, and Florence Margai, eds. *Race and Place: Equity Issues in Urban America.* New York: Westview, 2003.

Fuss, Diana. *Identification Papers.* New York: Routledge, 1995.

Gale, Lorena. *Angélique.* Toronto: Playwrights Press, 1999.

Garfield, Deborah M., and Rafia Zafar, eds. *Harriet Jacobs and Incidents in the Life of a Slave Girl.* Cambridge: Cambridge University Press, 1996.

Gasper, David Barry, and Darlene Clark Hine, eds. *More Than Chattel: Black Women and Slavery in the Americas.* Bloomington and Indianapolis: Indiana University Press, 1996.

Gates, Henry Louis Jr., ed. *Reading Black, Reading Feminist.* New York: Penguin, 1990.

———. *The Classic Slave Narratives.* New York: Mentor, 1987.

Germain, Annick, and Damaris Rose. *Montréal: The Quest for a Metropolis.* New York: John Wiley and Sons, 2000.

Gilmore, Ruth Wilson. "Fatal Couplings of Power and Difference: Notes on Racism and Geography." *The Professional Geographer* 54 no. 1 (2002): 15–24.

———. "Globalisation and U.S. Prison Growth." *Race and Class* 40 no. 2/3 (1998): 171–88.

———. "Public Enemies and Private Intellectuals." *Race and Class* 35 no. 1 (1993): 69–78.

———. "Terror Austerity Race Gender Excess Theatre." In Robert Gooding-Williams, ed., *Reading Rodney King/Reading Urban Uprising,* 23–37. New York and London: Routledge, 1993.

———. "'You Have Dislodged a Boulder': Mothers and Prisoners in the Post-Keynesian California Landscape." *Transforming Anthropology* 8 no. 1/2 (1999): 12–38.

Gilroy, Paul. *Against Race: Imagining Political Culture Beyond the Color Line.* Cambridge: Harvard University Press, 2000.

————. *The Black Atlantic: Modernity and Double Consciousness.* Cambridge: Harvard University Press, 1993.

————. "Living Memory: A Meeting with Toni Morrison." In *Small Acts: Thoughts on the Politics of Black Cultures,* 175–82. New York and London: Serpent's Tail, 1993.

————. *"There Ain't No Black in the Union Jack": The Cultural Politics of Race and Nation.* Chicago: University of Chicago Press, 1987.

Glissant, Édouard. *Caribbean Discourse: Selected Essays.* Trans. Michael M. Dash. Charlottesville: University Press of Virginia, 1989.

————. "Creolization and the Making of the Americas." In Vera Lawrence and Rex Nettleford, eds., *Race, Discourse, and the Origin of the Americas: A New World View,* 268–75. Washington and London: Smithsonian Institution Press, 1995.

————. "A Field of Islands." Trans. Jefferson Humphries. In Bainard Cohen and Jefferson Humphries, eds., *Poetics of the Americas: Race, Founding and Textuality,* 165–81. Baton Rouge: Louisiana State University Press, 1992.

Gmelch, George, and Walter P. Zenner, eds. *Urban Life: Readings in Urban Anthropology.* Prospect Heights, Ill.: Waveland, 1996.

Good, Judith G., and Edwin Eames. "An Anthropological Critique of the Culture of Poverty." In George Gmelch and Walter P. Zenner, eds., *Urban Life: Readings in Urban Anthropology,* 405–17. Prospect Heights, Ill.: Waveland, 1996.

Gordon, Avery F. *Ghostly Matters: Haunting and the Sociological Imagination.* Minneapolis and London: University of Minnesota Press, 1997.

————. "Globalisation and the Prison Industrial Complex: An Interview with Angela Davis." *Race and Class* 40 no. 2/3 (1998–99): 145–57.

Gordon, Lewis, ed. *Existence in Black: An Anthology of Black Existential Philosophy.* New York and London: Routledge, 1997.

Gould, L. Virginia. "Urban Slavery-Urban Freedom: The Manumission of Jacqueline Lemelle." In David Barry Gasper and Darlene Clark Hine, eds., *More Than Chattel: Black Women and Slavery in the Americas,* 298–314. Bloomington and Indianapolis: Indiana University Press, 1996.

Gray, Macy. *On How Life Is.* Sony Music, 1999.

————. *The Id.* Sony Music, 2001.

————. *The Trouble with Being Myself.* Sony Music, 2003.

Gregory, Derek. *Geographical Imaginations.* Cambridge and Harvard: Blackwell, 1994.

Hall, Stuart. "New Ethnicities." In David Morely and Kuan-Hsing Chen, eds., *Stuart Hall: Critical Dialogues in Cultural Studies,* 441–49. New York and London: Routledge, 1996.

————. "What Is This 'Black' in Popular Culture?" In David Morley and Kuan-Hsing Chen, eds., *Stuart Hall: Critical Dialogues in Cultural Studies,* 465–75. New York and London: Routledge, [1992] 1996.

Haraway, Donna J. *Simians, Cyborgs, and Women: The Reinvention of Nature.* New York: Routledge, 1991.

Hartman, Saidiya. *Scenes of Subjection: Terror, Slavery, and Self-Making in Nineteenth Century America.* Oxford: Oxford University Press, 1997.

Harvey, David. *Social Justice and the City.* London: Edward Arnold, 1973.

————. *Spaces of Hope.* Berkeley: University of California Press, 2000.

Henderson, Mae Gwendolyn. "Speaking in Tongues: Dialogics, Dialectics, and the Black Woman Writer's Literary Tradition." In Judith Butler and Joan W. Scott, eds., *Feminists Theorize the Political,* 144–66. New York and London: Routledge, 1992.

Henry, Francis. *The Caribbean Diaspora in Toronto: Learning to Live with Racism.* Toronto: University of Toronto Press, 1994.

Henry, Paget. *Caliban's Reason: Introducing Afro-Caribbean Philosophy.* New York and London: Routledge, 2000.

Higginbotham, Evelyn Brooks. *Righteous Discontent.* Cambridge and London: Harvard University Press, 1993.

Hill Collins, Patricia. *Black Feminist Thought.* New York: Routledge, 1990.

———. *Fighting Words: Black Women and the Search for Justice.* Minneapolis: University of Minnesota Press, 1998.

Hill, Daniel G. *The Freedom Seekers: Blacks in Early Canada.* Agincourt: Book Society of Canada, 1981.

Hoelscher, Steven. "Making Place, Making Race: Performances of Whiteness in the Jim Crow South." *Annals of the Association of American Geographers* 93 no. 3 (2003), 657–86.

hooks, bell. *Ain't I a Woman? Black Women and Feminism.* Boston: South End Press, 1981.

———. *Black Looks: Race and Representation.* Toronto: Between the Lines Press, 1990.

———. *Feminist Theory: From Margin to Center.* Boston: South End Press, 1984.

———. *Yearning: Race, Gender and Cultural Politics.* Toronto: Between the Lines Press, 1990.

Hull, Gloria T., Patricia Bell Scott, and Barbara Smith, eds. *All the Women Are White, All the Blacks Are Men, But Some of Us Are Brave.* New York: The Feminist Press, 1982.

Hurston, Zora Neale. "How It Feels to Be Colored Me." In Alice Walker, ed., *I Love Myself When I Am Laughing . . . The Zora Neale Hurston Reader,* 151–55. New York: The Feminist Press, 1979.

Inkster, Dana, dir. *Welcome to Africville.* Canada Video, 1999.

Jackson, Peter. "Constructions of 'Whiteness' in the Geographical Imagination." *Area* 30 no. 2 (1998): 99–106.

———. "Geography, 'Race' and Racism." In Nigel Thift and Richard Peet, eds., *New Models in Geography,* 176–96. vol. 2. London: Unwin Hyman, 1989.

———. "The Politics of the Streets: A Geography of Caribana." *Political Geography* 11 (1992): 130–57.

Jackson, Peter, and Jan Penrose. *Constructions of Race, Place and Nation.* Minneapolis: University of Minnesota Press, 1994.

Jacobs, Harriet. *Incidents in the Life of a Slave Girl: Written by Herself.* Jean Fagan Yellin, ed. Cambridge and London: Harvard University Press, [1861] 1987.

James, C. L. R. *American Civilization.* Cambridge and Oxford: Blackwell, 1993.

———. *Beyond a Boundary.* Durham: Duke University Press, 1963.

James, Joy, and T. Denean Sharpley-Whiting, eds. *The Black Feminist Reader.* Oxford: Blackwell, 2000.

James, Joy. *Transcending the Talented Tenth: Black Leaders and American Intellectuals.* New York: Routledge, 1997.

Johnson, Walter. "The Slave Trader, the White Slave, and the Politics of Racial Determination in the 1850s." *The Journal of American History* 87 no. 1 (June 2000): 13–38.
——. *Soul by Soul: Life Inside the Antebellum Slave Market.* London and Cambridge: Harvard University Press, 1999.

Jones, Gayle. *Eva's Man.* Boston: Beacon Press, 1976.

Jones III, John Paul, Heidi J. Nast, and Susan M. Roberts, eds. *Thresholds in Feminist Geography: Difference, Methodology, Representation.* New York: Rowman and Littlefield, 1997.

Keith, Michael, and Steve Pile, eds. *Place and the Politics of Identity.* New York and London: Routledge, 1993.

Kempadoo, Kamala. *Sun, Sex and Gold: Tourism and Sex Work in the Caribbean.* New York: Rowman and Littlefield, 1999.

Kirby, Kathleen. *Indifferent Boundaries: Spatial Concepts of Human Subjectivity.* New York and London: The Guilford Press, 1996.

Kobayashi, Audrey, and Linda Peake. "Unnatural Discourse: 'Race' and Gender in Geography." *Gender Place and Culture* 1 no. 2 (1994): 225–43.

Konadu-Agyemang, Kwadwo. "Characteristics and Migration Experience of Africans in Canada with Specific Reference to Ghanaians in Greater Toronto." *The Canadian Geographer* 43 no. 4 (1999): 400–14.

Lawrence, Bonita. *"Real" Indians and Others: Mixed Blood Urban Native Peoples and Indigenous Nationhood.* Vancouver: University of British Columbia Press, 2004.

Leacock, Eleanor, ed. *The Culture of Poverty: A Critique.* New York: Simon and Schuster, 1971.

Lefebvre, Henri. *The Production of Space.* Trans. Donald Nicholson-Smith. Oxford and Cambridge: Blackwell, [1974] 1991.

Lerner, Gerda. *Black Women in White America: A Documentary History.* New York: Vintage, 1972.

Lewis, Oscar. *La Vita: A Puerto Rican Family in the Culture of Poverty: San Juan and New York.* New York: Vintage, 1966.

Lorde, Audre. *Sister Outsider.* Freedom: The Crossing Press, 1984.

Lubiano, Wahneema. "Black Ladies, Welfare Queens, and State Minstrels: Ideological War by Narrative Means." In Toni Morrison, ed., *Race-ing Justice, En-Gendering Power: Essays on Anita Hill, Clarence Thomas, and the Construction of Social Reality,* 323–61. New York: Pantheon Books, 1992.

Madhubuti, Laini. "2001 BET Fashion Disaster Awards." http://www.bet.com/articles/.

Mahtani, Minelle. "Women Graduate Students of Colour in Geography: Increased Ethnic and Racial Diversity, or Maintenance of the Status Quo?" *The Great Lakes Geographer* 9 no. 1 (2002): 11–18.

Marsen, Jean-Claude. *Montreal in Evolution.* Montreal: McGill-Queens University Press, 1981.

Marston, Sallie A. "The Social Construction of Scale." *Progress in Human Geography* 24 no. 2 (2000): 219–42.

Martin, James. "Interview with James Martin." In *Born in Slavery: Slave Narratives from the Federal Writers' Project, 1936–1938,* vol. 16, no. 3. Washington: Library of Congress, 1937.

Massey, Doreen. *Space, Place, and Gender*. Minneapolis: University of Minnesota Press, 1994.

Mayhew, Robert J. "Was William Shakespeare an Eighteenth Century Geographer? Constructing Histories of Geographical Knowledge." *Transactions of the Institute of British Geographers* 23 (1998): 21–37.

McCauley, Robbie. "Sally's Rape." In Sydné Mahone, ed., *Moon Marked and Touched by the Sun: Plays By African-American Women*, 212–38. New York: Theatre Communications Group, 1994.

McClintock, Anne. *Imperial Leather: Race, Gender and Sexuality in the Colonial Contest*. New York and London: Routledge, 1995.

McDowell, Linda. *Gender, Identity and Place: Understanding Feminist Geographies*. Minneapolis: University of Minnesota Press, 1999.

———. "Spatializing Feminism: Geographic Perspectives." In Nancy Duncan, ed., *BodySpace: Destabilizing Geographies of Gender and Sexuality*, 28–44. New York and London: Routledge, 1996.

McKittrick, Katherine. "bell hooks." In Phil Hubbard, Rob Kitchin, and Gill Valentine, eds., *Key Contemporary Theorists on Space and Place*, 189–94. London: Sage, 2004.

———. "'Black and 'Cause I'm Black I'm Blue': Transverse Racial Geographies in Toni Morrison's *The Bluest Eye*," *Gender, Place and Culture* 7 no. 2 (2000): 125–42.

———. "'Their Blood Is There and You Can't Throw It Out': Honouring Black Canadian Geographies." *Topia* 7 (Spring 2002): 27–37.

———. "The Uncharted Geographies of Frantz Fanon in *The Wretched of the Earth*." Unpublished paper.

———. "'Who Do You Talk to, When a Body's in Trouble?' Marlene Nourbese Philip's (Un)Silencing of Black Bodies in the Diaspora." *Journal of Social and Cultural Geography* 1 no. 2 (2000): 223–36

McKittrick, Katherine, and Linda Peake. "What Difference Does Difference Make to Geography?" In Noel Castree, Alisdair Rogers, and Douglas Sherman, eds., *Questioning Geography*, 39–54. Oxford: Blackwell, 2005.

McLafferty, Sarah, and Barbara Templaski. "Restructuring Women's Reproductive Health: Implications of Low Birthweight in New York City." *Geoforum* 26 no. 3 (1995): 309–23.

Mensah, Joseph. *Black Canadians: History, Experiences, Social Conditions*. Halifax: Fernwood, 2002.

Mirza, Heidi Safia, ed. *Black British Feminism: A Reader*. New York and London: 1997.

Mitchell, Angelyn. *The Freedom to Remember: Narrative, Slavery and Gender in Contemporary Black Women's Fiction*. New Brunswick: Rutgers University Press, 2002.

Mitchell, Don. *Cultural Geography: A Critical Introduction*. London: Blackwell, 2000.

Monture-Okanee, Patricia. "The Violence We Women Do: A First Nations View." In Constance Backhouse and David Flaherty, eds., *Challenging Times: The Women's Movement in Canada and the United States*, 193–203. Montreal: McGill-Queen's University Press, 1992.

Morely, David, and Kuan-Hsing Chen, eds. *Stuart Hall: Critical Dialogues in Cultural Studies*. New York and London: Routledge, 1996.

Morrison, Toni. *Beloved.* New York: Penguin, 1987.

————. *The Bluest Eye.* New York: Washington Square Press, 1970.

————. "The Official Story: Dead Man Golfing." In Toni Morrison and Claudia Brodsky Lacour, eds., *Birth of a Nation'hood: Gaze, Script and Spectacle in the O. J. Simpson Case,* vii–xxviii New York: Pantheon, 1997.

————. *Paradise.* New York: Alfred A. Knopf, 1997.

————. *Playing in the Dark: Whiteness and the Literary Imagination.* New York: Vintage, 1992.

————, ed. *Race-ing Justice, En-Gendering Power: Essays on Anita Hill, Clarence Thomas, and the Construction of Social Reality.* New York: Pantheon Books, 1992.

————. "The Site of Memory." In Russell Ferguson, Martha Gever, Trinh T. Minh-ha, and Cornel West, eds., *Out There: Marginalization and Contemporary Cultures,* 299–305. Massachusetts: MIT Press, 1991.

Morrison, Toni, and Claudia Brodsky Lacour, eds. *Birth of a Nation'hood: Gaze, Script and Spectacle in the O. J. Simpson Case.* New York: Pantheon, 1997.

Nast, Heidi J. "Mapping the Unconscious: Racism and the Oedipal Family." *Annals of the Association of American Geographers* 90 no. 2 (2000): 215–55.

Nast, Heidi J. and Audrey Kobayashi. "Re-Corporealizing Vision." In Nancy Duncan, ed. *BodySpace: Destabilizing Geographies of Gender and Sexuality,* 75–93. New York and London: Routledge, 1996.

Nelson, Charmaine. "Slavery, Portraiture and the Colonial Limits of Canadian Art History." *Canadian Women's Studies* 23 no. 2 (Winter 2004): 22–28.

Nelson, Jennifer Jill. "The Space of Africville: Creating, Regulating, and Remembering the Urban 'Slum.'" In Sherene Razack, ed., *Race, Space and the Law: Unmapping a White Settler Society,* 211–32. Toronto: Between the Lines Press, 2002.

Nyman, Anne E. "'Sally's Rape': Robbie McCauley's Survival Art." *African American Review* 33 (Winter 1999): 577–87.

O'Breeden, James, ed. *Advice Among Masters: The Ideal Slave Management in the Old South.* London and Westport: Greenwood Press, 1980.

Outkast. *Big Boi and Dre Present . . . Outkast.* La Face/Arista, 2001.

Painter, Nell Irvin. "Hill, Thomas, and the Use of Racial Stereotype." In Toni Morrison, ed., *Race-ing Justice, En-Gendering Power: Essays on Anita Hill, Clarence Thomas, and the Construction of Social Reality,* 200–14. New York: Pantheon, 1992.

Peake, Linda. "Toward an Understanding of the Interconnectedness of Women's Lives: The 'Racial' Reproduction of Labour in Low-Income Urban Areas." *Urban Geography* 16 no. 5 (1995): 414–39.

Peake, Linda, and Audrey Kobayashi. "Policies and Practices for an Antiracist Geography." *The Professional Geographer* 54 no. 1 (2002): 50–61.

Peake, Linda, and Brian Ray. "Racializing the Canadian Landscape: Whiteness, Uneven Geographies and Social Justice." *The Canadian Geographer* 45 no. 1 (2001): 180–86.

Peake, Linda, and Richard H. Schein. "Racing Geography into the New Millennium: Studies of 'Race' and North American Geographies." *The Journal of Social and Cultural Geography* 1 no. 2 (2000): 133–41.

Peake, Linda, and Alissa Trotz. *Gender, Ethnicity and Place: Women and Identities in Guyana*. London: Routledge, 1999.

Peterson, Charles E. "The Historic American Buildings Survey Continued." *The Journal of the Society of Architectural Historians* 16 no. 3 (October 1957): 29–31.

Philip, Marlene Nourbese. *A Genealogy of Resistance and Other Essays*. Toronto: The Mercury Press, 1997.

———. *She Tries Her Tongue, Her Silence Softly Breaks*. Charlottetown: Ragweed, 1989.

Pile, Steve. *The Body and the City: Psychoanalysis, Space and Subjectivity*. New York and London: Routledge, 1996.

———. "The Troubled Spaces of Frantz Fanon." In Mike Crang and Nigel Thrift, eds., *Thinking Space*, 260–77. New York and London: Routledge.

Pile, Steve, and Nigel Thrift, eds. *Mapping the Subject: Geographies of Cultural Transformation*. London: Routledge, 1995.

Pulido, Laura. "Community, Place and Identity." In John Paul Jones III, Heidi J. Nast, and Susan M. Roberts, eds., *Thresholds in Feminist Geography: Difference, Methodology, Representation*, 11–28. New York: Rowman and Littlefield, 1997.

———. "A Critical Review of the Methodology of Environmental Racism Research." *Antipode* 28 no. 2 (1996): 142–49.

———. "Reflections on a White Discipline." *The Professional Geographer* 54 no. 1 (2002): 42–49.

———. "Rethinking Environmental Racism: White Privilege and Urban Development in Southern California." *Annals of the Association of American Geographers* 90 no. 1 (2000): 12–40.

Prince, Mary. *The History of Mary Prince, A West Indian Slave. Related by Herself*. In Henry Louis Gates Jr., ed., *The Classic Slave Narratives*, 187–238. New York: Mentor, [1831] 1987.

Pyle, Gerald F. "The Diffusion of HIV/AIDS and HIV Infection in an Archetypal Textile County." *Applied Geographic Studies* 1 no. 1 (1997): 63–81.

Rassool, Naz. "Fractured or Flexible Identities: Life Histories of 'Black' Diasporic Women in Britain." In Heidi Safia Mirza, ed., *Black British Feminism*. New York and London: Routledge, 1997.

Razack, Sherene. "Gendered Racial Violence and Spatialized Justice: The Murder of Pamela George." In Sherene Razack, ed., *Race, Space and the Law: Unmapping a White Settler Society*, 121–56. Toronto: Between the Lines Press, 2002.

———. *Looking White People in the Eye*. Toronto: University of Toronto Press, 1998.

Rich, Adrienne. "Notes Toward a Politics of Location." In *Blood Bread and Poetry: Selected Prose, 1979–1985*, 239–56. New York: W.W. Norton, 1986.

"Robbery Suspects Had Been Deported Twice." *The Globe and Mail*. February 14, 2003: A1.

Roberts, Dorothy. *Killing the Black Body: Race, Reproduction and the Meaning of Liberty*. New York: Random House, 1997.

Rose, Gillian. *Feminism and Geography: The Limits of Geographical Knowledge*. Cambridge and Oxford: Polity Press, 1993.

———. "Progress in Gender and Geography. Or Something Else." *Progress in Human Geography* 17 no. 4 (1993): 531–37.

Ruddick, Susan. "Constructing Difference in Public Spaces: Race, Class and Gender as Interlocking Systems." *Urban Geography* 17 no. 2 (1996): 132–51.

Sanders, Rickie. "Integrating Race and Ethnicity into Geographic Gender Studies." *The Professional Geographer* 42 no. 2 (1990): 228–31.

Scott, David. *Refashioning Futures: Criticism after Postcoloniality.* New Jersey: Princeton University Press, 1999.

Sekyi-Otu, Ato. *Fanon's Dialectic of Experience.* Cambridge and London: Harvard University Press, 1996.

Shadd, Adrienne. "300 Years of Black Women in Canadian History: circa 1700–1980." *Tiger Lily* 1 no. 2 (1987): 4–13.

Sharpe, Jenny. *Ghosts of Slavery: A Literary Archeology of Black Women's Lives.* Minneapolis: University of Minnesota Press, 2003.

Simpson-Freeman, Cheryl. "Green Hill Plantation Offers Look into Past." *The News and Daily Advance* (July 22, 1990): B1–2.

Singleton, Theresa A., ed. *"I, Too, Am American": Archaeological Studies of African-American Life.* Charlottesville and London: University Press of Virginia, 1999.

———, ed., *The Archaeology of Slavery and Plantation Life.* New York: Harcourt Brace Jovanovich, 1985.

Skelton, Tracey. "Ghetto Girls/Urban Music: Jamaican Ragga Music and Female Music." In Rosa Ainley, ed., *New Frontiers of Space, Bodies and Gender,* 142–54. New York: Routledge, 1998.

Smith, Neil. "Homeless/Global: Scaling Place." In Jon Bird, Barry Curtis, Tim Putnam, George Robertson, and Lisa Tickner, eds., *Mapping Futures: Local Cultures, Global Change,* 87–119. London: Routledge, 1993.

———. *Uneven Development: Nature, Capital and the Production of Space.* Oxford: Blackwell, 1990.

Smith, Susan J. "Immigration and Nation-Building in Canada and the United Kingdom." In Peter Jackson and Jan Penrose, eds., *Constructions of Race, Place and Nation,* 50–77. Minneapolis: University of Minnesota Press, 1993.

Smith, Valerie. "Black Feminist Theory and the Representation of the 'Other.'" In Cheryl A. Wall, ed., *Changing Our Words: Essays on Criticism, Theory and Writing by Black Women,* 38–58. New Brunswick and London: Rutgers University Press, 1989.

———. "'Loopholes of Retreat': Architecture and Ideology in Harriet Jacobs's *Incidents in the Life of a Slave Girl.*" In Henry Louis Gates Jr., ed., *Reading Black, Reading Feminist,* 212–26. New York: Penguin, 1990.

Soja, Edward, and Barbara Hooper. "The Space That Difference Makes: Some Notes on the Geographical Margins of the New Cultural Politics." In Michael Keith and Steve Pile, eds., *Place and the Politics of Identity,* 183–205. New York and London: Routledge, 1993.

Sparke, Matthew. "Mapped Bodies and Disembodied Maps: (Dis)placing Cartographic Struggle in Colonial Canada." In Steve Pile and Heidi Nast, eds., *Places Through the Body,* 305–36. New York and London: Routledge, 1998.

Spillers, Hortense. "Interstices: A Small Drama of Words." In Carole Vance, ed., *Pleasure and Danger: Exploring Female Sexuality,* 73–100. London: Pandora Press, 1992.

———. "Mama's Baby, Papa's Maybe: An American Grammar Book." In Angelyn

Mitchell, ed., *Within the Circle: An Anthology of African American Criticism from the Harlem Renaissance to the Present*, 454–81. Durham and London: Duke University Press, 1994.

Stewart, Lynn. "Louisiana Subjects: Power, Space and the Slave Body." *Ecumene* 2 no. 3 (1995): 227–45.

Tadman, Michael. *Speculators and Slaves: Masters, Traders, and Slaves in the Old South*. London and Madison: The University of Wisconsin Press, 1989.

Tater, Carol, Frances Henry, and Winston Mattis. *Challenging Racism in the Arts*. Toronto: University of Toronto Press, 1998.

Trinh, T. Minh-ha. *Woman, Native, Other*. Bloomington and Indianapolis: Indiana University Press, 1989.

Trudel, Marcel. *L'Esclavage au Canada Français: Histoire et Conditions De L'Esclavage*. Quebec: Presses Universitaires Laval, 1960.

Truth, Sojourner. "Ain't I a Woman?" In Miriam Schneir, ed., *Feminism: The Essential Historical Writings*, 93–95. New York: Vintage, 1972.

Walcott, Rinaldo. *Black Like Who?* Toronto: Insomniac Press, 1997.

———. "Caribbean Popular Culture in Canada; Or, the Impossibility of Belonging to the Nation." *Small Axe* 9 (March 2001): 123–39.

———. "Isaac Julien's Children: Black Queer Cinema after *Looking for Langston*." *Fuse Magazine* 24 no. 2 (July 2001): 10–17.

———. "Pedagogy and Trauma: The Middle Passage and the Problem of Creolization." In Roger I. Simon, Sharon Rosenberg, and Claudia Eppert, eds., *Between Hope and Despair: Pedagogy and the Remembrance of Historical Trauma*, 135–51. New York: Rowman and Littlefield, 2000.

———. "Rhetorics of Blackness, Rhetorics of Belonging: The Politics of Representation in Black Canadian Expressive Culture." *Canadian Review of American Studies* 29 no. 2 (1999): 1–26.

———, ed. *Rude: Contemporary Black Canadian Cultural Criticism*. Toronto: Insomniac, 2000.

———. "Who Is She and What Is She to You? Mary-Ann Shadd Cary and the (Im)Possibility of Black/Canadian Studies." In Rinaldo Walcott, ed., *Rude: Contemporary Black Canadian Cultural Criticism*, 27–47. Toronto: Insomniac, 2000.

Walker, Alice. *In Search of Our Mother's Gardens*. New York: Harcourt and Brace, 1983.

Werbner, Pnina. "The Materiality of the Diaspora: Between Aesthetic and 'Real' Politics." *Diaspora* 9 no. 1 (Spring 2000): 5–20.

White, Deborah Gray. *Ar'n't I a Woman? Female Slaves in the Plantation South*. New York and London: W. W. Norton, 1985.

White, E. Frances. *The Dark Continent of Our Bodies: Black Feminism and the Politics of Respectability*. Philadelphia: Temple University Press, 2001.

Williams, Sherley Anne. *Dessa Rose*. New York: William Morrow, 1986.

Wilson, Bobby M. "Critically Understanding Race-Connected Practices: A Reading of W. E. B. DuBois and Richard Wright." *The Professional Geographer* 54 no. 1 (2002): 31–41.

Winks, Robin W. *The Blacks in Canada: A History*. Montreal and Kingston: McGill-Queens University Press, 1997.

Wood, Marcus. *Blind Memory: Visual Representations of Slavery in England and America, 1780–1865.* New York: Routledge, 2000.

Woods, Clyde. *Development Arrested: The Blues and Plantation Power in the Mississippi Delta.* New York and London: Verso, 1998.

———. "Life After Death." *The Professional Geographer* 54 no. 1 (2002): 62–66.

Wylie, John. "New and Old Worlds: *The Tempest* and Early Colonial Discourse." *Social and Cultural Geography* 1 no. 1 (2000): 45–63.

Wynter, Sylvia. "1492: A New World View." In Vera Lawrence and Rex Nettleford, eds., *Race, Discourse, and the Origin of the Americas: A New World View*, 5–57. Washington and London: Smithsonian Institution Press, 1995.

———. "Africa, The West and the Analogy of Culture: The Cinematic Text after Man." In June Givanni, ed., *Symbolic Narratives/African Cinema: Audiences, Theory and the Moving Image*, 25–76. London: British Film Institute, 2000.

———. *Beyond Liberal and Marxist Leninist Feminisms: Towards and Autonomous Frame of Reference.* San Francisco: Institute for Research on Women and Gender, 1982.

———. "Beyond Miranda's Meanings: Un/Silencing the 'Demonic Ground' of Caliban's Women." In Carole Boyce Davies and Elaine Savory Fido, eds., *Out of the Kumbla: Caribbean Women and Literature*, 355–72. Trenton: Africa World Press, 1990.

———. "Beyond the Categories of the Master Conception: The Counterdoctrine of the Jamesian Poiesis." In Paget Henry and Paul Buhle, eds., *C. L. R. James's Caribbean*, 63–91. Durham, N.C.: Duke University Press, 1992.

———. "Beyond the Word of Man: Glissant and the New Discourse of the Antilles." *World Literature Today* 63 (Autumn 1989): 637–47.

———. "Breaking the Epistemological Contract on Black America." *Forum NHI*, 2 no. 1 (1995): 41–57, 64–70.

———. "But What Does Wonder Do? Meanings, Canons, Too? On Literary Texts, Cultural Contexts, and What It's Like to Be One/Not One of Us." *Stanford Humanities Review* 4 no. 1 (Spring 1994): 124–29.

———. "The Ceremony Must Be Found: After Humanism." *Boundary II* 12 no. 3/13 no. 1 (Spring/Fall 1984): 19–70.

———. "Columbus and the Poetics of the *Propter Nos*." *Annals of Scholarship* 8 no. 2 (Spring 1991): 251–86.

———. "'Columbus, The Ocean Blue and 'Fables that Stir the Mind': To Reinvent the Study of Letters." In Bainard Cohen and Jefferson Humphries, eds., *Poetics of the Americas: Race, Founding and Textuality*, 141–64. Baton Rouge: Louisiana State University Press, 1992.

———. "'A Different Kind of Creature': Caribbean Literature, the Cyclops Factor and the Second Poetics of the *Propter Nos.*" *Annals of Scholarship* 12 no. 1/2 (2001): 153–72.

———. *Do Not Call Us Negroes: How Multicultural Textbooks Perpetuate Racism.* San Francisco: Aspire, 1990.

———. "Ethno or Socio Poetics." *Alcheringa/Ethnopoetics* 2 (1976): 78–94.

———. "The Eye of the Other." In Miriam DeCosta, ed., *Blacks in Hispanic Literature: Critical Essays*, 8–19. New York and London: Kennikat Press, 1977.

———. "The Final Solution to the 'Nigger Question': Droppin' Some Science on the Bell Curve." *Forum NHI* 2 no. 1 (1995): 4–40, 64–70.

———. *The Hills of Hebron: A Jamaican Novel.* New York: Simon and Schuster, 1962.

———. "Is Development a Purely Empirical Concept, or also Teleological? A Perspective from 'We the Underdeveloped.'" In Aguibou Y. Yansané, ed., *Prospects for Recovery and Sustainable Development in Africa*, 299–316. Westport, Conn.: Greenwood Press, 1996.

———. "New Seville and the Conversion Experience of Bartolomé de Las Casas: Part One." *Jamaica Journal* 17 no. 2 (May 1984): 25–32.

———. "New Seville and the Conversion Experience of Bartolomé de Las Casas: Part Two." *Jamaica Journal* 17 no. 3 (August-October 1984): 46–55.

———. "'No Humans Involved': An open letter to my colleagues:" *Voices of the African. Diaspora* 8 no. 2 (Fall 1992): 13–16.

———. "Novel and History, Plot and Plantation." *Savacou* 5 (1971): 95–102.

———. "On Disenchanting Discourse: 'Minority' Literary Criticism and Beyond." In Abdul R. JanMohamed and David Lloyd, eds., *The Nature and Context of Minority Discourse*, 432–69. New York and Oxford: Oxford University Press, 1990.

———. "One-Love Rhetoric or Reality?—Aspects of Afro-Jamaicainism." *Caribbean Studies* 12 no. 3: 90–97.

———. "The Pope Must Be Drunk, The King of Castile a Madman: Culture as Actuality and the Caribbean Rethinking of Modernity." In Alvina Ruprecht and Cecilia Taiana, eds., *Reordering of Culture: Latin America, the Caribbean and Canada in the 'Hood*, 17–41. Ottawa: Carleton University Press, 1995.

———. "Rethinking Aesthetics." In Mbye Cham, ed., *Ex-iles: Essays on Caribbean Cinema*, 238–79. New Jersey: Africa World Press, 1992.

———. "Towards the Sociogenic Principle: Fanon, Identity, The Puzzle of Conscious Experience." In Mercedes F. Durán-Cogan and Antonio Gómez-Moriana, eds., *National Identities and Socio-Political Changes in Latin America*, 30–66. New York: Routledge, 2001.

———. "Unsettling the Coloniality of Being/Power/Truth/Freedom: Towards the Human, after Man, Its Overrepresentation—An Argument." *CR: The New Centennial Review* 3 no. 3 (Fall 2003): 257–337.

———. "A Utopia from the Semi-Periphery: Spain, Modernization, and the Enlightenment." *Science Fiction Studies* 6 (1979): 100–7.

———. "What It's Like to Be Black." In Mercedes F. Durán-Cogan and Antonio Gómez-Moriana, eds., *National Identities and Socio-Political Changes in Latin America*, 30–66. New York: Routledge, 2001.

Wynter, Sylvia, and David Scott. "The Re-Enchantment of Humanism: An Interview with Sylvia Wynter." *Small Axe* 8 (September 2000): 119–207.

Young, Iris Marion. *Justice and the Politics of Difference.* Princeton: Princeton University Press, 1990.

# Index

**Katherine McKittrick** is assistant professor of women's studies at Queen's University in Kingston, Ontario.